D1519655

TRANSCENDENCE
— and —
VIOLENCE

TRANSCENDENCE
— and —
VIOLENCE

The Encounter of
Buddhist, Christian and Primal
Traditions

John D'Arcy May

continuum
NEW YORK • LONDON

2003

The Continuum International Publishing Group Inc
15 East 26 Street, New York, NY 10010

The Continuum International Publishing Group Ltd
The Tower Building, 11 York Road, London SE1 7NX

Printed in the United States of America

Library of Congress Cataloging-in-Publication Data

May, John D'Arcy, 1942-
    Transcendence and violence : the encounter of Buddhist, Christian, and primal traditions / John May.
        p.   cm.
    Includes bibliographical references.
    ISBN 0-8264-1513-X (alk. paper)
    1. Christianity and other religions – Primitive. 2. Violence – Religious aspects – Christianity. 3. Australia – Religion. 4. Melanesia – Religion. 5. Buddhism – Relations. 6. Violence – Religious aspects – Buddhism. 7. Asia – Religion.   I. Title.
BR128.P75M39 2003
291.1'72 – dc21

2003001720

To my colleagues, north and south,
at the Irish School of Ecumenics, Trinity College Dublin,
who have created a working environment
that is both stimulating and enjoyable

The first time I heard about the white man's god, who was called GOD, was when we were walking through the forest with Robson. . . . Of course I knew it wasn't really this fellow God who made us. It was other ones who are secret, like everybody knew. I never did say this to Robson, though, as I didn't want to grieve him when he was kindly saving us. Besides, those things weren't for telling to some foreign stranger. Truly Robson's God was one puzzle to confound. Everybody knew where our real ones were as they could see them every night shining in the sky, but when I asked Robson where God was, he just said, "He is everywhere." He even said he was three people, which seemed some grievous mystery to confound. Also he told us that if we didn't believe God was everywhere then God would get angry and send us to some piss-poor place to get burnt, which was heinous, I did ponder. Our real ones never did care if you knew they were in the sky. They were just in the sky.

— Matthew Kneale, *English Passengers*

In the dark he continued speaking: "Even if you are a monk, like my brother, passion or slaughter will meet you someday. For you cannot survive as a monk if society does not exist. You renounce society, but to do so you must first be part of it, learn your decision from it. This is the paradox of retreat. My brother entered temple life. He escaped the world and the world came after him. He was seventy when he was killed by someone, perhaps someone from the time when he was breaking free — for that is the difficult stage, when you leave the world."

— Michael Ondaatje, *Anil's Ghost*

CONTENTS

FOREWORD

It is perhaps ironic that I should be asked to comment on this excellent study by John D'Arcy May. We both grew up in a small country town called Hamilton in the Western District of Victoria (Australia). We were both ignorant of the history of physical and cultural violence inflicted on the Aboriginal peoples of the place. We both defined ourselves in terms of a denominational "other" — Protestant and Catholic. John was the Catholic and I was the Protestant (Lutheran). And both of us have come to realize that our Christian heritage has failed in the way it has perpetuated violence, especially in its contact with primal peoples.

May explores with academic rigor the "failures of transcendence," that is, the way that followers of the highest moral ideals of transcendent faiths fail signally to act on them when faced with the unknown other, especially the primal other. The two faiths he explores are Christianity and Buddhism.

May faces us with the ugly reality that transcendent faiths like Christianity and Buddhism have perpetuated violence, not only during times of war, but in the very moment when they came into contact with a culture alien to their own. When they met the "other," they did not seek to understand it, but to suppress it, destroy it or transform it.

May shows us that both physical and spiritual violence are an integral part of our Christian and Buddhist heritage — both doctrinal and moral — and forces us to ask whether we can extract our very selves from this history of violence and spiritual failure. What we did to the "other" still haunts us. Ask the Indigenous peoples of Australia, Melanesia, Sri Lanka and Thailand about how transcendent religions brutalized them — body and soul.

May explores some of the reasons why these two religions did not forcefully oppose the cultural genocide and spiritual massacre of Indigenous peoples. The heart of the problem, according to May, is that followers of these two transcendent faiths encountered a repressed "otherness" in "themselves" with which they could not cope. One Aboriginal elder saw the inner violence of the white Christians when he said, "The whites came in here bloodthirsty.... They did not have love in their hearts." May wants us to consider seriously whether we still harbor the fear and violence of our heritage in our hearts — especially when we hear about a so-called Christian nation like America promoting war rather than peace.

1

The seemingly inherent violence in our transcendent tradition challenges the very heart of our theology. We can no longer live in isolation defining our faith over against other faiths, especially primal faiths. We can longer identify our grasp of transcendence as "superior" or the "other" as absolute. It is time to talk — to confess our crimes of spiritual violence and explore the depths of the transcendent in the archaic "other."

As we enter this decade against violence, May has thrown down the gauntlet of peace to religious thinkers. And as we begin dialogue between the religions of the world, May summons us to seek more than the similarities between our faiths, whether transcendent or primal. We are all called, May would say, to confess the failures of our faiths, failures that have — in the name of truth — led to violence against the other. And if we are to foster peace on earth, the religious thinkers must take the lead in respecting the other, learning from the other and developing peace-building theologies that actually "work" in practice.

Congratulations are in order! May has exposed clearly a great weakness in our respective religious histories. But he has not left us with a corpse. He offers us direction for "earthing" our respective faiths and thereby reviving them as "peace" agents in a violent world. Now we need a genuine will to talk as peacemakers with each other — Buddhist, Christian and primal believers. Who will motivate us to change our ways and talk this way, think this way, make peace this way? Perhaps, ironically, the very violence that surrounds us will shock us into action.

NORMAN C. HABEL

ACKNOWLEDGMENTS

This book had a long gestation, and there are many midwives to thank for its successful birth. It was conceived during four and a half fascinating years doing ecumenical work in Papua New Guinea (1983–87), where I remember with gratitude the enormous amount I learnt about the encounter of Christianity and Melanesian cultures from my colleagues at the Melanesian Council of Churches (as it was then called), the Melanesian Association of Theological Schools and the Melanesian Institute. An invaluable chance to reflect on this experience came when the originators of the innovative program *Theologie Interkulturell* in the Faculty of Catholic Theology at the University of Frankfurt invited me to give the lectures and seminars of the 1988 series, which resulted in the book *Christus Initiator: Theologie im Pazifik* (1990). Professors Hermann Pius Siller, Siegfried Wiedenhofer, Hans Kessler, Michael Raske, Johannes Hoffmann, Thomas Schreijäck and their colleagues have been a constant source of stimulus ever since. At the program's annual symposia I am particularly grateful to have met Professor Haruko Okano, who has been a most gracious guide to the subtle interplay of religion and Japanese culture, and Professor Karl-Wilhelm Merks of the Catholic Theological Faculty of the University of Tilburg in the Netherlands, whose invitations to participate in a similar program there have provided the opportunity to develop a number of key ideas.

The next step was: why not an English translation? But translating one's own work is not a good idea, and the project lapsed for several years, during which the seed slowly germinated. My former student Dr. Ulrich Dornberg organized a visit to Thailand for me in 1991 during which I first met Ajarn Sulak Sivaraksa, whose legendary capacity for friendship has been a source of encouragement ever since. The project began to come to fruition in 1998, when Professor Robert Gascoigne of Australian Catholic University in Sydney invited me to speak at a conference in January, which immediately suggested: why not Christmas at home followed by study leave? With the support of the then Director of the Irish School of Ecumenics, Dr. Geraldine Smyth, O.P., this was arranged.

Dr. Rod Lacey in Ballarat and Dr. Val Noone in Melbourne generously shared their enormous knowledge of things Melanesian and Australian, and thanks to the warm hospitality of Professor John Molony and his wife Denise I was able

3

to spend a month in Canberra at the Australian National University's Research School of Pacific and Asian Studies, whose then Director, Professor Merle Ricklefs, welcomed and encouraged me. Professors Donald Denoon, Brij Lal, Niel Gunson and Anthony Johns gave generously of their time. On my first ever visit to New Zealand, my former students Bruce and Diane Miller-Keeley introduced me to the quite unique ecumenical scene there. Finally, I was able to spend two weeks in the incomparable library of the University of Hawai'i at Hanoa, facilitated in every way by Professor David Chappell, who with his wife Stella made my stay there unforgettable. Thanks to my friends at the International Interfaith Center in Oxford, I was then invited to join a group from the UK hosted by *Rissho-kosei-kai* on a memorable first visit to Japan, to be followed by a second one at the invitation of Dr. Gene Reeves. This led to regular contacts with Professors David Loy, Joseph O'Leary, Michio Shinozaki and Makoto Ozaki, whose ideas and suggestions I value greatly.

Parts of the manuscript were read critically and helpfully by Dr. Frank Fletcher and Dr. Eugene Stockton, two Australian Catholic priests whose empathy with Aboriginal people is exemplary; by Professor Theo Ahrens, through whom my sojourn in Papua New Guinea first became possible and who has been a constant source of inspiration ever since; by Dr. Aloysius Pieris, S.J., who initiated me into the Buddhist-Christian dialogue in Sri Lanka in 1979 and whose theology I find unfailingly stimulating; by Professor Sallie King, who saved me from some misinterpretations of Thai Buddhism; by Professors Makoto Ozaki and David Loy, mentioned above; and by Professor Paul Knitter, whose perceptive criticisms salvaged some of my key insights from obscurity. Frank Oveis of Continuum never wavered in his commitment to the project and was helpful in every conceivable way as the manuscript became a book.

Anyone who ventures into so much unfamiliar territory in pursuit of an overarching theme is bound to make mistakes, and for those that remain I take full responsibility. I owe a great deal to a group of my students, who in 2001 took part in a research seminar in the course of which they read the entire manuscript and as intelligent readers searched out its weak points: Martin Rötting, Amanda Morrall, Charlotte Weber, Michael Wallace and John Clarke. You all helped me more than you realize. The same goes for my daughter Katrin, who recently spent three and a half years in Japan and gave me insights into that country which I would never have gained during my short visits. Finally, but always foremost in my own mind, I owe an incalculable debt to my wife, Margret, who accepted the upheaval of going to Papua New Guinea, acclimatized to Australia's ocker culture, accompanied me on most of the journeys mentioned above, and tempered my tendency to idealize the Asia-Pacific with a dose of realism. *Ich danke von Herzen!*

Note on Foreign Words

This book inevitably contains words from a variety of non-European languages. As these are used by way of illustration rather than to make philological points, it has been decided to dispense with all diacritical marks.

Introduction

WHY VIOLENCE?

*Traditions of Transcendence
and Their Failures*

When strangers meet, violence often results. That this is not always the case
is due to social conventions (smiling, avoiding eye contact, receptive gestures)
which reassure both parties that there is no danger of aggression. But when,
in an analogous sense, larger cultural, ethnic or social groups "encounter" one
another, the mechanisms of reassurance are more difficult to deploy. It is here
that the ambivalence of religious dispositions comes into play. It would seem that,
for every case where the religions inculcate attitudes that favor conciliation and
peace, there are many more in which it is precisely religious convictions that are
put at the service of aggression. Are the religions the main and abiding cause of
violence, or are they our greatest hope of finally overcoming the violence endemic
in most of our cultures? Put thus baldly, the question is probably misleading, but in
the light of widespread conflicts which, whatever their other causes, seem on the
face of it both ethnically and religiously motivated, it is a question that is close to
the surface of many people's minds. Those who are well enough informed to think
more closely about the matter might say that, whereas the "tribal" religions of self-
contained societies tend to be exclusivist and hostile to strangers, the "universal"
religions of the great traditions contain the seeds of an ethic of non-violence
which for the first time could be truly global. A further variant would claim
that it is the monotheisms — Judaism, Christianity and Islam, and with certain
qualifications also Hinduism — that have a history of violence, whereas religions
based on a divine essence or principle as distinct from a conscious transcendent
being, such as Taoism or Confucianism, are less inclined to violence but are by
the same token historically inconsequential.[1] These are aspects of the hypothesis
I wish to test in this book.

Without prejudice to religions such as Hinduism and Islam, about which I
know less, the two traditions that interest me most in this respect are Buddhism
and Christianity. I am myself a Roman Catholic Christian, and I have a long-
standing interest in Buddhism which has made me a different kind of Christian.

7

Christianity, after many inculturations which have produced both catholic variety and ecumenical tension, has a recent history of missionary encounter with the peoples of the Pacific Islands, including my native Australia. Buddhism, once virtually extinct and now still a tiny minority in India, the land of its birth, has been decisively shaped by its encounters with both east and south Asian cultures such as those of China, Korea, Japan, Sri Lanka, Thailand and Vietnam. In each case battles had to be fought — sometimes quite literally — to determine each religion's relationship with states and their governments, at times in the context of colonial interests and imperial ambitions. Even more important, however, from the perspective of this study, are the relationships which developed with the very different cultures and their distinctive religious traditions encountered by Buddhism and Christianity as they expanded into the Asia-Pacific region. The attitudes they adopted towards the religiously alien "other" and the disempowered poor can be reconstructed in a number of these contexts. My purpose in attempting this is not so much historical as dialogical: I wish to explore the ways in which these traditions — not only Buddhism and Christianity but equally the region's indigenous cultures — could relate today in the light of their past encounters. This should provide an index of their potential as forces for peace in the emerging global context.[2]

   Not everyone, of course, will accept this as a valid perspective. It may seem to beg the question whether religion of any kind has any intrinsic connection with morality. Indeed, it may smack of moral rigorism: only religions that meet certain ethical criteria independent of themselves will be permitted to collaborate on the tasks imposed from outside them by the new situation of globalization. Other readers may object to the implied equivalence of the two major traditions, the one theistic and personal, the other a-theistic and non-personal in conception, each of which regards itself as utterly unique and incommensurable with supposed alternatives. Some may want to insist that the so-called "primal" traditions of indigenous peoples also have a dimension of transcendence and can therefore contribute to the global task. Others again may be unhappy with the apparent assumption of some kind of immanence of religious transcendence which allows us to suppose that anything at all in the brutal arena of history could be influenced by religion in any decisive way. Here I merely wish to alert the reader to difficulties of this sort without attempting to discuss them further. Their solutions will, we may hope, come out in the wash, to be picked like flecks of gold from our prospector's pan in the concluding chapters. My primary interest is neither historical nor philological, but I hope to reconstruct some at least of the spiritual, intellectual and ethical achievements — and failures — of Buddhism and Christianity and the indigenous traditions they encountered in Asia and the Pacific as they each faced and coped with the unknown. Only then will we be in a position to assess whether they are still capable of doing so.

In considering a region as vast and complex as the Asia-Pacific, of course, we must be extremely selective. Indeed, some would doubt whether any such coherent geopolitical entity exists at all. My response to this has always been that it is a new constellation of countries and cultures that is still in the early stages of formation, but is recognizable nonetheless.[3] When we learn to look at the Pacific Ocean as the new Mediterranean, the "central sea" which, thanks to the new media of communication and ease of travel, is now binding together the very disparate peoples it once separated by its immense distances, we find many stories of encounter and conflict involving both Buddhism, the ancient presence, and Christianity, the recent arrival. How does the Buddhist *sangha* come to be implicated in the ongoing violence in Sri Lanka? What explains its ambivalence under the military regime in Burma (Myanmar)? What is its role in Cambodia, and how was it able to mount a morally credible alternative to the opposing ideologies in Vietnam? With what success have the Buddhists of Tibet been able to respond to the Dalai Lama's exhortations to resist Chinese occupation nonviolently? To what extent do the quite drastic differences between these Buddhist sub-traditions influence their responses to violence and oppression? What status do "scripture" and "practice" have in particular traditions? While the answers to these and many more questions are urgently required within the overall framework of my project, I have chosen to concentrate on two countries where the historic roles played by Buddhism have an intrinsic interest and which I have been able to visit to collect impressions and information: Thailand and Japan. These are studied in Part II.

Similarly, the missionary history of Christianity throughout the Pacific yields many stories of missed opportunities and lasting achievements. Polynesia, in particular, is rich in examples of both coercion and cooperation, from the virtual extinction of the indigenous religion of Hawai'i to the remarkable independence with which the Maori of Aotearoa (New Zealand) originally responded to Christianity and which they still display in their autonomous churches and cultural revivals. Here too I have preferred to concentrate on the home ground with which I am most familiar: Australia and Melanesia, studies of which make up Part I; and here too we can only scratch the surface of the research that needs to be done. What theologies were held by the individual missionaries, who came from a wide variety of denominational backgrounds? How did they read scripture? What role did the authority structures of their churches and mission boards play in their missionary strategies? Was their undoubted piety characterized by distinctive spiritualities? And what was the contribution of the Pacific Islands converts who themselves became missionaries?

In each case, I propose that a study of the failures of the great traditions in their encounters with alien cultures may provide us with a "back door" to dialogue, a new basis on which to assess the Buddhist and Christian contributions to humanity's collaborative tasks and the potential of their own developing relationship. Such a mutual confrontation with past and present inadequacies in dialogue, of course, presupposes a considerable maturity. I believe this is now being achieved in Buddhist-Christian dialogue and that it will be significantly enhanced if both traditions attend more to the attitudes they have adopted towards the "primal" religious traditions encountered in the course of their missionary expansion.

Having examined at least a selection of the available data on such encounters, there remains the even more challenging task of reflecting on it constructively in a post-colonial, post-modern intellectual context dominated by projects of deconstruction. Whose historical perspective are we adopting when "we" — predominantly, I assume here, Europeans, Americans and Australians with some kind of Christian background — venture to reconstruct what happened in intercultural encounters and interpret their significance? That of the Chinese puzzling over the ways of life and forms of expression of Indian Buddhists? Of Pacific Islanders adapting their myths to explain what was happening to them as they rapidly came under Western Christian influence? But who is authorized to recount such histories? Using which methodologies? Where does "objectivity" lie in such cases, and what is the role of the "subjectivity" of those involved in research?[4] These are issues we shall have to bear in mind as we embark on the empirical studies of Parts I and II. They will recur as we draw the results together in Part III, where we try to sort out the categories and strategies employed by all parties to the intercultural encounters (chapter 5) and draw conclusions about the ways in which their capacity for transcendence equips them to avoid or resolve conflicts, especially when these turn violent (chapter 6 and Conclusion).

The word "transcendence" is used frequently in texts about religion, but what does it actually mean? And what relationship could it have to violence? We need to reflect briefly on this before we begin (section 1). In doing so we need to be aware that the sets of presuppositions we inherit from the Western philosophical tradition may no longer be adequate — may in fact even be counterproductive — if we are to engage seriously with other people's views of transcendence. Secondly, we need to prepare our minds for what I shall call "failures of transcendence": for the realization that religious traditions, which derive from their awareness of transcendence the noblest moral ideals, can fail signally to act on them when faced with the unknown other, the stranger who could so easily become an enemy (section 2).

1. The Enigma of Transcendence

To propose some kind of linkage between transcendence and violence is to suggest a study of such thinkers as Nietzsche, Freud, Foucault, Girard and others who have thought deeply about the nature of violence and its relationship with religion and ideology. My project is not such an exercise in high theory, but a study of how particular religious traditions, as they entered particular regions of the Asia-Pacific, have encountered cultures that were strange to them, how indigenous cultures have coped with the incursion of these universalist traditions, and how each encounter raised or lowered the potential for conflict and violence.

My own early training in the scholastic philosophy and theology of the Middle Ages, especially the thought of St. Thomas Aquinas, has left me with the profound conviction that transcendence is nothing less than the defining dynamic of human intellect.[5] Whether transcendence, thus understood, remains intentional, as most modern European and Japanese subjectivist philosophy has conceived it, or whether it can be objectified as a transcendent Being or Reality that exists beyond our range of perception but whose existence is presupposed by every act of intellection, as the critical realism of medieval scholasticism maintained, is a question sharpened by contemporary linguistic philosophy but disallowed by post-modern deconstructionism.

The perennial human quest for wisdom and understanding, palpable in the most ancient myths of primal peoples and reflectively present in the active pursuit of knowledge by the Greeks, Indians and Chinese, has become transformed in the modern era into the single-minded development of science and technology as ends in themselves. The results of such "development" on the living spaces of indigenous peoples and natural species are apparent. Our understanding of the world may have increased in proportion to our success in explaining it, but this has not necessarily enhanced our capacity to relate to one another and to our natural environment. It has become a truism that knowledge has not increased wisdom.

We are used to the idea of an expanding physical universe; it is less common to think of the inevitable working out of the intellect's dynamic of transcendence in terms of a constantly expanding mental universe. In saying this we have already made the connection between transcendence and violence. It is our capacity for transcendence, for always being already "beyond" in anticipation what we grasp conceptually, that allows us to form the concept of a "whole," a universe of possible knowledge to which our actual knowledge is merely the preamble. In the era of modernity we seem to have restricted this capacity to the pragmatic pursuit of knowledge-for-use in the hope of solving particular problems *in* the world, neglecting the classical metaphysical problem *of* the world: why there should be

existence rather than not. In doing so we have lost a sense of what Gregory
Bateson called an "ecology of mind," a sense of the wider, interlocking and over-
lapping contexts as well as the moral purposes of knowledge, not just those that
happen to be useful for technological ends, as is now apparent in the field of
bioethics. From this angle of approach we see that transcendence, as a defining
characteristic of intellect, *always* has a moral dimension. Though knowledge is
an end and a value in itself, the marriage of science and technology has made
us realize that the constant expansion of knowledge brings with it the question
of the responsible *use* of that knowledge. Once transcendence is transposed into
technology it confronts us even more immediately with responsibility for human
and ecological integrity, projected into the future, as thinkers such as E. F. Schu-
macher and Hans Jonas have made clear. Technology, too, always has a moral
dimension, precisely because it participates in the human intellectual dynamic of
transcendence.

In such an intellectual atmosphere it becomes difficult to appreciate that historically it has been the religions that have continually produced powerful symbols of
transcendence and practices for "realizing" it in both senses of the word: grasping
it intellectually and acting in its light. The religions have been sources of "limit
concepts" — God, nothingness, infinity, eternity — which, when internalized,
have the effect of relativizing interests, curbing desire and making us content
with little. Though ethics can be constructed rationally as a philosophy of the
good and the means to attain it by right action, the deeper sources of morality
were first intuited by and remain embedded in the narrative traditions of the
religions. Today, however, as these traditions confront one another in conscious
awareness of their differences, we are losing confidence in "grand narratives"
(François Lyotard) which purport to contain or explain the whole. There is no
basis for universal principles in unchanging essences; we are aware of the all-
pervasiveness of change and the self-referentiality of language. But more recently
it has become possible to see that this "deconstructionist" critique, though it has
certain affinities with the late medieval nominalism of William of Ockham, was
anticipated and indeed surpassed by Buddhist dialectics many centuries earlier,
and this not from purely philosophical, but from religious motives.

There is a potential for misunderstanding here because of the very different
roles philosophy has played in Buddhist and Christian traditions. Jan van Bragt
has put the contrast well:

> There is no such thing as Christian philosophy, and the West knows no
> logic of religion. Christianity never constructed a philosophy of its own,
> but was content to adopt Greek philosophy without changing its original
> orientation and basic categories. Western philosophy is not concerned with

explaining religious experience but with grounding the natural phenomena of everyday consciousness. Our Western culture never attempted to develop a logic radically founded upon Christian revelation, whereas Nagarjuna and other Buddhist philosophers took care to make the Four Noble Truths of the Buddha the starting point of their philosophy.[6]

It is becoming apparent that the natural dialogue partner for Western "post-modernism" is not Christianity, which finds itself trapped in static philosophies and immutable dogmas, but Buddhism, so that a conversation between Derrida and Nagarjuna (ca. 200 C.E.), such as that set up by Joseph O'Leary, seems perfectly natural.[7] Derrida, intent on exposing the great ontological systems as self-refuting rhetorical exercises which conceal their own lack of foundations, is seen to be engaged on a quest not dissimilar to that of the Buddhist philosopher, though certainly not in conscious dependence on him and without his spiritual purpose of clarifying what the meditator needs to know if the journey towards inner liberation is not to be thrown off course.

The other obvious dialogue partner for philosophical Buddhism is Western existential psychotherapy, and this has been taken up from a Buddhist perspective by David Loy.[8] In Loy's view Buddhism, in a way much more radical than Heidegger's phenomenology of time as awareness of death, yet complementary to Ernest Becker's interpretation of our "symbolic immortality projects" as a "denial of death," interprets our fear of nonbeing and our fundamental sense of "lack" as our refusal to confront the illusion that "I am real."[9] This opens up the — to Westerners — unfamiliar prospect of transcendence as emptiness (*sunyata*). In Nagarjuna's radical interpretation, this applies even to *nirvana* itself. From this perspective, *every* attempt to establish a teleology which would give "meaning" and "purpose" to our lives, assuring us that there is a future worth striving for, puts "me" and "mine" back into the picture and reintroduces dualism.[10] Human activity in its entirety becomes a flight from the realization of our own unreality.

These are some indications of the "meta-dialogue" that must be developed to make explicit the presuppositions of interreligious encounters. "Transcendence" takes radically different forms in the "universalist" cultures of India, Israel and Greece and in the "immanentist" civilizations of China, Egypt and Japan.[11] The differences are sharpened still more when we introduce the concept of violence as a correlate of transcendence. Is violence merely a moral issue, or does it have, as Nietzsche thought, an ontological dimension: *is reality itself violent and founded on some ultimate principle of violence?* To some, Darwin's theory of natural selection, at least in its quasi-mythical forms of "survival of the fittest" and "social Darwinism," seems to confirm this. Does it therefore make sense to speak, not just of religious motivation as one of a cluster of psycho-social causes of violence, but of *violence as itself religious?* Did religion and social order arise conjointly in some primordial sacrificial ritual which *uses violence to gain control of violence* as the continual result of rivalry and retribution?[12] Such disturbing questions will leer at us between the lines as we proceed with the empirical studies of Parts I and II, and they will be taken up again in Part III.

2. Confronting the Failures of Transcendence

When Thich Nhat Hanh left Vietnam at the height of the war with America to try to explain the Buddhist resistance movement to an uncomprehending West, one of those with whom he reached an immediate rapport was Thomas Merton.[13] Their mutual understanding rested in part on the realization that each of their traditions was failing to come to grips with the moral and spiritual challenge of the war. To be able to discuss such failures openly with a spiritual friend from another tradition presupposes a high degree of maturity. The example of the Vietnamese Buddhist and the American Trappist prompts the question: has Buddhist-Christian dialogue reached this degree of maturity?[14]

"Failure" in such contexts means in the first instance the moral failure of individuals. It is this that allows the decisions to be made which lead to violence, and it is this that prompts rationalizations of violence drawn, however spuriously, from religious traditions. But things are not that simple. Knowledge has a social dimension, and there is a sense in which such decisions are also collective. Both leaders and led, especially in times of crisis, are shaped by an already existing social consensus, however tacit and implicit, that certain things are true for the society in question and that certain courses of action are right for it. It is here that religious traditions *as such,* as distinctive systems of belief, can have a historical responsibility for predisposing collectivities towards particular ways of acting and towards finding justifications for these in traditional beliefs. The study of the moral guilt of individuals makes sense in such contexts, but the structuring of the contexts themselves also needs to be considered. We are concerned in what follows not just with "human error," but with "systems failure." Here religious traditions can play a decisive role.

In the course of the twentieth century both Christian and Buddhist traditions have been challenged to confront violence and have failed in ways that are paradigmatic for our theme. I shall give brief consideration to two of them as a prelude to our consideration of the two traditions' Asia-Pacific encounters.

2(a). The Failure of European Christianity in the Shoah

The Holocaust of six million European Jews in Nazi extermination camps marks a deep crisis for both Judaism and Christianity as faith traditions.[15] For religious

Jews, with their sense of the immediacy of God's actions in history, this threat to the very existence of the covenant people causes a theological anguish which is scarcely imaginable to Christians, with their somewhat more detached view of divine involvement. Even so, the German Catholic theologian Johann Baptist Metz, echoing the dictum of the philosopher Theodor W. Adorno that there could be no poetry after Auschwitz, said that we could no longer do theology "with our backs to Auschwitz."[16] Despite the protests of the Confessing Church, inspired by the great Swiss Reformed theologian Karl Barth, and the German Lutheran Dietrich Bonhoeffer's courageous attempts to maintain ecumenical contacts abroad and support the attempt on Hitler's life, and notwithstanding the objections raised by Bishop von Galen in Münster or Cardinal Faulhaber in Munich against specific Nazi measures such as euthanasia, the question of Christian "responsibility" for the Holocaust hangs heavy over both Catholic and Protestant churches.[17] Centuries of anti-Jewish indoctrination in Europe, going back to the acrimonious split between the infant Christian community and its Jewish parent in the first century and leaving traces in the New Testament itself, left a legacy of resentment against Jews which even the emancipation of the eighteenth and nineteenth centuries could not obliterate; on the contrary, the spectacle of Jews seeking baptism in order to become acceptable in business and professional circles only increased it.[18] Christianity might be said to have repressed its original Jewish identity, only to project its remorse at having done so back onto the Jews, despised as "Asians on the streets of Europe" and made into scapegoats for Christianity's own failures and shortcomings. Christianity's limited ability to acknowledge the "otherness" first of the Jews, then of the Muslims, then of the peoples "discovered" by Europeans in the New World, may be traced back to its unresolved theological relationship with the Jews, which Karl Barth called "the only great ecumenical question."[19]

Over all this hangs the shadow of Auschwitz.[20] Auschwitz, the abiding symbol of the *Shoah* (catastrophe) that befell Europe's Jews at the hands of Christians, is unique, not so much because it is a specifically modern atrocity in which all available technological means were directed to the single end of annihilating a people, but because of its "theological" quality: the Jews were targeted not because of anything they had *done* but solely on account of what they *were*. "Not all the victims were Jews, but all Jews were victims" (Elie Wiesel). "Not all Christians were perpetrators, but all the perpetrators were Christians" (Robert McAfee Brown). Together, the two sentences mark out the parameters of "Holocaust theology." But is theology possible at all after Auschwitz? Auschwitz takes the problem of evil — how God can be simultaneously all-powerful, all-knowing and all-compassionate and yet allow Auschwitz to happen — beyond the reach of both reason and revelation. The *Shoah* unilaterally breaks God's covenant with Israel, unless it be interpreted as "just punishment" or "historical necessity" (as some of the early post-war statements by German Christians unfortunately tried to do). If Auschwitz "means" anything, it means a total rupture of religious faith and Enlightenment rationality. This realization led some American Jewish thinkers (Richard Rubenstein, Emil Fackenheim) to abandon belief in the God of the biblical covenant, though others (Eliezer Berkovits) felt able to affirm God's simultaneous presence and absence in Auschwitz, leaving Jews with a 614th commandment: survive! Deny Hitler a posthumous victory! For these authors Auschwitz discloses the powerlessness of a suffering God who had no choice but to remain silent (Hans Jonas). Jewish faith after Auschwitz must contain a "yes" and a "no"; Jews must now take responsibility for their own destiny (Irving Greenberg). For Elie Wiesel, the legacy of Auschwitz is the residual formula: "Jews do not hate"; the rest is silence.

For Christians the temptation has been to "interpret" Auschwitz by inserting it into the Christian story and transposing it into the categories of Christian theology. Even Jürgen Moltmann's daring attempt to have God participate in our pain through Jesus' suffering and death has been accused of this, though it was one of the earliest attempts to make any kind of theological "sense" of Auschwitz. Coming to terms with the *Shoah* forced Christians to accept the untraditional idea of a God who suffers in solidarity with victims, a "self-limiting" God on the model of the Kabbalistic *zimzum*, a "self-emptying" God as portrayed in Jesus' renunciation of divine sonship in Phil 2:6–8 (*kenosis*). Christians have been forced to question traditional ideas such as the immutability of God, the atonement and the redemptive value of suffering and sacrifice. Even more difficult, however, has been the acknowledgment of a failure that goes right to the heart of Christian faith and doctrine and which may have left traces in the New Testament itself. But the challenge of Auschwitz has also opened up unsuspected lines of approach to central Buddhist concepts such as "emptiness" (*sunyata*) and "compassion" (*metta-karuna*).[21]

2(b). The Failure of Theravada Buddhism in Sri Lanka

For Buddhists the recent history of the *sangha* in Sri Lanka is similarly problematic, even when viewed in full awareness of Christianity's complicity in Ceylonese colonial history. Like other such divided islands (Cyprus, Ireland), the island of Lanka, which became Buddhist in the time of the Indian emperor Asoka (ca. 268–239 B.C.E.), has always had to contend with a substantial minority, in this case Hindu Tamils. Viewed as part of the large Tamil population of neighboring south India, this minority can easily be seen as the advance guard of an overwhelming alien majority. The earliest evidence of Buddhism in Sri Lanka coincides with the reign of a Tamil king in Anuradhapura, and the campaign against him led by Dutthagamani (101–77 or 161–137 B.C.E.), who slew his enemy in single combat, was portrayed as a Buddhist revival. "These events are the recorded beginning of Singhalese Buddhist nationalism. From now on Sinhalese kings were regarded as defenders of the faith, and Buddhism acquired official trappings."[22] The king's remorse after this slaughter was assuaged by "some Enlightened monks" thus:

> That deed presents no obstacle on your path to heaven. You caused the deaths of just one and a half people, O king. One had taken the Refuges, the other the Five Precepts as well. The rest were wicked men of wrong views who died like (or: are considered as) beasts. You will in many ways illuminate the Buddha's Teaching, so stop worrying.[23]

The whole problem of the relationship between Buddhism and power, *sangha* and state, inherited from the Indian Buddhist emperor Asoka, thus arises at the very beginning of Singhalese Buddhism.

Tamil invasions were repulsed throughout Sri Lanka's history (notably in the fifth, ninth, tenth, eleventh and thirteenth centuries), in each case strengthening the ties between the *sangha* and its royal protectors. Buddhism became the symbol of ethnic identity and the willing ally of Sinhala nationalism, and this ideologization of the religion robbed it of much of its critical potential.[24] Senior monks became the functional equivalent of court Brahmins; indeed, in the Anuradhapura period (fourth century B.C.E.–ninth century C.E.) the Singhalese king was chosen by the Indian *purohita* fire ritual, and the power struggles between *brahmana* and *ksatriya* castes at court led to the establishment of an absolute monarchy. Brahmin influence was finally eliminated by an alliance of monks and pious laypeople, thereby restoring somewhat the credibility of the *sangha* and the symbolic significance of the ancient Mahavihara monastic complex. Theravada Buddhism allows little scope for "popular" religion,[25] and "by and large Buddhism in Sri Lanka had no clear theory of other religions," because it is unable to see them in the context of a transcendental unity such as is conceivable in Hinduism or Christianity.[26]

This profound ambiguity attaches to the role of the *sangha* right through the successive colonial epochs of the modern period: under the Portuguese (1505–1658), the Dutch (1658–1795) and the British (1795–1948), Singhalese national identity crystallized around the *sangha*, and it was often *bhikkhus* (monks) who inspired or supported revolts such as the Great Rebellion (Kandy, 1848) and the independence movement a century later. Because the British had protected the Christian churches and separated *sangha* and state, the pent-up resentment of the Buddhists exploded in bitter post-independence controversies over proselytizing, the language question and control of the schools. Though the secular, Western-educated nationalists who achieved political independence wanted a religiously neutral state, all, even the Marxists, learnt to respect the anger and influence of the monks. But the "Sinhala Only Act" (1956) and the nationalization of Catholic schools (1961) could not prevent the Youth Rebellion of the Singhalese Buddhist "Aspiring Rural Youth" (1971), which was ruthlessly crushed. Thus began the militarization of the conflict and its polarization along race lines, with the *sangha* firmly on the side of Singhalese nationalism, even to the point of supporting the paramilitary JVP (*Janatha Vimukthi Peramuna*, "People's Liberation Front'), whose massacre of Tamils in 1983 prompted the formation of the countermovement *Tamil Eelam* for a "Tamil Homeland."[27]

The "Modernist" or "Protestant" Buddhism that developed during this period, though contemptuous of popular syncretism and bitterly opposed to the Christian elite, effectively used the techniques of missionary Christianity to produce its own propaganda and its own brand of fundamentalism.[28] The reforms of the Anagarika Dharmapala, who wore the white robe of a lay renunciant without becoming a monk, sprang from nationalism and culture rather than religion and philosophy, "ostensibly Buddhist but in fact an innovative departure from the religious system of classical Singhalese Buddhism."[29] In the face of the threat to Singhalese identity posed by British Christianity and Tamil Hinduism, the ancient chronicles and traditional Buddhism were reconstructed as a dualistic national myth. The resulting fundamentalism

> is not religious in the classical sense of that term but rather a variant of a secular faith couched in religious language and elevating traditional religious symbols stripped of their symbolic power to evoke a multiplicity of meanings. . . . In other words, the specifically Buddhist character of the myths and legends is subservient to the personal and social identity both threatened and affirmed in the texts. Cultural identity in effect becomes a "religious fetish, an idol, a thing which has self-contained magical properties," rather than a transcendent and transforming moral and spiritual ideal in terms of which all systems and institutions are judged as limited or only a partial embodiment. Religions thus harnessed to nationalism are often regarded as more pure and orthodox than the traditional forms they seek to supplant; in turn, nationalism readily takes on the character of a fervid, absolutistic revival of religion.[30]

It is thus not difficult to understand how Buddhist purists gave way to Buddhist extremists, for whom violence was not too high a price to pay for complete political domination of the island by Singhalese Buddhists, equating nation, race and religion.[31] Buddhism in Sri Lanka is now engulfed by this militant Singhalese nationalism, no longer motivated by the anti-colonial struggle but by the racist ethnocentrism referred to on the subcontinent as communalism.[32]

We have looked briefly at two examples of the moral and spiritual failure of great traditions. In each case the key element was an inability to rise above an ancient heritage of hatred and alienation: European Christians persecuting the Jews, Singhalese Buddhists demonizing the Tamils. Before we can contemplate the possibility of a "global ethic" to which the "united religions" of the world could contribute, we need to have a better understanding of how such distortions can happen — unless we have already concluded that they are not distortions at all but the inevitable result of trying to forge relationships with the "transcendent." Does the conviction that Jesus is the revelation of God or that Gautama's enlightenment shows the way to peace outweigh the historical evidence of atrocities committed in their names?

The appalling events of 11 September 2001 and the downward spiral of violence in the Middle East have shown us the depths to which religiously fueled violence can descend, and the "war on terrorism" declared by the West in response rings hollow when measured against the atrocities of Western imperialism throughout the modern era. Have the religions a credible and effective answer to violence other than Jihad or Crusade? In order to demonstrate that they have, they must confront not only their lasting achievements in transforming and being transformed by cultures foreign to them, but their historical failures as well. This will be our dual focus in the studies that follow.

Part I

CHRISTIANITY'S PACIFIC VOYAGE

Prologue

It was while preparing the lecture on which chapter 1 is based that it occurred to me that I did not even know the names of the Aboriginal peoples who lived in the part of Australia (the Western District of Victoria in the southeastern corner of the continent) where I grew up. On a visit home from Europe in 1977 a cousin took me to see a stately home known as Ercildoun on a property adjoining her husband's sheep farm at Burrumbeet, beside which was a small cabin, identified as "The First House," built above an embankment in which a stone cellar with a stout door had been constructed. It was here, I was told, that the first Scottish settlers defended themselves against attacks by the Aborigines. On another visit in 1979, after losing my way in that spur of the Great Dividing Range known as The Grampians, within sight of which I had spent my boyhood, I came across cave paintings on a remote ridge which gave me my first inkling of the atmosphere and significance of a sacred site.

Why had I heard and seen nothing of the Aborigines all the years I had lived in the little town of Hamilton, known to the earliest settlers as The Grange after the creek that flowed through it? The first article I ever published, prompted by my embarrassment at being Australian in the racially aware Europe of the late sixties, records that I had only ever seen Aborigines being used as punching bags for the local whites in the boxing tent at the annual agricultural show.[1] Why was it apparently a matter of indifference to me that Aboriginal people had once inhabited the area — place names such as Warrnambool, Terang and Byaduk were sufficient evidence of that — and that they had been so comprehensively exterminated? Why did nobody else seem in the least interested in the matter?

Why was it our main preoccupation as Catholics to convince ourselves how superior we were to Protestants while scrupulously observing the laws of our church concerning Sunday Mass attendance, Friday abstinence from meat, and sexual morality? Was there no place in the Catholic Social Teaching to which I was introduced in secondary school, some of it admirably concerned with questioning the notorious White Australia policy, for at least a mention of the churches' shared responsibility for what had happened and was still happening to Aboriginal people? (we now know that Aboriginal children were being forcibly removed from their families in order to be civilized and Christianized up to and well beyond the referendum that gave Aborigines the franchise in 1967).

Now at last, after all these years, I have access to research which tells me why there were streets in my home town named after Gray, Cox, Brown and Thompson and reveals what the pioneers did in order to take possession of the district.[2] The story that unfolds is described as "that of a great human drama, of two races brought face to face and forced to come to terms with each other, for neither could go away."[3] As the area then known as the Portland Bay District rapidly filled up, violence increased, usually starting soon after settlers first arrived in a given locality.[4] Though they occasionally fought among themselves and practiced severe punishments for moral and ritual deviations, the Aborigines were not warlike in the European sense of using violence to obtain land, property and resources. Yet in the Western District during the 1840s violence reached levels which alarmed the colonial government and led to interventions in Westminster, for "the honor of England, whose colony this distant field of murder is," was at stake.[5] Critchett estimates that by 1848 only thirty-five Europeans had been killed, yet the Aboriginal death toll was probably ten times as many.[6] One protracted conflict in 1845–47 was dubbed "The Eumeralla War" by the writer Rolf Boldrewood.[7] At The Grange (later Hamilton), where various European settlers had a particularly bad reputation for their treatment of Aborigines, especially women, they mounted "a small swivel gun, loaded with musket balls" to ward off outraged Aborigines; Patrick Codd, one of the worst perpetrators, was murdered.[8]

The scant remaining evidence reveals that the Aborigines of the Western District had achieved a level of culture and technology that set them apart from their northern Australian relatives. They constructed weirs to create eel and fish traps and they survived the harsh winters by remaining sedentary in huts, some built of stone, which held anything from a dozen to 40 people. When these were destroyed or rendered unusable by the whites they fell victim to influenza, smallpox and venereal disease and rapidly died off.[9] They have been described as "complex hunter-gatherers" whose motive for the "outrages" they perpetrated on white settlers, some of which involved cannibalism, was most probably their indignation at losing their life-giving water holes and not receiving a share in the prosperity already being flaunted by Europeans.[10] Those who lived along the rivers I used to fish in — the Wannon and the Grange Burn — and gathered near the mountains I used to climb — Mt. Napier, Mt. Sturgeon and Mt. Abrupt — and roamed the beaches at Portland and Port Fairy where I used to swim, would have belonged to the Gunditjmara and Djabwurong language groups, comprised of the Bung Bung.gel, the Tucalut, the Tolelemit, the Wanedeet, the Tapper, the Kolor, the Wallowerer, the Moonwer, the Yarre.her.beer, the Pi.ye.kil.beer and the Yarrer tribes, among others.[11] It is with a feeling of mixed exhilaration and helplessness that I am finally able to put names to these peoples in that far corner of a distant continent whose memory had been so thoroughly erased in the hundred years between first contact and my family's move from Melbourne to Hamilton in 1944, when I was aged two. My question now, half a century further on, is: what role did Christianity play in all this? And what implications does this have for Christianity's credibility as a force for peace today?

Chapter One

INTERNALIZING
THE PRIMAL OTHER

*The Christian Encounter
with Aboriginal Religion*

There exist records — photographic and even cinematographic — of the moment of contact between Europeans and peoples who had hitherto had no knowledge of a world outside their own geographical areas.[1] These pictures, capturing expressions of mingled fear and curiosity, of limitless wonderment and the courage to face the radically new, invite profound meditation. In the case of the arrival of European colonists in what was variously known two centuries ago as *terra australis incognita, Tierra Austrialia del Espiritu Santo,* or simply New Holland, only written records survive alongside some pen and ink drawings, but they enable us to reconstruct much of what was thought and done in those first fatal weeks and months after the landing of the First Fleet at Botany Bay on 18 January 1788. The outer story of first contact is instructive enough, and we will return to it presently; the historian of the convict settlements, Robert Hughes, speaks of Europeans discovering their "geographical unconscious."[2] But the real aim of this chapter[3] is to penetrate to the inner story of contact between Europeans and Aboriginals. We will see that in a very real sense *this* first contact is only now beginning to take place.[4]

The Europeans in question were almost exclusively inhabitants of the islands which, because of the sensitivities of the one I presently live on, I have learned *not* to call the "British Isles." They were almost all adherents of the main Protestant Christian traditions (though there were also some Jews; the first Irish Catholic convicts left on the *Queen* in 1791, and fifty thousand had been transported by 1852).[5] We shall look first at the challenge presented by the very existence of the Aborigines to the worldview of nineteenth-century European Christians (section 1), then at the resilience of Aboriginal religious culture (section 2), and finally at the implications of the encounter for both Europeans and Aborigines today (section 3).

25

1. The Failure of European Theology

We need have no illusions about the Christian convictions of those whom the First Fleet under Governor Phillip deposited on the "fatal shore" of Botany Bay on that January day in 1788. His successor, Governor Hunter, wrote that "a more wicked, abandoned and irreligious set of people have never been brought together in any part of the world."[6] The officers were as appalled as the convicts at the harshness of the landscape, the severity of the climate, and their inability to make contact with the New Hollanders, as the Aborigines were then called. The best educated and most idealistic among the settlers were children of the Enlightenment; indeed, they were self-conscious in their application of its humanitarian principles, and Phillip was under explicit instructions "by every possible means to open an intercourse" with the Aborigines and to "conciliate their affections," enjoining everyone to "live in amity and kindness with them" and punishing anyone who should "wantonly destroy them."[7] This he conscientiously tried to do, and his admiration for them was as genuine as his ignorance was profound. The result was tragedy. As the weeks slipped by and incomprehension turned into exasperation, some of the convicts reacted violently to what, in their fear of the unknown, they took to be provocations by the Aborigines, who promptly retaliated by spearing cattle and men. According to John Harris,

> Although it can no longer be proven, it is virtually certain that the first acts of aggression in the long war between whites and blacks were committed by white colonists, and that the first deaths were Aboriginal, unrecorded like the majority of subsequent Aboriginal deaths.... It was the general opinion...that "the natives are not the aggressors."[8]

The Governor resorted to that well-tried standby of colonial rulers, the punitive expedition. The officer entrusted with carrying out the first of these, Captain Watkin Tench, was a humane and thoughtful Christian. He remonstrated with Phillip about the morality of such harsh retaliation, and when he failed to find any culprits in the impenetrable bush, nothing more was said.[9] But two precedents had been set: crime, even on the part of ignorant savages, merited punishment; but under the extraordinary circumstances then prevailing, such retribution raised moral issues which had yet to be debated. It also raised the issue of simply understanding a way of life so utterly different from anything Europeans had encountered before, even after three centuries of colonialism.

Two fundamental misconceptions bedeviled the "theology" which marked out the first settlers as children of their time, and they continued to characterize the much more explicit theology of the first missionaries to the Aborigines, who did not arrive till more than thirty years later. The first was the Enlightenment ideal of the Noble Savage, the child of nature unspoiled by what a later author was to call "the first taint of civilization" in the Pacific.[10] This idea of an ideal humanity proved impossible to reconcile with the reality of Aboriginal life. That the whites, even the most highly principled among them, saw the Aborigines in overwhelmingly negative terms is abundantly documented. The Aborigines were almost unanimously located at the lower end of the Chain of Being. There was earnest debate about whether they were human at all.[11]

The second misconception concerned the relationship between civilization and evangelization.[12] There were those who debated which should come first, but most of the educated Christians simply assumed their interdependence and regarded civilization — which invariably meant Europeanization; attempts were soon made to "Europeanize" even the landscape and the fauna — as the indispensable precondition for receiving the Gospel. The conclusion was easy to draw that the Aborigines were "as yet beyond the power of Christ to save." Samuel Marsden, the most forceful and influential clergyman of Sydney's early days, declared:

> The Aborigines are the most degraded of the human race ... the time is not yet arrived for them to receive the great blessings of civilization and the knowledge of Christianity.[13]

To their credit, the missionaries never went to the length of exonerating the brutality of pastoralists and the hostility of the secular press by acquiescing in the prevailing view that the Aborigines were sub-human and could therefore be disposed of like the native flora and fauna. Archbishop Polding, among others, firmly asserted that they had immortal souls, and the verse from the Acts of the Apostles, "God hath made of one blood all nations of men for to dwell on all the face of the earth" (17:26), is cited again and again in letters and diaries of the period.[14] There were even those who raised the question of the Europeans' right to invade the continent in the first place.[15] The standard biblical apology for racism was that the darker races stand under the curse of Ham (Gen 9, 10), which was given a global interpretation, and the imagery of black for evil, white for virtue occurs frequently.[16] The terminology of denigration was often taken directly from the simian imagery used to portray the Irish as brutish savages.[17] The Aborigines, in short, had to be civilized, and the best means to achieve this was to take people away from their land, on which they performed unspeakable ceremonies, and to "rescue" children from their benighted parents. Thus began the sorry story of the "stolen generations," the forcible removal of Aboriginal children from their parents, who remained in Aboriginal reserves or shanty towns while their children were placed in homes. The unquestioned assumption that assimilation was a prerequisite for salvation never ceased to determine both missionary and government policy towards Aborigines. This practice, which contravenes human rights conventions to which Australia is a signatory, continued well beyond the granting of voting rights to indigenous Australians in 1967 and such removals, in the name of "social welfare," still take place today.[18]

The enormity of the tragedy that sprang from this failure to recognize the humanity of the Aborigines and the integrity of their culture is only now being revealed. As Harris rightly points out, "[t]he missionaries' own belief system presented them with an almost insurmountable barrier to the achievement of their aims,"[19] just as their instinctive ethnocentricity prevented them from understanding Aboriginal culture. No one in the early nineteenth century had any clear conception that the small bands which made up the kinship and language groups had to keep moving in order to follow the seasons and the location of game, for they were nomadic hunter-gatherers who had no need of agriculture or the domestication of animals.[20] In the eyes of the settlers, however, this fact alone made them uncivilized, for everyone knew that, as Marsden put it, people who had no material wants and lived by sharing rather than owning property must be savages.[21] The invaders, in Harris's words, "wanted it all," and the squatters' maxim was "niggers and cattle don't mix."[22]

The Enlightenment had proclaimed the equality of all, and the figure of the Noble Savage was comprehensible because it fitted this European preconception. Aboriginal reality, however, was incomprehensible, which is why even the more humane among the settlers looked upon the Aborigines as sub-human.[23] As white settlement inexorably progressed and the Aborigines sank into despair dulled by alcohol, this too was rationalized as further proof that they were lazy and degenerate, a view the clergy reinforced by preaching that it was obviously the hand of Providence that was causing them to "fade," "melt away" and "perish" as a "doomed race."[24] The few Aborigines who became Christians learned to cherish hope for the next life, not for this. By the middle of the nineteenth century it was widely felt that Australians should "draw the veil" over the atrocities of the early years of settlement, thus inaugurating what the anthropologist Stanner was later to call "the great Australian silence," "a cult of forgetfulness practiced on a national scale."[25]

The men and women who thus dismally failed to understand the Aboriginal cultures they had stumbled upon were, in many cases, "the best the nineteenth century had to offer," and "without them, the plight of Aboriginal people would have been immeasurably worse."[26] They were for a long time utterly unable to grasp that *the primary aggression was white presence itself*, with its thoughtless invasion of the land that was life to Aboriginal people and the immediate introduction of venereal and other diseases against which the Aborigines had no resistance (Governor Phillip recorded that half the population of the Sydney area died of chickenpox in the first fourteen months of settlement).[27] Over and above the outright violence of "punitive expeditions," poisonings and random shootings, there was the *cognitive violence* which eroded and largely destroyed an intact and functioning view of the world. As Aboriginal theologians have succinctly put it: "Stealing our land is murder" and amounts to "cultural genocide."[28] This raises questions of profound religious import:

> Granted that collective identity and land, whether possessed or desired, are deeply implicated with one another, how does *transcendence* bear upon the question of land, that is, upon the *immanence* of the earth? In short, what does God have to do with it? God owns the land. It is only leased, with conditions he stipulates, to the Israelites.[29]

But in the nineteenth century, Christians read the Biblical story in terms of legitimate conquest. Yet in the Biblical context, it was the actual possession of the promised land, not the promise itself or the eventual loss of the land, that raised ethical problems for the Israelites, for they were not natives but strangers:

> In the end, whether the people who generated the myth were empowered or disempowered — and making ethics contingent upon power makes a mockery of ethics as an independent court of judgment — whether they were conquerors or oppressed victims seeking liberation, they have bequeathed a myth to future generations that is ethically problematic at best, a myth that advocates the wholesale annihilation of indigenous peoples and their land.[30]

This, too, is a part of the Biblical legacy that nineteenth-century Christian settlers took to heart.

By the middle of the nineteenth century the Aboriginal birth rate had plummeted as people literally lost the will to live and the motivation to reproduce. In the area around Port Phillip "it was reported that there was an 'indifference to prolonging their race, on the ground as they state of having no country they can call their own.'"[31]

> In the area around Melbourne where European settlement was greatest William Thomas, Assistant Protector for the Westernport District, reported that for the six months from 1 September 1841 to 1 March 1842 there were no births in his District. In the years that followed he noticed that few children were born and these "seldom lived one month." In June 1845 only one child remained of those born in the preceding six years: "one chief has acknowledged to me," he wrote, "that he has no power to stop it [infanticide]; the blacks say, 'no country, no good have it pickanineys' [babies]."[32]

It is time to ask ourselves how we react to this story ("we" meaning both Europeans and Euro-Australians and Americans). If we are honest, I suggest that we will find ourselves saying that it is all very tragic, but understandable in view of the mentality of the time. But to what extent is *their* time *our* time; how much of their mentality do we still share? These nineteenth-century Christians were "enlightened," and their knowledge of and dedication to the gospel were at least as great those of contemporary Christians. There may well be lessons to be learned from their failure. Let us see if we can understand Aboriginal religion any better than they.

2. The Resilience of Aboriginal Religion

The memory is only now being retrieved of just how tenaciously Aboriginal groups in many parts of Australia fought to defend their land against the incursions of whites.[33] Even more interesting is the probability that they had already developed cultural strategies to deal with their contacts with Melanesians in northern Cape York (adjacent to the Torres Strait) and with the Indonesians who regularly visited Arnhem Land (further west along the north coast) well before the "great white flood" of invasion arrived in the southeast.[34] The land was their life, and against overwhelming odds they clung to it and the stories and rituals associated with it until they were forcibly removed or, anticipating the cost of resistance, acquiesced in relocation and drowned their despair in drink. It is only now that the realization is beginning to dawn on white Australians that the land has *religious* significance for Aborigines; that although they probably never numbered more than a few hundred thousand at any one time[35] they had humanized the entire continent, covering it with a seamless web of meaning which, though invisible to whites, on the latest archaeological evidence may have endured for a hundred thousand years.[36]

For most nineteenth-century Christians, religion meant theism of a morally robust kind (unless they preferred the more abstract and rationalistic deism proposed in the previous century). In the face of what they saw as the moral depravity and infantile intelligence of the Aborigines, they could not imagine that they were dealing with anything remotely resembling "religion." The young science of anthropology, for its part, was equally incapable of seeing anything religious in Aboriginal culture, for different but related reasons. There were those — notably the German anthropologist Wilhelm Schmidt, S.V.D., — who assumed that religion, if discernible at all in such uncouth savages, would consist in faint traces of the monotheism from which all religion originally derived, and the most zealous researchers uncovered evidence of "high gods" or "supreme beings" (among them Baiame and Daramulun) on the deist pattern; but as a student of this period remarks, "the place these beings have found in anthropological literature is disproportionate to their place in Aboriginal religion."[37] It is now becoming clear that it was contacts with other cultures — Melanesian, Indonesian and European — which wrought subtle changes in the Aboriginal relationship to place, modifying their "ontology of space" by first suggesting that detachment from land and entry into historical time might be possible and giving rise to the Hero Cult in the northeast, the Fertility Mother in the northwest, and the Sky Being in the southeast.[38]

For the pioneers of anthropology such as Tylor and Frazer, the religion of "primitive" peoples remained fixated at the childish stage of evolution and was more properly categorized as "magic." Durkheim, utilizing the earliest first-hand reports of Aboriginal customs and ceremonies supplied from central Australia by Spencer and Gillen, tested his theories of the origin of society on what he took to be these "elementary forms" of religion and thus of society. Though his was "the first attempt to take Aboriginal religion seriously," he was compelled by his own theory to present Aboriginal religion as a function of society, thereby postponing for many years the fundamental insight that virtually the opposite is the case: "one might almost say that society exists for the sake of religion rather than religion for the sake of society."[39] Malinowski's functionalism, in the modified form of the structural-functionalism proposed by Radcliffe-Brown, Australia's first professor of anthropology, set the pattern for the scientific investigation of Aboriginal cultures in the first half of the twentieth century. Research was directed to the reconstruction of Aboriginal society rather than an appreciation of its meaning for Aborigines themselves.

Religiously sensitive anthropologists such as Strehlow, Elkin and Stanner were eventually able to transcend the Durkheimian premises of functionalism and to discern a non-theistic religion which, while vividly aware of transcendence and couched in terms of spirit beings, is primarily centered on Life, Land and Community as its preeminent *religious* values. Elkin was prepared to speak of Aboriginal "philosophy," Stanner to use the word "sacrament" of the Aboriginal relationship to the land.[40] This epoch-making paradigm shift opened the way towards the realization that Aboriginal religion flows through the physical landscape as the symbolic-sacramental point of contact with the deeds of ancestral beings whose emergence from a timeless state beyond yet encompassing human time established the Law and brought into being the present order of things.

Stanner called this timeless state "what many Aborigines call it in English: The Dreaming" (deriving from Spencer and Gillen's translation of the central Australian Aranda word *alcheringa*).[41] Remarking that he had never found Aboriginal words for "time" or "history," he characterized this time-beyond-time as an "everywhen." Each individual and each lineage group has a specific Dreaming, which can be symbolized by virtually any aspect of physical nature but is usually a plant or animal (which thereby falls under a taboo for the individuals concerned). In traditional culture people carried a kind of "Dreaming map" in their memories, imparted as secret-sacred knowledge at the time of initiation, which defined their relationship to a particular stretch of country and allowed them to negotiate kinship relationships with neighboring groups and rights to travel through their country. The continent was thus "a world full of signs,"[42] a "speaking land."[43]

Our present situation vis-à-vis Aboriginal religion is well summarized by Charlesworth:

> Australian Aboriginal religion is a non-theistic religion based on the sacred and sacramental character of the land, and it requires a considerable effort of mind and imagination for a European to come to grips with it.[44]

It may help us to make this effort if we remember that the mythical stories are not so much ontological statements about the nature of the universe as what the Berndts call "guides for action," distillations of traditional wisdom designed to address the perennial choice between good and evil and provide "a charter for the whole pattern of human existence."[45]

Today, we see the emergence of a post-traditional Aboriginal culture which calls itself "Aboriginality" (comparable perhaps to the *négritude* of West Africa or the "black consciousness" of South Africa) and is coming to terms with a more mobile urban lifestyle. According to Swain, "it seems Aborigines today increasingly define Aboriginality in terms of *how* they relate to land rather than *to which* lands they are related. Theirs is a *sense* of place rather than a *knowledge* of their specific site."[46] The tough political battles over land rights, better health care and humane treatment in prisons have brought about a new sense of emancipation and self-confidence. This is producing Aboriginal literature, including theology. But before we proceed to a brief review of this, we need to pause and take stock of our position as European Christians with regard to this remarkable story of apparent cultural eclipse and unexpected renewal. Now that we are painfully learning to decipher the meaning of Aboriginal religion, can *we* — *may* we, Europeans and Australians with our historical responsibility for the Aboriginal tragedy — transpose that meaning into Christian theology in a wider ecumenical context?

3. Confronting the Primal Other

The Australian priest-archaeologist Eugene Stockton is surely not far wrong when he says that the arrival of Europeans in Australia initiated "the most severe culture clash in history."[47] The scale of the physical violence may have been greater in Latin America or East Africa, but in the case of the Aborigines the cognitive violence was extreme, the cultural incompatibility almost incalculable. Even if we allow for the extraordinary situation in which Europeans from distant islands of the North Atlantic found themselves, we must ask what lay at the root of their failure to comprehend. In particular, where was their implicit or explicit Christian theology deficient in ways that might still have something to teach us? Can we probe the subconscious depths of their dilemma and learn something about our own relationship to "primal" religion — which is, after all, in some sense *our* religion, the way in which the vast majority of humankind *is* religious?[48]

We begin to discern a dialectic of "sameness" and "otherness": in the nineteenth century, the European urge was to make what was different the *same* as us and what we are used to; today, in an era variously termed "post-modern" and "post-colonial," we are happier to assert the uniqueness of what is *other* as a rationale for incompatibility and incommunicability, thereby absolving ourselves from trying to establish a relationship. In reacting as they did to Aboriginal reality as they perceived it, the colonists, I suggest, were encountering *themselves*, but to a degree of "otherness" greater than they could cope with. Their inability to acknowledge this "other" as in some sense an undiscovered, repressed or forgotten dimension of themselves very soon led them to project their terror of it onto the Aborigines — and the land itself — in the form of naked aggression and destruction. There are testimonies by Aborigines who preserved the memory of what the encounter looked like from their side which reveal their moral outrage at these strange beings who were as helpless as children in a land where sustenance abounded, yet would listen to no advice and lashed out vengefully at every Aboriginal protest against their wanton selfishness:

> When whites first came to this land ... they did not come to it as proper human beings. They came in here bloodthirsty. They fought their way across the whole island of Australia. The missionaries, also, who took up positions here — they were not real Christians because most had hatred in their hearts for the Aboriginal people. When I think back over the stories of my grandfather and great-grandfather, I know the whites did not have love in their hearts.[49]

It has taken two centuries for this irreparable hurt to begin to be understood. Once again, the contribution Aboriginal theologians could have made was stifled:

> Jesus was thrust down my throat. I was not encouraged to think for myself or allow a theology to grow from within me as an Aboriginal. I had to get rid of the "dependency baggage." I was told what to do, what to think, where to live. I was not free. I now need to think things through, to feel my

own needs, work through my own faith, and develop my own Aboriginal theology.[50]

It is only now beginning to be appreciated that this task "is literally a matter of life and death," that "the tragedy of many Aboriginal communities" has a direct relationship to the "deep spiritual crisis" brought about by "a deep sense of shame, a lack of worth and a feeling of being lost" as a result of "the approach of many missionaries and the attitude of non-indigenous Australians in general."[51]

White Australian artists have begun to fathom the depths of this psychic "first contact."[52] Their imaginative encounters with the primal Other invite the criticism that they are "appropriating" Aboriginal culture and spirituality for "therapeutic" use as a cure or complement for supposed crises and deficiencies in white Australian consciousness, thereby colonizing the land and its people imaginatively all over again.[53] But they also invite Euro-Australian theologians, for the first time, to embark on a true *dialogue* with Aboriginal religion in which the Enlightenment sensibility of the European Christian confronts the repressed and forgotten "archaic Other," the "cosmic religion" which, though it lacks virtually all the characteristics of European civilization, may turn out to be crucial for humanity's survival.[54]

To take just two examples, Eugene Stockton reminds all "new Australians" that they are "grafted like a branch on to a living mature stock," the native gum tree of Aboriginal culture, which implies "not only participating in the social, political and economic life of the nation, but also a deliberate effort, a sort of spiritual conversion — what I have elsewhere described as 'coming home to this land.' "[55] Aboriginal religion still holds in readiness a "spiritual gift" which could make the once so self-confident "lucky country" from a merely "clever country" into a "wise country."[56]

Frank Fletcher sets out to create

> a framework that, whilst it includes the outer Euro-Australian history of social policies and of cultures, also seeks to understand the inner "soul" story that has accompanied them. In that framework I discern that the inner story reveals an affliction of soul, and that this affliction of soul ties in closely with the historical treatment of the Aborigines.[57]

The pre-modern European culture of the settlers, particularly the Irish, whose "spirituality depended broadly upon participation-in-nature for its sense of the sacred and the spiritual," retreated into self-consciously conceptual assertions of orthodoxy in the new minority situation, isolated far from home and roots. Fletcher calls this the "sealing off of the primal by the modern colonial mentality," which "has been at a price, the sense of loss affecting both psyche and spirituality":

In so far as the sense of the sacred and of spiritual influences were felt in the land, and in so far as such were connected with the Aborigines, they were treated with suspicion and often condemned as pagan.[58]

As a result,

The early settlers were unready culturally and psychically for the depths where the *Tremendum* awaited them in this land, the numinous snake beneath the waterhole ready to arch up into the clouds to bring earth and heaven together. The affliction of the Euro-Australian soul has been in the ongoing frustration of the primal sacredness, the loss of the earth-heaven passion. As such we remain still colonialist strangers in dread of the Mystery that is here.[59]

In the words of Denis Edwards, we are all "in apprenticeship to the Aboriginal view of the land."[60]

What of the Aborigines themselves? What did they "internalize" apart from the oppression they suffered?[61] On the burnt-out stump of their culture the fresh shoots of new growth are appearing. The pope's phrase in his speech at Alice Springs, "you have endured the flames," has become a catch-cry among Aboriginal activists. The immemorial rock carvings and cave paintings, the body and bark decorations have been successfully transposed from traditional ceremonies to more durable media such as acrylic paint and screen printing. Though by no means all levels of meaning in these paintings are disclosed to whites, "Aborigines appear more adept at expressing themselves in painting than in words, when it comes to deeply felt convictions."[62] The poetry of Oodgeroo Noonuccal (Kath Walker) has compelled the attention of Australians for decades, but now there are vigorous new voices such as Bill Nedjie, whose *Story About Feeling* is widely read by concerned Australians, as is Sally Morgan's autobiography *My Place*. In theology, the patient work of the Anglican and Uniting Churches at Nungalinya College near Darwin has produced leaders such as Bishop Arthur Malcolm and Moderator Djiniyini Gondarra, who have been able to interpret the religious significance of land rights claims and the Christian revivalism among northern Aborigines to white Australian Christians.[63] Patrick Dodson, the first Aboriginal Catholic priest, who left the Church to become a key figure in Aboriginal politics, has made a powerful theological interpretation of the religious basis of land rights.[64] Miriam Rose Ungunmerr, an Aboriginal Catholic artist, besides giving us Aboriginal stations of the cross which have become a subject of meditation for many Australian Christians, has beautifully explained an Aboriginal term for contemplation, *dadirri*, as "listening to the stillness" in order to learn the language of the sacred land.[65]

It has been claimed that there is a higher proportion of Aboriginal people actively engaged in "publishable theological reflection" than whites.[66] Aboriginal theology still bears the conservative stamp given it by missionary teaching, which is sometimes expressed in evangelistic or Pentecostal revival movements.[67] But a "story-telling theology" is also developing, "a non-western, non-intellectualized model of teaching transcendent truths about creation and life."[68] It will be a test of the authenticity of Euro-Australian reflection on Aboriginal identity that it practice *dadirri*, attentive listening, towards these newly articulate voices of Aboriginal Christians. In this way we may yet be able to receive the rejected gift of Aboriginal spirituality and achieve "a breakthrough, out of the ordinary, where the soul is brought to a spiritual experience for which the land is a sacrament."[69] One of the most striking evidences of this is the *Rainbow Spirit Theology* which "affirms our past spirituality as the work of the Creator Spirit" in the conviction that "God was already speaking to us through the law revealed in the land."[70]

Appreciating the challenge presented by this encounter is difficult for Europeans in much the same way that psychological counseling or psycho-analysis is difficult: one can no longer take refuge in generalities! One must confront oneself in all one's particularity, minus the masks, and face the memories one would prefer to leave buried; in short, one must see one's "self" *as Other*. Now that Aboriginals at last have a voice in the public sphere, Euro-Australians hear the repressed primal Other speaking back, proclaiming an unfamiliar and unwelcome version of Western selfhood. We are able to gauge the depth of the hurt and anger caused by the attitude of "assimilation," which justified the removal of children from their families and people from their land and obliterated memories of language and culture. It is no exaggeration to call this attempted genocide:

> The Australian practice of indigenous child removal involved both systematic racial discrimination and genocide as defined by international law. Yet it continued to be practiced as official policy long after being clearly prohibited by treaties to which Australia had voluntarily subscribed.[71]

The policy contravened the rights of the child and of indigenous peoples, the right to minimum standards of health care and the right to retain culture, religion and identity, among others.[72] It has been described as a "systematic attempt at social and biological engineering," willingly aided by Christians who saw their cooperation as a work of charity: " . . . the inculcation of Christian 'moral values' was seen [by the government] as a way of promoting assimilation."[73] The Aborigines bitterly resisted the policy of assimilation and in the end frustrated it, just as they never agreed to the dispossession of their land and defended it by every means at their disposal. The policy flowed directly from racist assumptions of European (and Christian) moral and cultural superiority. Aboriginal children of mixed descent had to be "protected" from "contamination" by their own culture and "assimilated" to the European way of life; the paler their skins, the more likely they were to be selected for this "privilege." They realized very early what was being done to them:

> You have almost exterminated our people, but there are enough of us remaining to expose the humbug of your claim, as white Australians, to be a civilized, progressive, kindly and humane nation.... If you would openly admit that the purpose of your Aborigines Legislation has been, and now is, to exterminate the Aborigines completely... we could describe you as brutal, but honest. But you dare not admit openly that what you hope and wish for is our death! You hypocritically claim that you are trying to "protect" us; but your modern policy of "protection" (so-called) is killing us off just as surely as the pioneer policy of giving us poisoned damper and shooting us down like dingoes![74]

The legal basis for regulating the lives, breaking up the families and removing the children of Aboriginal people was, and still is, welfare. Poverty is taken to mean neglect; Aboriginality is regarded as being synonymous with irresponsibility:

> ...being Aboriginal was in itself reason to regard children as "neglected." Even on the rare occasions when officials did not regard Aboriginal culture with contempt and fear, the emphasis on marriage and having fixed housing and employment in definitions of "neglect" was inherently biased towards seeing all Aboriginal family life as neglectful.[75]

The stories told in the report *Bringing Them Home* of "the attacks inflicted on our hearts, minds, bodies and souls, by caretakers who thought their mission was to eliminate us as Aboriginals"[76] bear witness to the depths of the deprivation involved:

> It's all the non-material stuff I don't have — the lineage. It's like you're the first human being at times. You know, you've just come out of nowhere, there you are....[77]

Those who survived are known as the "stolen generations":

> I guess the most traumatic thing for me is that, though I don't like missionaries being criticized — the only criticism I have is that you forbade us to speak our own language and we had no communication with our family.... Once that language was taken away, we lost a part of that very soul. It meant our culture was gone, our family was gone, everything that was dear to us was gone.[78]

> We didn't know anything about our culture. We were completely brain-
> washed to think only like a white person.... They were simply a lost
> generation of children. I know. I was one of them.[79]
>
> I didn't know any Aboriginal people at all — none at all.... How can
> you be proud of being Aboriginal after all the humiliation and the anger
> and the hatred you have?[80]

The results of this misguided policy, actively supported by the Christian churches,
include "genealogical bewilderment," the fear of unwittingly committing incest
because kinship relationships are no longer known; the loss of any basis for claims
to native land title; catastrophic mental and psychological effects; and consequent
low standards of health coupled with rates of imprisonment 26 times the average
for non-indigenous Australians.[81]

Though the more radical Aboriginal activists campaign for a treaty with white
Australia as a recognition of their sovereignty as a First Nation, Aborigines
are generally less interested in reparations than in a simple apology for what
was done.[82] The churches have gone a long way towards admitting that they
were "unconsciously complicit"[83] in disinheriting Aborigines, "... that the church
thought it was acting in a loving way by providing them [Aboriginal children]
with homes, but was blind to the racist assumptions that underlay the policy and
the practice."[84] "With the wisdom of hindsight we can only wonder how as a
nation, and as a Church, we failed to see the violence of what we were doing."[85]
The thirteen member churches of the National Council of Churches in Australia
have endorsed the *Bringing Them Home* report:

> Christians must try to understand what happened from the perspective
> of the Christian faith. As church leaders, we commit ourselves to reflect
> theologically on the trauma experienced by the Stolen Generations and by
> the nation as a whole, and on our calling to be bearers of reconciliation.[86]

The challenge now is to unearth the full unpleasant truth about the past, work for
the human rights and land rights of Aboriginal people, construct a new theology
in collaboration with Aboriginal theologians, cooperate in making church records
available, and demand an official apology and reparations.

Confronting the pain of the stolen generations are the hostility and resentment of many whites, who do not feel themselves responsible for past and present
atrocities and do not want to be reminded of them. It seems obvious to me that
this confrontation has a psycho-social dimension which must be addressed by
both sides *together* if there is to be any hope of national reconciliation and healing as the prerequisite to a treaty (*makarrata*) between the people of Australia

and the Aboriginal "First Nation." This would demand a public apology by the government for past atrocities and effective redress for present injustices, including some form of land rights based on Aboriginal relationships to the Land as sacred.[87] Strictly speaking, nothing can or may be compared with the *Shoah*, the Nazi Holocaust of European Jewry; but it may be permissible to make the point that for Australians, coming to terms with the atrocities perpetrated on the Aborigines and the land that was their life is something like the moral equivalent of European Christianity's responsibility to the Jews.

This brings us to the threshold of theology, which must go even deeper than psychology. The dialogue with Aboriginal religion and spirituality as expressions of the "primal Other" which is unique in its integrity yet constitutive of all humanity must first of all be internalized, must become — in Raimon Panikkar's felicitous phrase — "*intra*-religious dialogue." The recognition of Aboriginal otherness implies critique of European completeness. Really listening to the "discourse of the others" means the end of European intellectual sovereignty, for the Others, borrowing from the West but drawing mainly on their own resources, *have* succeeded in surviving humanly and socially and in shaping and reshaping those "universes of meaning" or "webs of significance" which have allowed them to live meaningful lives and survive the encounter with an alien culture. But Aboriginal humanity is not *absolutely* "other," nor have a century and a half of "assimilation" made Aboriginal culture in any fundamental way the "same" as European. Neither Aboriginal nor European can lay absolute claim on transcendence, on what Emmanuel Levinas calls "the Infinite," which transcends yet relates both. From the point of their meeting on, whether they like it or not, they are in relationship, and henceforth the Infinite is mediated to them *both* by the quality of that relationship. The short cut of the one's reducing the other to "the same as us" or "incompatible with us" is no longer available to either.

Lest we imagine that only European thought is capable of constructing a "basis" for dialogue in this way, let it be remembered that Aboriginal religion had a profound sense of transcendence (in Stanner's view it was one of the most transcendent of all religions) and a practice of something like mystical contemplation (*dadirri*). The difficulty it presents to Europeans is the essentially aesthetic quality of its awareness, the mythic consciousness embodied in the metaphorical structures of its stories, the forms of its music and dancing and the symbolism of its art. Our problem as Europeans is that we do not begin to understand the levels of meaning in these. If we did, there is evidence that we would find experiences of transcendence, principles of morality and orderings of society which *in and of themselves*, without any well-meaning condescension as from "developed" world religions towards "primitive" primal religion, deserve to be listened to with the utmost seriousness as ways of completing what other traditions lack. Aboriginal religion *is* world religion, one of the "ways along the path to peace and order" with its distinctive "methodology of accessing the non-discursive."[88]

What European Christians need to consider is the loss to all humanity if this consciousness is finally obliterated, and the moral and theological implications for Christianity, regarded as "superior" because it allied itself with the historical "winners," if it can be shown to have been implicated in the obliteration. It has been the burden of this chapter that in such a case not only would something of our (European) selves and our relationship to nature be irreparably damaged at the very time when we are beginning to realize the universal importance of this relationship, but also that our moral claim to formulate the ethic that would secure universal peace would be compromised from the outset. As the incipient and tentative European-Aboriginal collaboration on constructing an Australian theology indicates, this questioning may extend to the most basic levels of Christian symbolization and conceptualization, to doctrines such as creation and incarnation, and to the relationship between symbol and concept itself.[89] If Christianity is ever to break loose from its European captivity, the Aboriginal contribution will be pivotal, but by the same token it is also extremely vulnerable. If this "spiritual gift" that has been spurned for so long is ultimately rejected, we must ask whether we are morally justified in continuing to assert the "universality" of our tradition and its claim to ecumenical relevance. The supposition that we are entitled to "usc" Aboriginal religion for some larger purpose must itself be subjected to moral scrutiny. This way of thinking does violence to the integrity of Aboriginal religion and runs the risk of overlooking its intrinsic potential for non-violence. The problem thus becomes one of form rather than content: perhaps "universalist" Christianity can supply to "particularist" Aboriginal religion not so much alternative core beliefs and moral attitudes but a medium in which those of Aboriginal religion can be communicated ecumenically to a wider humanity.

The Christian encounter with the "other" is no longer exclusively subject to European definitions of this encounter. In the words of the Rainbow Spirit Elders:

> In the past, unfortunately, we allowed the European missionaries, who did not know our culture, to determine what was alien to the Christian faith within our culture.... The time has come for Aboriginal, not Western, Christians to identify both the good and the bad in our traditional culture, and discover where our God is in our recent experiences of oppression. It is also important that we ... identify those features of European and Western Christianity which have alienated us from the very Gospel the missionaries were preaching.[90]

Our study of the relationship between transcendence and violence thereby takes a first step towards identifying the problem that will preoccupy us as we proceed. Aboriginal resources for resistance to injustice and reconciliation of conflict initially owed nothing to Christian theology or European humanism. The Aborigines' route from an ontology of space into historical time may be a two-way street leading us Europeans back to a lost immediacy with the self and the earth, our repressed Archaic Other. Can this route be traveled without illegitimate appropriation, cognitive violence and the colonization of culture? In each and every case, the quality of the relationship to the alien Other becomes a moral test of the relationship to the Infinite variously symbolized by the religious traditions, whether Aboriginal or European. To what extent do our mutual "horizontal" relationships depend on such "vertical" relationships to the transcendent? How does the transcendence apparent in the contemplative side of Aboriginal cultures — the Dreaming, *dadirri* — differ from the "absolutist" transcendence of Christian faith as expressed in doctrines such as incarnation and revelation? Can these be a hidden source of violence, as seems to have been the case in the encounter with the Aborigines? The following study of the comparable but significantly different Christian encounter with Melanesian cultures may shed further light on these questions.

Chapter Two

INITIATION INTO THE FUTURE

Christianity and Modernity in Melanesia

When I mentioned to Garry Trompf, a well-known Australian Melanesianist who had spent many years in Papua New Guinea, that I was going to start working there in 1983, he exclaimed: "It's the most exciting country on earth!" And so it is. Though it is also probably the most evangelized country on earth and had a relatively straightforward passage to independence in 1975, it is wracked by social tensions, ethnic differences and regional disputes. Though its mountains, forests and seas are rich in natural resources, its natural environment is under threat and the island of Bougainville was devastated for eight years by a guerilla war of secession over the huge copper mine at Panguna. Papua New Guinea's political system is riddled with patronage, yet it is a functioning, if colorful, democracy. In my four and a half years there I cannot remember one single day when I did not learn something new about our common humanity.

Because of the inhabitants' dark skins but also, perhaps, because of their menacing aspect, the islands to the north west of Fiji were given the collective name Melanesia ("the black islands") by the explorer Dumont d'Urville in 1832, and the term has been inherited by ethnologists.[1] These islands seemed to form a striking contrast to the parts of the Pacific thus far discovered by Europeans, for the individual peoples, not unlike the Celts in Europe, had scarcely ever come together to form overarching or hierarchical political structures. In the heartland of the largest island, the highlands of New Guinea, there were neither hereditary chiefs nor priests. Leadership, whether in war or peace, fell to the ablest, and when they failed it was taken from them. Ritual warfare had made these peoples virtually impervious to one another, and their languages and cultural peculiarities deviated sharply.[2] Nevertheless they maintained trade routes such as the Kula Ring in the New Guinea islands and the Moka Ring in the highlands. Along the Papuan coast and between the coasts and the highlands, too, trade was carried on. Canoes are mentioned in the myths of some highland peoples, and even today shells are highly prized among them as *bilas* or decoration. It is now thought that the ancestors of the present-day Melanesians occupied the main island of New

Guinea as long as fifty thousand years ago, and they were among the first human beings to discover gardening some nine thousand years ago. Their religious practices, inasmuch as they can be distinguished from everyday living, are not directed towards bringing about the intervention of high gods, but at tapping the sources of *gutpela sindaun,* the good life in all its dimensions.

The encounter with Christianity in the persons of white missionaries had an irreversible impact on all the peoples of Melanesia. For Melanesian Christians the existential question is not the dialogue of European denominations but how to live their new faith while preserving their cultural identity as they face the social and ecological problems which inevitably accompany modernity. At an equally fundamental level they are asking "how much 'harmless' or non-violent plurality can be tolerated within Melanesian nations, and which actions are to be taken when divisions fester into the worst forms of negative payback,"[3] as they have recently in Papua New Guinea, West Papua, East Timor, the Solomon Islands and Fiji. For Pacific Islanders economics and politics are preeminently "religious" matters; in the everyday life of modernizing societies this becomes most apparent in the search for humanly responsible "development."

Melanesian Christians, in particular, have at times been preoccupied with the missions and their history, especially their own experiences with missionaries.[4] The verdict is ambivalent. The great missionaries are honored, and in some cases they have already been incorporated into legend as quasi-mythical figures. But the residue of resentment is unmistakable. There is no doubt that individual missionaries lorded it over the people and failed or refused to understand their customs. In the end, however, that is not what counts. The basic problem has more to do with the deeply felt foreignness of the whites and their ways together with the overwhelming superiority of the technical side of their culture. For Pacific peoples, this is closely bound up with an underlying spiritual power (*mana* in Polynesia, *paua* in Melanesia). Have the whites really revealed the secret of this power, or have they withheld it, as the Islanders themselves would do with their ritual secrets? This is probably the most basic question of all Melanesian theology. As long as this suspicion remains the people see no reason why they should disclose the secret mysteries from which they draw life, even if this means that their secrets die with them. How can this mutual mistrust be broken down, thus initiating a real dialogue? Once again we are faced with the task of trying to understand why the "village-Christian dialogue"[5] had so much trouble getting started in Melanesia.

This is the setting in which we must try to understand the reactions of Melanesians to the European Christian presence using their own cultural forms of expression (section 1). These in turn have implications for economic and political development, which became manifest in the "cargo cults" (section 2), and they also present to nascent Melanesian theology the challenge of coping with unequal development and its potential for violence by reconciling the "logic of retribution" intrinsic to their own cultures with the eschatological vision of redemption transmitted by Christianity (section 3).

1. Myth and Magic:
World Construction and Social Discernment

The Australian Aborigines seem to move through their country as through a mythic landscape with which they, their human interrelationships and their moral dramas are organically one.[6] In Melanesia, whose peoples are digging-stick cultivators rather than hunter-gatherers, the politics of land use interpose themselves, and in some cases there is an ever-present threat of being driven out of one's ancestral territory by recurrent tribal fighting, especially where population density makes land scarce and boundary disputes readily give rise to conflict. In a heavily populated region such as the Enga in the western highlands of Papua New Guinea it is therefore little wonder that the spirits of the forest can be antagonistic and the spirits of the dead must be scrupulously placated.[7] The ordering of relationships in the community (village, clan) thus becomes a matter of crucial importance, for each social group is in effect a tightly organized survival unit, directly dependent on its success in wresting a livelihood from the land and linguistically and culturally sealed off from other ethnic groups (tribes).[8] The coherence of the community, the custody of ritual secrets and the demonstration of wealth and power thus become moral and political priorities of the first order.[9]

Not only the living belong to this community, but also the spirits of the ancestors (*tumbuna*) and of nature (*masalai*). The bonds with this "meta-society,"[10] like those within the village community itself, are cemented by exchange relationships which are much more than merely economic. They are intensely human in that they form the matrix of all relationships in the life of the village, including marital and ritual ones. The instinctive attitude to life becomes: keep others in your debt. I return a gift of five coconuts by giving more: then my partner in exchange again owes me something. If someone steals five of my pigs, I make sure I find out who did it and get my own back with interest. This forms the basis of the law of retribution (*bekim* in Melanesian Pidgin, usually referred to as "payback"), which dominates all aspects of Melanesian life, the "retributive logic"[11] which determines Melanesian thinking even in its religious dimension. Missionaries tell how the Highlanders, after being told that Christ died for them, took an intensive part in church life until they judged they had paid back the debt, after which they turned their backs on the church.[12]

Just as the law of exchange regulates relationships between individuals in the villages and the clan groups and villages among one another, similar relationships hold among peoples themselves. Most prominent of all is the relationship to the land. There are certainly claims to ownership, but these must be carefully distinguished from rights to use, which have arisen traditionally and in some circumstances can acquire precedence over rights of ownership.[13] Because there is no precise boundary marking, but rather a tacit acknowledgment of the traditionally recognized rights of ownership or use, there is ample scope for conflicts over land, especially when members of one group believe that neighbors are encroaching on their area. If a member of the group is killed or injured in the course of these disputes, this must be "paid back" by killing one of the enemy's warriors or abducting one of their women. This lies completely within the logic of payback, for otherwise one would concede to one's opponents a permanent advantage, which they could then proceed to convert into increasing power over one's own people, and that would be the beginning of the end.

It would be wrong, however, to convey the impression that for this reason Melanesian life is nothing but a web of enmities and intrigues. Rather, the exchange and retribution arrangements serve the purpose of maintaining personal relationships, whether among human beings or with the spirits. Community consists in these relationships, and the well-being and ultimate survival of all depends on their being maintained. Relationships to nature and its phenomena are included in this network of I-Thou relationships, whereas in Western civilization the position is almost reversed: the I-It relationship with nature determines the relationships between human beings.[14] The perception of the body is "at one and the same time empirical, aesthetic and mythic," and it is referred to in language derived from the mineral and vegetable world.[15] The relationship to nature is thus the opposite of anthropomorphic; the characteristic absence of distance between body and world is more appropriately called "cosmomorphic."[16] The structure of the cosmos reproduces the structure of human community, and the cosmos is contained within the shared perceptual world of the social group.[17]

With this we reach the threshold of the Melanesian understanding of religion, which we will cross shortly. When I implied above that it was "right" to carry out retribution I touched on an underlying ethical principle. If the cohesion of the social group is the primary imperative of common survival, it follows that the elimination of every threat, whether internal or external, can only be "good," because this alone redounds to "our" well-being. A "big man," who has accumulated sufficient wealth and influence in the form of effective leadership, impressive oratory, pigs and women (roughly in that order!), can allow himself a great deal of license without incurring obligations to the community. If he overdraws his "credit," however, or fails to achieve the success that brings prestige to the group, he can be called to account and deposed. Malformed children and in some cases twins can be disposed of as evidence of malign intervention by hostile spirits. Sorcerers who divert their evil powers from the traditional enemies onto their own people can incur penalties, even death. Whatever furthers the good life (*gutpela sindaun*) of "our" people is morally "good"; what detracts from it is "evil."[18] One often hears it said that Melanesians are "pragmatists." But just as their "survival ethic" is closely bound up with their relationship to land, this ethic in its turn is based on a value system which lays bare the religious foundations of their cultures.

The coastal fish festival[19] or the highlands pig festival[20] is a single great celebration involving the whole community in the renewal of and participation in cosmic life. If there is any point at which one can compare and generalize Pacific religions, this is it. The Melanesians know "gods" in the sense of sky beings aloof from the world, from whom culture heroes came forth and who are prepared to call to order offended ancestors or spirits bent on evil. But the great celebrations, which are at the very heart of these peoples' lives, are not directed towards the heavenly beings nor even to the totem spirits as such, but have the purpose of symbolizing, bringing about and sharing in the overflowing life of river and ocean, forest and garden, and not least of one's own women who have a sacred responsibility for fertility and nurture. The "big man" among the Simbu or the Enga, surrounded by several wives and their rich bride price of pigs and ornaments, is in a position to organize the slaughter of staggering numbers of pigs and to distribute their meat among his people in ways that entrench his political status. He thus represents the living assurance that the sources of life remain open to his people.

This is the reason — ultimately a "religious" one — why it is absolutely necessary to maintain human relationships and those between humans and spirits, and to resolve any conflicts which may arise by initiating appropriate exchange relationships as soon as possible. The social order of the village and the kinship bonds of the clan are very closely bound up with relationships towards the "meta-village" of the spirits, and this social order is simultaneously reproduced in the cosmic order of nature. Every unusual event in nature, every sickness, every unsuccessful hunt has a personal cause and signals the imminent breakdown of the vitally important harmony with the forces of nature. Legal and social relationships are thus intertwined with cosmic.[21] In the light of this it is understandable that it took a long time for the Christian missionaries to achieve any insight into the religious dimension of Melanesian ritual and society. This is due at least as much to the anthropological deficit of nineteenth-century Western theology as to the theological illiteracy of small ethnic groups. The destruction of these societies, apart from being immoral in itself and thus an indictment of Christian ethics and Western humanism, deprives "us" — Europeans of whatever provenance — of indispensable sources for understanding how a relationship to land which cares for the earth and fulfills human beings is closely bound up with the renewal of community and thus touches the question of peace, which is becoming more acute as economic globalization fosters cultural regionalization and societies become more multicultural.[22] The "transcendent" aspect of Melanesian religion, we begin to realize, must be sought not in abstract concepts or moral ideals but in the immediacy of intra- and inter-group relationships. Not only do these relationships always have a cosmic reference, they also incorporate skilful techniques for conflict resolution and peacemaking.

The ubiquity of magic in the cultures of the South Pacific and its obvious power over people is at the root of the accusation — which causes many problems in education, development and health work — that their mythical view of the world is fundamentally irrational. In the nineteenth century anthropologists distinguished sharply between "mere" magic as a lower stage of development, and the higher stage of "genuine" religion, and peoples were assigned to one or other according to exclusively European criteria.[23] On the other hand, magic is indeed incompatible with the "hard" empirical sciences on which our technological civilization is based. It simply has no place in the worldview of modernity (which is possibly one of the reasons for the emergence of "post-modernity"), yet for the Melanesian cultures of the South Pacific in the missionary period it was all-determining. Our task is to make intelligible how magic in its original social context, as an expression of the mythic consciousness, is just as "rational" as modern science in its quite different context.

If we think in terms of a society which includes the "meta-community" of the spirits it becomes apparent that magic is a medium of social communication and control, a means of resolving conflicts and establishing rights. Patrick Gesch calls magic "a process of social discernment,"[24] which includes both normative and cognitive elements, and for Mary MacDonald it is

> a dramatic statement, sometimes tragic, sometimes comic, about the nature of life and how to share most things in life. Magic appears in Melanesia as a complex symbol of life pervading both the ordinary and the more significant events of life. In this sense magic may be regarded as the characteristic form of religion in Melanesia.[25]

Melanesians know how to distinguish between "good" and "evil" magic, and sorcerers who no longer operate within the tight social network of tribal society can do a great deal of harm.[26]

It is noticeable how often the word "life" occurs in the quotation from Mary MacDonald. The central significance of magic throughout the Pacific is closely bound up with the all-determining reality of all-encompassing Life. The rituals employed routinely in fishing and hunting, tending the garden or making love are meant to increase Life, and when Life is in any way threatened people's thoughts turn to sorcery. "Any life-threatening illness . . . is attributed to the aggression of people or spirits," and this holds always and without exception.[27] Concepts such as "accident" or "objective cause" play a very subordinate role in the Melanesian view of the world. More than once Melanesians explained to me that when people suffer harm or when even slightly unusual sicknesses occur the relevant question is not "*What* was the cause?" but "*Who* was the cause?." The imperative of maintaining the tribal group in existence, of sustaining the Life manifested in the community imposes the unconditional demand to find an unambiguous answer to this question. Somewhere someone has broken a taboo or a relationship. The fundamental task of the sorcerer is to act as the antenna of the community and discover the identity of the person concerned, whether human or spirit. The law of retribution then demands that there be "payback." The consensus of those concerned is that these are moral necessities; "laws of nature" and "objective proof" play no part. It is not hard to imagine how this system of social control functioned in intact tribal societies. It is the cause of considerable difficulties, however, when it continues to function alongside Western medicine and jurisprudence without any attempt being made to mediate the mythic and the modern worldviews.[28]

What matters in the end for Pacific people is control of that power (*paua* in Melanesia, *mana* in Polynesia) which enables them to shield their communities from harm and overcome the hostile power of evil spirits and hereditary enemies. The magic necessary for this is the people's most precious secret, closely guarded by the men and kept even from their own women, for even they constitute a threat because of the dark powers connected with menstrual blood in the coming into being of new life. In the practice of magic under the presuppositions of the mythic view of the world lies the most sensitive point of contact with Christian faith. In this perspective, what Christians call "salvation" is perhaps best epitomized as "wholeness" (both are translated by the German word *Heil*).

Wholeness, in this sense, does not suggest any dichotomy between "material" and "spiritual" realms, for human beings and spirits maintain active relationships which include the land and the life of the natural world. The individual cannot experience this wholeness independently of the community in which he or she lives.[29] Wholeness — or, in Christian terms, "salvation" — is mediated by *lo* (derived from, but more comprehensive than, "law") which means meeting all the demands of harmonious life in community. The *bikman* ("big man" or clan leader) not only watches out to see that this happens, he takes care that the potential of *lo* is fully exploited for the well-being of all, especially by means of the great festivals, which strengthen exchange relationships and demonstrate overflowing life. Of the one who participates fully in all this it can be said: *I stap stret*, he or she fulfills all obligations, with the result for the individual and the whole community that *I stap gut, I gat bel isi, I gat gutpela sindaun*, harmony and prosperity reign. Should someone destroy relationships, however — *kalapim lo* — there result *sin* or *rong* together with *wari* and *sem*, feelings of unease because members of the group as well as the spirits have been angered.[30] It is here that Melanesians seek the causes of *sik*, illness. Melanesian Christians have been able to make the connection between the concept of *lo* and the New Testament vision of the Kingdom of God.[31] Because of their understanding of *lo*, however, Melanesians are inclined to think of God as an angry, jealous and vengeful master who can be influenced by keeping his commandments and the use of ritual. Sin is understood as infringing a taboo or making a mistake in performing a rite. The central New Testament idea of justification by grace alone is completely absent, as is the conviction that relationships could be an end in themselves rather than a means to obtain the good life — salvation — from God.[32] And yet, since the very first contact with the whites, there is a kind of holy restlessness among the people of Melanesia, a strained anticipation of a healing and wholeness which, as conceived by their cultures, would go far beyond mere curative medicine or economic development. If they have to come to terms with this strange new world which has broken in upon them unbidden, then they want the whole story, the whole "secret," the ritual magic that must lie behind such phenomenal material success. They do not want crumbs from the master's table, but the right to partake of the same meal, and without delay. If the secret turns out to be connected with the Christian faith, then they expect its representatives to solve the riddle. Even when they have arrived at the insight that Christian faith means much more than this, and after having adopted it in all seriousness through conversion and renewal, they insert it into their fundamentally different worldview and demand more than just hymns and doctrines. But this worldview itself has been changed considerably in reaction to its penetration by Western civilization. Its expectations and plausibility structures, even its underlying values, remain relatively untouched, but the cosmos of conscious experience and acquired knowledge has expanded and become many-sided and many-leveled. Far from being "passive" or "static," this worldview turns out to be dynamic, resilient and adaptable.[33] In turning to the manifestations of these tensions throughout the period of white contact, which have become world famous under the misleading name "cargo cults," we realize that we are no longer concerned with the anthropological preliminaries to Melanesian theology but are directly engaging with it.

2. The Cult of "Cargo" as Rite of Passage

At about the same time as the first contacts with white colonial officials and missionaries and — with interruptions and regional variations — right up to the present, indigenous popular movements have been recorded in all parts of Melanesia which were a cause of concern and dismay to the authorities, whether colonial or post-colonial.[34] These movements seemed to have something to do with deep-seated expectations (dubbed "millenarian hopes" by those who suspected the influence of biblical instruction by missionaries) that the cargoes disgorged from ships and planes were really destined for the peoples of Melanesia, if only they could fulfill certain conditions and recognize certain signs. The movements therefore received the quite misleading name "cargo cults," thereby depriving social scientists of an apt description for the consumer societies of the West, whose technological and economic frenzy can be seen as an attempt to compensate for the loss of their spiritual roots.[35] The term, which was no doubt supposed to connote the "materialism of the primitives," has only a limited application to the actual phenomena in Melanesia. The most common assumption was that the people were in the grip of some lunatic frenzy; one of the first such movements to be studied by the government anthropologist in Papua entered history as the Vailala Madness.[36] Observers were inclined to put these phenomena down to the psychic instability of the primitives. Later interpretations saw in them prototypes of Western economic and political structures and apostrophized them as emancipation and adjustment movements.[37] The missionaries rarely took any interest in the movements over and above disciplinary action and moral condemnation. It took a long time before any of the whites were in a position to recognize their religious core.

This was unfortunate, because the real beginnings of Melanesian Christian theology lie precisely here, in what Pat Gesch calls the "village-Christian dialogue" with the cult movements.[38] Pastors and seminary students repeatedly assured me that concerns close to the hearts of their fellow-Christians were more likely to be expressed in the village context, often with cargoist overtones, than in the conscientious sermons of evangelists or the dutiful dissertations of seminarians, even if the cults are officially regarded in church circles as works of the devil. Even where they have died out as cult movements, they have bequeathed what John Strelan called a "cargoist mentality" to significant sections of economic, administrative and political life. In the modern sector this subterranean presence of the cults causes problems, but the Melanesians have their own agenda with different priorities. It is necessary to decipher this hidden agenda, for otherwise Christian faith and Melanesian culture will only appear to be in dialogue without ever really engaging.

We have already seen that for most Pacific Islanders, to enter into a relation-ship is to set up a pattern of exchanges. We have also been able to picture just how traumatic the first contacts with white explorers, convicts, traders and colo-nial officials were, especially for Melanesians. But after the initial fear and shock had given way to curiosity and the prospect of political or economic advantages, people were naturally interested in forming relationships with the newcomers. Even at this early stage, however, fateful misunderstandings arose. The Islanders were happy to exchange with the Europeans for the few baubles offered by the whites the right to use certain pieces of land, without being able to imagine why the Europeans understood that the land itself had been transferred to their ownership.[39] Once buildings had been erected and plantations laid out, the men indentured as laborers and the women driven from their villages and gardens, the people were appalled. Confronted with the full panoply of white colonization, what could they offer in order to balance the already distorted relationship? What were they to make of the ever more oppressive superiority of these beings, who had at their disposal apparently unlimited quantities of all imaginable commodi-ties, which unerringly found their way to the white masters from the bellies of their ships?

The whites usually left the Islanders in no doubt that they regarded them as inferior, and this attitude is still perceptible today, especially in business circles. Not even missionaries were always able to keep their Western feelings of supe-riority and their evangelical mandate in balance. They too sometimes reached decisions without taking any account of the indigenous people who were affected by them. There was always something to criticize about the people's customs. Some Europeans proceeded as if the natives counted for nothing, and that is the way many Islanders soon came to see themselves. There was an urgent need to discover the meaning of this primordial event, the arrival of the whites, and to take control of it, otherwise their fate was sealed. It is important to make clear that they aimed at no less than this. From the very beginning all their efforts were bent towards discovering the secret of the whites' supremacy. They could only conceive of such an undertaking by integrating the new reality of the whites' world into the framework of their myths, so that they could detect clues to the appropriate rites which would allow them to influence it.

A myth widely dispersed along the north coast of New Guinea and the islands to the northeast played an important role in the search.[40] It tells of two brothers, Manub and Kilibob, who are in strife because one tries to seduce the other's wife (the roles are reversed in different versions). The cleverer brother sets off in his canoe, visiting islands and avoiding reefs, and creates tools and fruits for the people as he goes along, while the slower brother remains behind. The arrival of the whites — triggered by Mikloucho-Maclay's landing on the Rai Coast south of

Madang, the very heartland of the myth's distribution — immediately suggested an interpretation: the cleverer brother, who was often portrayed as being white, had finally returned from beyond the horizon, i.e., from the land of the ancestors, bringing gifts in abundance for his less endowed brown brothers. In other words, people were firmly convinced that the whites' goods were theirs by right. Why then did the whites persistently refuse to share them with the indigenes? Why did they frustrate every attempt to enter into appropriate exchange relationships?

To that there could only be one answer: because of their stupidity the descendants of the brown brother had forgotten or overlooked the rituals which, it went without saying, were essential for gaining access to the cargo. It therefore became an urgent necessity for the people to discover these rituals, which had been kept secret by the whites. In the framework of the "rationality of magic" explored above, this train of thought is perfectly logical. Whenever the people's frustrations and tensions at being excluded from the new era became unbearable, "social experiments" were carried out in order to find the ritual that would bring about the breakthrough into the world of the whites. These were the "cargo cults." They represented an enormous intellectual effort in a cultural context in which thinking assumes communal and ritual forms. It is true that there was usually a leader, a visionary, who created symbols for the already present yearnings of the people. But the movements themselves were entirely the people's own creations.

The activities that resulted could only appear absurd to the outside observer: people mimed the use of the radio or the raising of the flag, the reading of books or the drilling of recruits, hoping that in one of these practices — which must have appeared equally absurd to the Melanesians — the ritual secret lay hidden. Money, the magical totem of the whites par excellence, was buried, cooked, mixed or placed in "money machines" — red boxes or disused cash registers — in the expectation that it would increase; perhaps most significantly of all, sexual intercourse, the token of fertility and the source of prosperity, was practiced, often in cemeteries, where it could influence the spirits of the ancestors. The Mount Rurun Movement of Matias Yaliwan in the East Sepik area is one of Melanesia's classic cults.[41] Yaliwan had a tense relationship with the local Catholic Church in his village, Yangoru. Once he found a key whose religious embellishment suggested that it belonged to a tabernacle. For Yaliwan, however, this key evoked the eschatological symbolism of the Book of Revelation, and when a Catholic priest, to whom Yaliwan had given the key, refused to give it back to him, Yaliwan became convinced that an important secret was being withheld from him. His disturbed feelings crystallized around two stone markers erected on the summit of Mount Rurun by the Americans during the war, which for Yaliwan were foreign bodies intruding on the sacred mountain. The dramatic removal of the stones on 17 July 1971, which attracted attention around the Pacific, was only one chapter in Yaliwan's stubborn search for the key to the whites' secret.[42] Gesch, who has studied the movement's roots in village religion, where the central ritual was initiation, proves conclusively that Yaliwan was seeking nothing less than the rite that would initiate him into the modern world. It was Yaliwan and his followers who seized the initiative and made the attempt to understand modernity with their own cultural means — not intellectually or theoretically, but communally, in such a way that they could expect practical results for the whole people. The mutual misunderstanding between Yaliwan and the Western sector, to which he longed to have access, was total and tragic. Incitement to or membership of a cargo cult has become illegal in contemporary Papua New Guinea, but the heritage of Yaliwan and many of the other cult leaders is anything but extinguished.

The introduction of a money economy by the colonizers reduced the personal and group relationships at the heart of Melanesian economic exchanges to a purely abstract measure of exchange value utterly detached from life contexts. This value in itself becomes a "thing" which can be "owned," whereas in traditional Melanesia the land and its produce were always understood as things an individual or a group was permitted to *use* in a context of community well-being, but never to *own* as the exclusive possession of an individual. This led to many misunderstandings between Melanesians, who thought they were negotiating the temporary transfer of usufruct, and Europeans, who thought they had acquired legal title to land. It also causes serious problems for those Melanesians who operate in the Western sector today, for back in their villages there is scant respect for individual ownership of the bank accounts, homes and cars which are regarded as "private property" in the urban setting. Individual ownership brings freedom from the obligation to share generously with one's *wantoks* ("one-talks," those with whom one identifies because of language and culture), which would automatically be incurred in the village, but it also erodes the reciprocity which was the cornerstone of Melanesian social life.[43] Individual enterprise is thus shackled by the immediate imperative of sharing wealth with one's relatives and creating obligations in return for one's largesse, which is why many a trade store or transport company has gone bankrupt before it could accumulate enough capital to expand. Neither acquisition nor accumulation but redistribution and reciprocation are the watchwords of Melanesian economics. Added to this is the "cargoist mentality," which makes both business and politics in Melanesia a mixture of economic rationality and quasi-magical expectation.[44] If it is true that money, in a certain sense, secularizes and even replaces "magic," it is also seen as the "holy spirit" of the new religion of modernity.[45] The obligation of sharing to which it immediately gives rise originates as a culturally legitimate concern for the local interests of one's *wantoks*, but in both church and politics it can easily pass over into what the Europeans castigate as "corruption," leading in the end to what

Trompf calls "sophisticated techniques of dishonesty," both post-Christian and neo-traditional, which are the cause of endless controversy and conflict.[46]

Money is thus an alien innovation, though one to which the Melanesians have adapted with gusto. Though the Islanders possessed various media of exchange long before the appearance of the whites (shells, pigs' and dogs' teeth, bird plumage), these were embedded in ritual exchanges designed to strengthen relationships and were thus "religious." The idea that exchange relationships could be made so abstract as to become completely depersonalized and objectified was not only foreign, but threatening.[47] It was thus not by chance that Yaliwan's followers, once the movement transformed itself into the Peli Association, developed a regular cult of money, in which "flower maidens" shook money boxes back and forth while young men held their breasts from behind and the boxes were then buried in the cemetery. A table ritual for the multiplication of money, possibly reminiscent of the Catholic mass, formed part of the most famous of all the cargo cults, that of Yali from Sor on the Rai Coast near Madang. Like other cult leaders, Yali had worked away from his home area and experienced at first hand the effects of the economic difficulties of the 1920s, including the strikes and disturbances among the dock workers in Rabaul. During the war he rendered the Allies valuable service, and by the time he returned to his village he had definite plans to help his people attain economic self-sufficiency. But a cult from Madang, the Letub Movement, which arose in 1937 and spread quickly during the war in the course of a Christian adaptation of the Manub-Kilibob myth and the incorporation of the Letub dance,[48] still claimed the allegiance of the people, and Yali's reforms inexorably took on the characteristics of a cult. After allowing himself to be proclaimed messiah and king in 1949 he was arrested, but neither prison nor a trip to Sydney, organized by the administration before his arrest to enable him to see the origins of cargo in factories, diverted Yali from his Melanesian-millenarian ideas, though he did renounce his cult shortly before his death in 1973.[49] Nevertheless his movement continues as *wok bilong Yali* or *lo bos* under the leadership of Beig Wen in Madang town and along the Rai Coast even today.[50]

Paliau Maloat, a former policeman who drew up comprehensive plans for the social and economic reform of his home island of Manus after the war, also took over certain elements from a local cult leader called Wapei and was arrested for a time. His efforts were always directed towards political activity, however, and he wanted his movement to be understood as a reform movement, not a cult.[51] On the other hand, he founded his own church, with a liturgy resembling parliamentary proceedings and a confession of faith in the form of a political manifesto.[52] Another example of the fusion of cultic and commercial interests is the economic cooperative founded in Lae in the early seventies to develop the rural area around Pindiu in Morobe Province. It bore the name "Pitenamu

Association" (made up of the initial letters of the names of the participating districts), but it too degenerated into a cult of money under the apparent influence of earlier cults such as the *"Skin Guria* Movement" of the 1940s and the more recent Tanget cult.[53]

It is thus not surprising that the cargo cults have been interpreted as proto-political protest movements directed against the colonial powers, above all by Worsley.[54] Lawrence's study of the Yali movement showed, however, that one does not do justice to their religious character when one claims they are "nothing but" protest movements. According to more recent accounts[55] it is not enough to explain the cults as "safety valves for frustrations" or "manifestations of psychic instability." There are cases in which the people who incited to cult activity were suffering from psychic illness, and such outbreaks of emotion will always attract the volatile, but the significance of these cults for the majority of their adherents goes much further than this. Underlying the cults is a genuine Melanesian "ideology," which Schwarz summarizes thus:

1. The belief that Melanesians have lost their true identity and with it the fullness of life through some foolish or sinful act of an ancestor.

2. The expectation of the return of an ancestor (or ancestors), who will restore their lost identity and bring back the Golden Age.

3. The vision of a this-worldly salvation — salvation as something to be experienced here and now in a concrete, material way, and as embracing the whole community and the whole creation.

4. The belief that knowledge of the correct ritual and its correct performance will open the way for the advent of the day of salvation.[56]

Cargo, in short, became a very Melanesian symbol, adapted to modern conditions, of salvation, i.e., of Life as comprehensive wholeness and healing.[57]

Quite early in the colonial period there were in fact movements with a religious and even explicitly Christian motivation. After the departure of the Lutheran missionary Christian Keysser from New Guinea in 1920 tension developed between the people and his successor at Sattelberg above Finschhafen on the Huon Peninsula.[58] A community leader named Selembe, who had spent some years in the service of the government at Rabaul, received a message from the Holy Spirit and initiated a revival movement which came to be called *Eemasang* ("house cleaning").[59] By 1933 Eemasang had achieved its goal of renewing the community, but two further returnees from Rabaul, Tutumang and Mutari, who had experienced the 1929 strike in which the disturbances of the twenties culminated, stirred up a regular money-cult. Although this had been under way since 1922, the Europeans only noticed it in 1927. Its discovery unleashed a spiritual crisis in the church,

but from 1930 on the purification rituals of Eemasang tended to serve the purposes of the cult: spiritual purity would bring forth money. In the end, there was
a public showdown between the missionaries and the cultists, from whom Keysser
demanded and got a public apology. But in 1946 a movement called *Skin Guria*
("body shaking") broke out among the Hube, followed by various phases of the
Tanget movement (named after a plant with magic properties), which since its
first appearance in 1947 and further outbreaks in 1956, 1960, 1968 and 1970
continues to this day.[60]

The movements, then, attempted to come to terms not only with the external influences of the modern world, but also with the Christian faith, which was
seen as part and parcel of this new world. Both they, and the countermeasures
which the churches felt obliged to undertake, contain theological impulses which
must be taken seriously. Certain cult leaders were elevated to the status of a
"Melanesian Jesus," the myth of the two brothers was occasionally reinterpreted
so that Jesus could take his place among the ancestors, and the eschatological passages of the Bible occasionally inspired people to neglect their work in
expectation of the end of the world. Now that Holy Spirit movements with their
"theology of experience" are so predominant, it is easy to overlook that in the
difficult post-war, pre-independence years the foundations for a contextual Christology were laid, not only in Papua New Guinea but in other parts of the Pacific
as well.[61] Those in positions of responsibility, whether indigenous or expatriate,
were strongly inclined to reject the cargo movements as "pagan" and rely on disciplinary measures. But those who spoke for the village communities themselves
were not lacking in theological judgment:

> It is rather they who raise the implicit, almost unconscious dialogue carried
> on with the tradition by the individual Christian in his or her daily life to
> the level of explicit awareness, thus helping to lay the foundation on which
> Christian faith, against the background of Melanesian traditions and under
> challenge from social change, achieves a profile of its own by which it also
> acquires ecumenical relevance.

The crucial question is thus: Did Christ present himself to these peoples as the
"initiator of faith" or as a new "culture hero"?[62]

The millenarian movements of Melanesia have brought forth a whole series
of indigenous "prophets" whose concern was to lead their people on the journey of discovery into the strange new world while preserving their identity and
integrity.[63] The very first encounter with white civilization — at a distance, as it
were, under the alienating conditions of the colonial and mandate periods — was
disorientating and painful. The Melanesians at once saw themselves compelled
to reshape their entire view of the world in the only medium available to them,

that of communal and ritual action. It is a great pity that the whites felt any such need very late in the piece, if at all. Very early on the devout Christians from the mission stations discovered the other side of white culture while working in the towns and on plantations: cynicism not only about native customs, but about Christianity itself, coupled with immorality and lawbreaking.[64] In between came the utterly confusing events of the Second World War, when the Japanese and the Americans appeared from nowhere, devastated large parts of the country, and just as suddenly disappeared. But even in the context of everyday life it is scarcely less traumatic to experience the polarization between village and town[65] and what Lynn Giddings has called the "*kaukau* (sweet potato, i.e., traditional) ethic" of tribal culture as against the "coffee ethic" (i.e., plantation-based) of the business world.[66] Even if one is of the opinion that the indigenous religious movements have ultimately failed in their attempt to integrate the new experiences into their traditional view of the world, it is equally obvious that Christian preaching and moralizing are not coping with the profound effects of the new era on marriage and the family, the upbringing of young people and not least on political morality.[67] It is not only Melanesian cultures that are being put to the test but the Western and Christian ideas and structures that have been imposed on them. The real dialogue of the unequal partners is only now getting under way, after many peoples have been culturally, if not physically, destroyed. What are the implications of this for Christian theological and ethical claims?

3. "Biocosmic" Religion and the Sacralization of Violence

In the Melanesian view of the world space is "essentially qualitative,"[68] and time is undifferentiated, without past or future, except at the point of action.[69] The *ego* stands in relationship with the totem, the spirit ancestor, the uterine group, and the mysterious powers of passion: it is this complex that constitutes mythic time and the existence of the individual. The kinship structure of society derives directly from this existence in mythic time, and it is sustained by the ancestral story handed down by tradition and guarded in ritual. The "word" in which this story is transmitted is related to both "thing" and "thought" and is in the first instance "act": it is thus that tradition and myth are able to comprehend the whole of existence over generations.[70] In this context of mythic time, so difficult for Europeans to grasp, the body merely "supports" the living person (*kamo*, as distinct from the dead person, *bao*) and is otherwise ignored, for self-knowledge arises in the course of social relationships. The person has no one single name, but a complex of names deriving from various roles; he or she only exists to the extent that these roles are played out. The person is intrinsically "participative."[71] The trauma involved in detaching the person, thus conceived, from its social-natural, anthropomorphic-cosmomorphic, "mythic" matrix becomes apparent. The complementarity of *mythos* and *logos*, the conclusion that they are equally primordial in the constitution of thought, also becomes inescapable.[72] Myth and person are mutually constitutive for all human beings, whether Melanesian or modern.

In religious terms, the introduction of Christian faith with its Trinitarian theology into this milieu of what is sometimes called "primal"[73] religion in Melanesia was necessarily traumatic. At the risk of over-simplification, if non-theistic Melanesian religion could be classified, with Mantovani, as "biocosmic" because of its immediacy, through myth and ritual, to the sources of physical life in the rhythms of nature,[74] then theistic Christianity, which — in this respect like Buddhism — offers a definitive end to the state of alienation biblically known as "sin," might be described as "metacosmic," transcendent as opposed to immanent.[75] Though the burden of this book is to demonstrate the fundamental continuity between the two, the contrast in a situation such as that of Melanesia encountering Western Christianity is immediately apparent. When we — Westerners — are told that "Life" is the central religious value of Melanesian cultures, we almost inevitably interpret this as some kind of idealization. But what is meant is nothing more or less than physical survival (*sur-vivre, Über-leben*), the primordial continuity of human participation in the processes of nature.[76] There is a widespread myth known as *dema,* a term originating with the Marind-Anim of West Papua, in which a culture-hero dies so that the means of life in the form of pigs, crops or a significant plant are assured for the community.[77] Attempts have been made to find in this a connection with redemptive suffering as embodied in the story which interprets Jesus' death as "sacrifice," though others see the *dema* ritual as a straightforward exchange to secure the continuity of Life.[78] We thus discern a possible tension between transcendence conceptualized as the Christian God and transcendence discerned as immanent within the relationships renewed by the *dema* ritual.[79]

Though its media of expression are oral rather than scriptural, ritual rather than dogmatic, and collective rather than individual, the biocosmic religion of Melanesia has been able to accept the metacosmic perspectives opened up by Christianity as complementary to its own innate orientation to a transcendence of a different sort, manifested not in concepts and ideals but in communal and cosmic relationships. The greatest challenge it had to face was not in the area of protology (the story of creation) but of eschatology (the anticipation of the "last things," *ta eschata,* especially the revolutionary concept of a future which is ultimately in God's hands yet can be influenced by human action). This new perspective, I believe, was one of the factors that triggered the cargo cults by awakening expectations of qualitatively different human well-being, symbolized by consumer goods, in the context of new and more efficacious rituals. But it also laid the foundation for overcoming the warrior ethic of ritual violence in perpetual tribal fighting. The transformation, however, has been anything but complete. All too often the Melanesians received this "good news" in a context of violence: contempt for their cultures, social upheaval, economic exploitation, physical punishment. As we have seen, the dynamic of persons-as-relationships characteristic of the Christian doctrine of the trinity cannot simply be imposed on Melanesian ideas of community belonging and exchange. Can the teaching of redemptive sacrifice nevertheless be imposed on the *dema* myths?[80] According to Ahrens such attempts run the risk of "re-paganizing Christianity" by short-circuiting the dialectic of grace and freedom that "interrupts" the logic of retribution and the "scapegoat mechanism" of institutionalized vengeance, while Mantovani denies that he ever interpreted the *dema* ritual as a sacrifice.[81]

If the Christian gospel was the revelation of a non-violent God who in some sense stood against the law of retributive logic (payback),[82] can the sacrificial interpretation of Christ's death function as a kind of "Christian decoder" for the Melanesian *dema* myths of life-from-death, or are we laboring under a misapprehension in thinking that either phenomenon involves specifically *sacrificial* violence? Neither the lynching of Jesus of Nazareth as a common criminal nor the ritual death of the *dema* is intrinsically sacrificial, unless by virtue of an interpretation from a certain religious perspective.[83] If the Bible can portray God in an "unsophisticated" and "anthropomorphic" way as "violently egocentric," thereby linking monotheism to "the formation of collective identity" and the legitimation of nationalism by transcendence,[84] does the portrayal of Jesus Christ as "the incarnation of God's love, not as victimizer but as the divine victim of human violence," an innocent victim rather than the bearer of communal guilt, definitively transcend this?[85] Does the law of Christ merely *interpret*, or does it definitively *interrupt* the law of retribution and violence?

Ahrens concludes his critique of Melanesian "sacrificial" rituals by asserting:

> The naked violence which people face not only in Melanesia, but in fact everywhere is the cutting edge of future ecumenical theology. . . . If violence is — to a larger or lesser degree — conditioned by religion, then Christianity should make this its major concern in Melanesia. Indeed, it must discover the violence/culture/religion triangle as the cutting edge of a future Melanesian theology.[86]

What has been added to the Melanesian "religion of the garden," i.e., of fertility and retribution, in this view, is the "eschatological vision" brought by Christianity:

> The religion of the garden has been infected with an eschatological virus.
> ...In the process of their interaction the truth of their stories is being
> tested.... It may be that Christianity will be shed like poorly glued veneer.
> ...But it may also be possible that something new is growing, real wood.[87]

That the relationship between biocosmic and metacosmic, immanent and transcendent was never satisfactorily resolved is in my view a large part of the
explanation for the rapid spread of fundamentalist varieties of Christianity
throughout the region.[88] This prompts the question: In what does the "transcendence" implicit in Christian faith consist? Has it passed the test of containing and
transforming the violence which Westerners take to be endemic in Melanesian
religion, though it is present in all cultures structured by the logic of retribution?
Or is Christianity's pretension to transcendence itself a fundamental cause of violence because it inevitably frustrates human aspirations and capacities? What is
the religious significance of physical life in its human embodiment and in nature
for the relationship between self and others, self and transcendence in Melanesian
cultures? We shall return to these questions too in Part III.

Part II

BUDDHISM'S
ASIAN JOURNEY

Prologue

For many Australians of my generation, the Vietnam War was a political coming of age. For me it was also a religious one. It was not the quest for spirituality which initially led me to Buddhism, but the enigma of Vietnam. When the war started I was a Catholic seminarian (and thus, by one of history's little ironies, exempt from conscription in secularist Australia).[1] Spirituality was not my primary need — I was having an overdose of that! — but I was ill-prepared for the questions which began to penetrate the cloistered seclusion of Sacred Heart Monastery in Croydon, an outer suburb of Melbourne. Was it right that young men of my age were being called up by an invidious lottery system and sent into active combat in Vietnam while we were excluded? When the first conscientious objectors were harassed by the civil and military authorities, my discomfort increased: could this really be happening in democratic Australia, and how was my automatic exemption justified in comparison with what these young men went through?[2] The Catholic community was increasingly — and publicly — split on the issue of the morality of the war, not just its strategic justification by the "domino theory" of communist domination of Asia. Though communism had no attraction for me and I had been kept ignorant of Marxist theory, there was a certain integrity, not just opportunism, about those who were organizing anti-war demonstrations and boycotts in the Trade Union movement. What really lay behind the frenzied anti-communism of many Catholics, led by prominent lay intellectual B. A. Santamaria in his paper *News Weekly?*[3] My instincts tended strongly in the opposite direction indicated by the rival *Catholic Worker* under the influence of equally committed Catholics such as the philosopher Max Charlesworth. Dared I follow these instincts to the point of open opposition to the war or even pacifism?

My dilemma was solved to a certain extent by my being sent to Rome for further study in 1967. But even more unfamiliar questions had been stirring, only to be reawakened years later when I finally became master of my own intellectual development. Why was it so imperative to support America in fighting such a massive war in Asia so soon after the carnage of Korea? Who were these Vietnamese that the Americans seemed to have no problem ridiculing and killing? What had they been guilty of to deserve this? And above all: what was Buddhism, which in stark contrast to the wholly compromised Catholicism of President Ngo Dinh Diem and his brother, Archbishop Ngo Dinh Thuc of Hue, was patiently inspiring the Vietnamese to resist with non-violent means *both* their oppressors, the National Liberation Front *and* the Americans with their puppet regimes? What sort of religion could justify the self-immolation of Thich Quang Duc in Saigon on 11 June 1966, to be followed by a number of other Buddhist monks and nuns?[4]

It took me many years more to realize that the Viet Minh, portrayed as the specter of communism by American propaganda, were the people's movement, standing in a centuries-old tradition of resistance to Chinese, Japanese and French imperialism.[5] It was their utter failure to comprehend this, and not the power of international communism, that led to the Americans' ultimate defeat. But an even greater enigma for the West at this time was the all-pervading influence of Buddhism in Asia. Its history in Vietnam is a microcosm of its Asian journey: introduced as an already Sinicized version of an Indian religious tradition, harmonized to the point of symbiosis with indigenous religion, able to accommodate itself to the mystic-magic heritage of Taoism and the authority of Confucianism without losing its identity or its independence, Vietnamese Buddhism was able to demonstrate a remarkable vitality at the hour of its greatest test.[6] Whence did it draw this inspiration? What were the sources of this immensely practical yet utterly peaceful resistance? In what relationship did this endlessly resourceful mainstream Buddhism stand to the political pressures operating on it from all sides and to the sectarian movements which claimed to derive from it, such as Hoa Hao and Cao Dai? What light did these Buddhists' heroism throw on the potential of Buddhism in other parts of Asia for non-violent development and the peaceful pursuit of justice?

Much later, I discovered in the thought of Thich Nhat Hanh that both Buddhists and Christians can find ways of resolving these tensions in the course of socially engaged spiritual practice. For the Vietnamese monk "you cannot practice peace without time," and "Time lies in Love."[7] Fruitful practice depends on attentiveness; however, "we are all much too busy."[8] Though there is no such thing as absolute non-violence, we will meet violence with violence as long as we accept violence as a way of dealing with problems. Nhat Hanh's bedrock principle, which has sustained him in the most difficult situations, is therefore: "If you want peace, peace is with you immediately."[9] Out of this practice grows "strength for a life of action," for then past, present and future interpenetrate, diversity *is* unity, death *is* life, and we have a real prospect of making the future possible.[10] In our morbid fascination with armaments and military might we see the externalization of our inner disposition towards violence;[11] the same surely applies to the destructive aspects of the grand project of one-sidedly economic "development." Transcendence, for the Buddhist, is not a theoretical problem but a practical task.

The need to seek answers to such questions has been with me for a long time. Now that interreligious dialogue has become commonplace and attempts are being made to formulate a "global ethic," they have become if anything more acute. The place to begin, I believe, is Indian Buddhism's original encounters with the very different cultures of East and Southeast Asia. How did this Buddhism, already ramifying into major and minor traditions, manage to accommodate itself to such alien ways of thought and life without apparent recourse to domination and violence? It is difficult, perhaps to the point of presumption, for a Western Christian to put this question to Asian Buddhism, yet I am convinced that by reason of the very unfamiliarity of the contexts the gain in knowledge about the connections between transcendence, violence and peacemaking may be all the more significant.

In the following chapters it is therefore my aim to take as close a look as the inaccessibility of the sources and my lack of linguistic tools allow at Buddhism's encounters with Chinese, Japanese and Thai cultures. It is my hope that these stories have much to teach us about Buddhism's possible contribution to an inter-religious ethic appropriate for the radically transformed global situation we face in the new millennium. Whereas, in Part I, I felt I could assume a general knowledge of the European history of Christianity and the nineteenth-century background on the part of most readers, here I need to establish a greater depth of historical perspective if the bearing of Buddhism's Asian inculturations on its present-day potential for peace is to be fully appreciated.

Chapter Three

THE BUDDHA IN SACRED SPACE
Japanese Buddhism in War and Peace

Buddhism came to Japan in the sixth and seventh centuries c.e. as a doubly foreign religion: originating in far distant India, though with the visiting card of Chinese civilization. Its doctrines and practices, forged in a thousand years of debate and interaction with the other religious "ways" of India, had been to a greater or lesser extent Sinicized before the Japanese came to know of them through their contacts with Korea. What they made of them is the subject of this chapter.

The Zen Master Dogen (1200–1253) still thought of Japan as a "peripheral small country" at the very fringes of the civilized world, far from the centers of religion and culture in India and China.[1] Dogen constantly upbraids not only Japanese but most Chinese teachers for having failed to grasp the insights of the great Indian masters like Nagarjuna and Bodhidharma. In particular, he deplores the view, currently widespread in China, that the teachings of Confucius, Lao-tzu and the Buddha are equivalent in profundity. "In the teachings of both Confucius and Lao-tzu there is nothing that can be compared with the merit of the Buddha's wisdom. . . . Even if they really were Bodhisattvas, they would still be unequal to the Buddha. . . . We should clearly realize that Confucius and Lao-tzu were unaware of both the three stages of time and the law of causality."[2] The implication is that the pure teachings of Indian Buddhism have been adulterated in China by harmonizers and syncretists who see the "three religions" (san-chiao) as equivalent and proclaim that "the three traditions are one" (han san wei i).[3] The Japanese should be on their guard against any such tendencies.

There is implicit in this attitude towards Buddhism an assumption, discernible even in the earliest texts of the Pali canon, that this is a universal religion, a truth that can be grasped by anyone of sufficient intelligence and a way that can be followed by men and women everywhere, regardless of race or station. This is astonishing in view of Buddhism's antiquity and the ethnic roots of its Vedic forebears and Brahmin contemporaries. But universality in principle is one thing; coming to terms with the utter strangeness of a hitherto unknown culture is another, and this is the test that various Theravada and Mahayana forms of Indian Buddhism faced when they began to take hold in China. The Chinese, for their part, were both baffled and stimulated by this alien cult with its bewildering array of texts, its communities of celibate ascetics and its insistence that monks should not do reverence to the emperor, yet which offered them "a staggering intellectual experience" by widening the range of their imaginative powers and narrative traditions.[4] The resulting epic of inculturation was to last five centuries, until the terminology of the texts was to some extent understood and the practices they advocated were assimilated.[5] We shall look first at the ways in which the Japanese assimilated this Sinicized Buddhism and the price Buddhism had to pay for cultural acceptance in Japan (section 1) before going on to look in more detail at the responses — or lack of them — of Japanese Buddhism to the challenges of early and late modernity: imperialism and militarism (section 2), individualism and democracy, ecology and technology (section 3). Our focus will be the putative failure of Japanese Buddhism to come to grips with the problem of violence, explicitly in its support for imperialism and implicitly in its inability to respond to the destructive effects of economic success.

1. Japan's Embrace of the "Civilizing Religion"

Korea, predestined by geography to be the link between China and Japan, had itself entered into an uneasy relationship with Buddhism as a result of Chinese colonization. The first records of Buddhist monks coming to Korea date from the late fourth century (Shun-tao, 372; Malananda, 384). Of the three Korean kingdoms at that time, Silla, which had been least enthusiastic in welcoming the Buddhists, eventually dominated the peninsula (688–935), while Paekche, wishing to establish good relations with the neighboring Japanese, sent gifts of Buddha images and scriptures to the Japanese court (538 or 552), intimating that these were potent sources of national well-being.[6] With the introduction of Buddhism came Chinese art and culture, literature and philosophy, science and medicine. In order to participate in the benefits of Buddhism, the Japanese became literate: "Buddhism was seen as a source of instant culture." Moreover, in the Buddhist scriptures "the Japanese found an ethic of tolerance, compassion, and nonviolence, which eliminated much of the cruelty and harshness of the people."[7] This meant, however, that from the very beginning Buddhism was seen by the Japanese as an instrument of civilization, and whether it was accepted or rejected by the rulers of a given period, it remained closely tied to their interests.

Whereas in Korea and northern Vietnam Chinese influence led to the setting up of quasi-imperial states administered by literati on the Confucianist model, the Japanese, in attempting to consolidate a system of centralized government by the imperial clan based on penal law (*ritsu*) and administrative statutes (*ryo*, hence *ritsuryo*) in the seventh century, again went their own way. When the outward-looking immigrant Soga clan was permitted by emperor Yomei (r. 585–87) to practice Buddhism over the objections of the indigenous Mononobe and Nakatomi, this meant little more than the adoption of a superior *kami* with magical powers for "protecting the kingdom" on the Korean model.[8] Confucianism was not accepted as an administrative system but was used for the education of traditional rulers and is strongly reflected in Prince Regent Shotoku Taishi's Seventeen Article Constitution (604); but Japan never became Confucianist in its social structures and political institutions.[9] Whereas the Chinese emperors ruled under the Mandate of Heaven, of which they had to prove themselves worthy, the Japanese *Tenno*, as the descendant of the mythical sun goddess Amaterasu Omikami, the genetrix of the divine nation, was the embodiment of this sacred collectivity and was therefore beyond criticism. Real power may have shifted to the *Shogun* (clan overlords) and *Daimyo* (landed gentry) as the court became isolated and ineffectual towards the end of the Heian period, but the authority symbolically invested in the sacred person of the emperor was unchallengeable, even under the Tokugawa Shogunate (or *bakufu*, "military government"). It was this mythical authority of the emperor, rather than Confucian ethics or Buddhist doctrine, that was invoked to legitimate all subsequent historical developments, however radical.[10]

As the new unified Japan was shaped by measures such as the Taika Reforms (645), which abolished serfdom, and the Taiho Code (701), the Buddhist religion was actively promoted as a necessary complement to the cults of localized *kami*. Regionalism was superseded by nationalism as the emperor Shomu decreed in 741 that state-subsidized temples be erected in each province and in 749 that a bronze statue of Vairocana, the universal or "sun" Buddha, be cast for the great Todai-ji temple in the new capital, Heijokyo (modern Nara). "Completed and consecrated with ceremonial pomp three years later, this Vairocana Buddha was at once the symbol of the magnificent universe and of the centralized state."[11] But as the six Nara Schools, of both Theravada and Mahayana provenance, developed, their monasteries became too powerful, and as a result the capital was moved to Heiankyo (present-day Kyoto) in 794. Thus was initiated the Heian era, which was to last till 1185, and with it Japan's feudal period as the landowning clans — especially the Fujiwara, who dominated the court by securing marriage alliances with the imperial house, thus infiltrating government officialdom — reasserted themselves and the emperor's power became largely symbolic. During this period the role of Buddhism, as depicted in splendid works of literature such as Murasaki Shikibu's *The Tale of Genji* and *The Pillow Book of Sei Shonagon*, seems to have been to provide the aristocracy with efficacious rituals consonant with their amorous and aesthetic pursuits. Its impact on the general populace is less easy to define.

Early in this period two innovative monks laid the foundations for the future course of Buddhism in Japan. Saicho (Dengyo Daishi, 767–822) and Kukai (Kobo Daishi, 774–835) were permitted to study in China. Each was on a personal quest. Saicho, said to have been born in answer to his father's prayers to Hie Sanno, the *kami* of Mt. Hiei overlooking Kyoto, received Buddhist ordination at Todai-ji in Nara in 785. It was a time of unrest following the Ezo rebellion in the north, the weakening of the *ritsuryo* system of centralized government, and the temporary removal of the capital to Nagaoka in 784. Saicho spent the next twelve years meditating on the impermanence of things on Mt. Hiei. He saw that "The three realms, floating in boundless time, are filled with suffering from which there is no respite" and he vowed "that all beings of the world will together reach the wonderful enlightenment."[12] The doctrinal position presupposed by this vow is no longer that of the Hosso sect in which Saicho had been trained, for he places no restrictions on the universal presence of the Buddha-nature and the capacity of all beings to attain enlightenment. It is thus not surprising that he was drawn to the teachings attributed to the school then flourishing on Mt. T'ien-t'ai in China, where he was able to study in 804. There he received ordination and dharma transmission in the Mahayana tradition, and for the rest of his life he strove to obtain permission to carry out T'ien-t'ai (Jap. Tendai) ordinations on Mt. Hiei. What he had in mind was greater independence of religious organizations from government control, but the bodhisattva precepts he had been given on Mt. T'ien-t'ai were regarded by the Nara authorities as suitable for lay devotees only, and permission was denied until after Saicho's death. "Saicho's movement for independent Mahayana ordination was an exercise of the same order as Shinran's decisions to eat meat and to marry."[13] Saicho already appreciated the importance of the *Lotus Sutra*'s teaching that there is "one vehicle" (*ekayana*) of universal salvation, which was to influence all subsequent forms of Buddhism in Japan.

Kukai, a gifted student of the Chinese classics, was destined for a brilliant career at court until a meeting with an unknown Buddhist priest led him to become a mountain ascetic. He too visited China in 804, making straight for the T'ang capital Ch'ang-an where he first mastered Sanskrit and then received initiation into esoteric (Tantric) Buddhism under Hui-kuo. Kukai was both confident and charismatic and was evidently much loved by the Japanese people, as is shown by his success in organizing public works where the ailing *ritsuryo* government failed. Whereas Saicho rejected the earlier Japanese schools and clung to his independence on Mt. Hiei, Kukai founded his center of Shingon learning at Kongobu-ji on Mt. Koya, south of Nara, under imperial patronage. In 823 he was granted a further temple, To-ji, at the gates of Kyoto, even establishing a Shingon chapel inside the great Todai-ji in Nara in 822. His inclusive tolerance, far from combating the established Nara sects, eventually absorbed them and embraced Confucianist and Taoist doctrines as well. "As far as Kukai was concerned, even making tea and writing poems in the company of the emperor and nobles were forms of religious activity. The fact that he was so eminently popular among the people can be considered a further expression of his religious outlook."[14] Both Saicho and Kukai, in their very different ways, accepted an already Sinicized Buddhism as a means of deepening and refining the Japanese religious sensibility.

With the inauguration of the Kamakura Shogunate by a group of *samurai* in 1192 after bloody battles in which they destroyed rival clans, civil power was finally transferred from the degenerate Heian court to a new center, which was to be the catalyst of many new and characteristically Japanese developments. In the latter part of the Heian period, despite its cultural brilliance, "the general state of Buddhism was one of continued corruption, ambition, and cynicism. Increasing rivalry between schools of Buddhism, which by now had their own armies of monk-soldiers, led to bloody fights, burning of temples, and perpetual intrigue."[15] Popular Buddhism went its own way, inspired by holy men (*hijiri*) who became less and less like traditional monks and seized upon devotion to Amida Buddha as a way of concentrating people's yearning for assurance of salvation in the simple practice of invoking Amida's name. Popular at court as a means of consoling the spirits of the dead and alleviating anxiety about the afterlife, the cult spread widely under the inspiration of *hijiri* such as Kuya (903–72) and Genshin (942–1017). Though Kuya eventually received official ordination as a Tendai priest on Mt. Hiei in 948, this was possibly a tactical move on his part to ensure the completion of his great project of copying the *Great Perfection of Wisdom Sutra,* which was dedicated with a splendid ceremony in 963, for he retained the name by which the people knew him as an unorthodox wandering ascetic who buried the dead and organized relief for those afflicted by poverty and plague. His motivation for copying the *sutra* was its reputed power to protect against disasters and epidemics.

On the very day of the *sutra*'s dedication the Tendai priest Ryogen defeated the Hosso priest Hozo at a public debate in the emperor's palace by defending the teaching of the *Lotus Sutra* that all living things contain the potential of reaching Buddhahood in this life. Ryogen's motivation was to increase his fame and consolidate his power at court. The concurrent events bring the role of Buddhism in Japanese culture into sharp focus. In the eyes of the people, it was Kuya's embodiment of the *bodhisattva's* compassion that lent authenticity to his advocacy of Pure Land faith and practice.[16] Ryogen, on the other hand, the rebuilder of Enryaku-ji after fire had devastated Mt. Hiei, used his prowess at interpreting the *Lotus Sutra* and performing efficacious rituals to ingratiate himself with the all-powerful Fujiwara family. Such knowledge was power; indeed, the *Lotus Sutra* "served as the coinage by which Tendai monks purchased power," for

> in tenth-century Japan, Buddhism and politics, religion and politics, were not two different phenomena — to do religion was to do politics, and vice versa . . . in early Japanese society the *Lotus Sutra* was, at least in function, a "political" text.[17]

Buddhism, it seems, was polarized between its role as the guarantor of good fortune amidst the intrigues of the court and its role as a protector of the people from the disasters that accompanied the demise of *ritsuryo* administration.

From the Chinese the Japanese had learned not only to classify the Buddhist texts and teachings in such a way that the *Lotus Sutra* and its doctrine of universal Buddhahood were made to appear definitive, but also to view their own age as the period of Buddhism's predicted and definitive decline (*mappo*). The Kamakura Shogunate provided a new context in which these convictions could flourish independently of the constraints of Tendai and Shingon orthodoxy, fed by the growing popularity of devotion to Amida and the practice of invoking his name (*nembutsu*). The great innovator in this regard was Honen (1133–1212). Constantly persecuted by the Nara sects and the Mt. Hiei authorities, Honen left Mt. Hiei when he realized the true significance of the invocation of Amida while reading the Chinese master Shan-tao: "Do not cease thinking upon his name even for a moment. This is an act that ensures rebirth in the Pure Land, for it is in accordance with the vow of that Buddha."[18] This was a practice open to the most ignorant among the poor. As Honen's influence grew, so did opposition to his movement on Mt. Hiei, and he eventually died in exile on Shikoku. His followers became known as the *Jodo* or Pure Land sect, which advocated the exclusive practice of the *nembutsu* as the only sure way to rebirth in the Pure Land in accordance with the Buddha's vow.

One of those most profoundly affected by Honen's spirit of compassion and constancy of conviction was Shinran (1173–1262). Observing the widespread hypocrisy of Buddhist priests who found excuses to marry and eat meat, Shinran, to whom the Bodhisattva Kannon had appeared in female form, felt himself religiously justified in doing both in the age of Buddhism's all too evident decline (*mappo*). From being an insignificant temple priest on Mt. Hiei he became a devout follower of Honen, protesting against the latter's exile, with unusual courage and directness, as "illegal" and contrary to dharma, only to suffer the same fate himself. In his *Teaching, Practice, Faith, Attainment* he recorded how "he had wakened to the need for absolute dependence on the power of Amida," thereby reaching "the ultimate point of unshakable realization of 'other power,' the true heart and mind given by Amida, the diamond-like mind that is inde-structible."[19] The source of his popularity was his teaching that Amida's power is available especially to the exploited lower classes of both town and countryside, even those who oppose the *nembutsu*. He founded the *Jodo Shin* or True Pure Land sect, and his insistence that human nature is corrupt and that Amida's compassion extends all the more to those who do evil reminds one of Luther's *simul justus et peccator.*

The true religious drama of the period, against a backdrop of warring clans, natural disasters and threatened invasions, becomes fully apparent when we find Nichiren (1222–82), whose very name combines words of Chinese and Japanese origin, vehemently opposing not only the established sects but also the contempo-rary innovations just described. Unlike all the other religious leaders of the time, Nichiren was not a member of the nobility or the landed gentry but was born of poor fisher folk in Awa Province, far to the east of both Kyoto and Kamakura, and was therefore regarded as an outcast and a commoner. His low birth would have been painfully obvious when, as a priest of his local Tendai temple and a *nembutsu* practitioner, he visited all the main temples of Nara and Kyoto in 1242 after a period in Kamakura. He found relief from his growing disillusionment with Court Buddhism when he read in the *Nirvana Sutra:* "Follow the dharma, not man; follow those sutras that reveal the whole meaning of the dharma, not those that reveal only a part."[20]

Only the *Lotus Sutra,* he now believed, fulfilled this promise, but it was being undermined by the spread of Pure Land and esoteric teachings. These Nichiren uncompromisingly attacked in his own home temple, with the result that he was driven out of town. Undeterred, he responded to a series of natural calamities between 1257 and 1260 by boldly presenting to the former regent Hojo Tokiyori his *Treatise on the Establishment of the True Dharma and the Peace of the Nation,* link-ing both past and impending disasters to the decline of the dharma and making propagation of the *Lotus Sutra* the indispensable precondition of national survival. He was ignored, and when an envoy from Kublai Khan in 1268 raised the specter of Mongol invasion, Nichiren was arrested in 1271 as himself a threat to national security, condemned to death and eventually exiled. His followers were ruthlessly dispersed. Amid the rigors of exile he became convinced that he was the embod-iment of the Bodhisattva Eminent Conduct as portrayed in the *Lotus Sutra* and that his bitter lot was the one foretold there for its faithful devotees. He vowed: "I will be the pillar of Japan; I will be the eyes of Japan; I will be the ship of Japan," and he signed his treatise *The True Object of Devotion* simply, "Nichiren, a priest of Japan."[21] The true object of devotion was the *Sutra* itself and the one practice he demanded to the exclusion of all others was the faithful chanting of its title: "By intoning '*Name Myoho Renge-kyo*' ['Taking refuge in the *Lotus Sutra*'] you are assured of buddhahood; what is most important is your depth of faith. The root of the Buddha-Dharma is faith."[22] Rejecting the teachings of all other sects as implicitly supporting the corrupt ethics of the ruling class, Nichiren appealed directly to the downtrodden with his single-minded adherence to the *Lotus Sutra* and his strict refutation (*shakubuku*) of all other practices. Once again, the subtleties of Buddhist philosophy and the diversity of practices inherited from China had been reduced to a single exclusive doctrine. But Buddhism, from being the preserve of the elitist scholastic traditions of Nara and Mt. Hiei, was now well and truly in the hands of the people.

The fact that Eisai (1141–1215) entitled his major work *Propagation of Zen as a Defense of the Nation* sheds further light on the "use" of Buddhism in the Kamakura period. Eisai wished to reinvigorate Tendai Buddhism in the tradition of Saicho by introducing the Rinzai Zen he had brought back from China. Even Dogen (1200–1253), a much more independent figure who eschewed sectarianism yet was unsparing in his criticism of Tendai compromises with power politics and popular religion, presented to the emperor Gosaga a treatise entitled *The Method of Pacifying the State by the True Law*.[23] He had to contend with mounting opposition from Mt. Hiei and competition from a Tendai-Shingon-Zen syncretism introduced by Enni Bennen in 1243.[24] Almost alone among his contemporaries, Dogen rejected the notion of an age of decline (*mappo*), and instead emphasized the Right Dharma (*shobo*), which transcends time and space yet is to be realized here and now. He taught the oneness of practice and attainment; that the "just sitting" (*zazen*) meditation of Soto Zen to which he had been introduced in China is *in itself* attainment. This, and not the unsolvable paradoxes (*koan*) employed by the Rinzai lineage, is the true *koan*: "...the *koan* themselves are enlightenment, and vice versa...enlightenment is practice. Therefore single-hearted practice of zazen is already the undisguised manifestation of the *koan* themselves."[25] For him,

> the Buddha nature is not a potentiality but an actuality...applicable not only to sentient beings but to all beings, nonsentient as well as sentient. ...Buddha nature is understood by Dogen not as an unchanging, substantial entity but as an ever changing, nonsubstantial reality that is realized inseparably from the transiency common to all beings.... Dogen insists that impermanence, the undeniable reality common to all beings, is Buddha nature.[26]

These are the daring intellectual moves of a religious genius, authenticated by the consistency by which Dogen sought out the true meaning of Buddhism and resolutely put it into practice as a monastic founder and philosopher.[27]

Today, Dogen's thought, especially his tendency to identify Zen and the state, monks and lay people, is being scrutinized by critical Soto thinkers who wish to question the identification of Buddhism with "Japaneseness" (*Nihonjinron*).[28] Dogen therefore becomes a pivotal figure in assessing the Japanese assimilation of Chinese Buddhism and the authenticity of the resulting Japanese Buddhist synthesis.[29] This evaluation, in turn, is of crucial importance in scrutinizing the roles various types of Buddhism have played in early and late modern Japan.

2. The Buddha in the "Sacred Nation"

Saicho and Kukai introduced to Japan the radical notion that Buddhahood, far from being virtually unattainable as the Hosso sect had taught, was available to all "in this very body" by the "rapid path" (*jikido*) to "rapid enlightenment" (*sokushin-jobutsu*). For Saicho, basing himself on the story in the *Lotus Sutra* XII about the enlightenment of the Dragon King's daughter, this included women and all sentient beings.[30] At first sight this seems to be an admirable testimony to the universality of Buddhism, but in the context of the political "use" of Buddhism then and now it demands further scrutiny. From about the ninth century on the *honji-suijaku* theory "became the basis for the combinations and associations of Shinto and Buddhist divinities" (derived from *hon-jaku,* the "temporary manifestation of a higher principle").[31] It was on this basis that the Buddha could be seen as a *kami* and the *kami* as avatars of the Buddha, e.g., the god Hachiman as the Buddha Amitabha (Amida), the goddess Amaterasu as the universal Buddha Mahavairocana. Bound up with this from the thirteenth century on was the doctrine of an innate enlightenment (*hongaku*) already present in all beings and only needing to be awakened by practice, which allowed the "hypostasis" (*suijaku,* i.e., the *kami*) to be interpreted as superior to the "essence" (*honji,* i.e., the Buddha). This was allegedly handed down by oral transmission, whose secret documents (*kiroku,* strips of paper recording mystical experiences) were interpreted by the "chroniclers" (*kike*) of Mt. Hiei. For them the Buddhas and Bodhisattvas were manifested as the seven divinities of the Hie shrine, i.e., "as *kami* in order to protect the state and its history. In other words, the ultimate duty of the chroniclers was the study of the *hon-jaku* combinatory Shinto-Buddhist system of the Hie shrines at the foot of Mt. Hiei . . . known as Sanno Shinto."[32]

This analysis opens up some remarkable perspectives on the "Japanization" of Chinese Buddhism. Firstly, it shows how local the *kami* cults, as invocations of clan deities, were and remained, even after being ennobled by the superimposition of Buddhism, which in fact amounted to the "localization" of Buddhist figures. Indeed, the reception of Buddhism seems to have varied throughout Japan according to the "mindscape" of each place, which itself became a representation of some aspect of Buddhism "incarnate" in the local deity. The Kunisaki Peninsula, for instance, as described in Allan Grapard's fascinating study, was transformed physically into a "textualized mountain," the geographically "enmountained text" of the *Lotus Sutra*, its twin peaks representing the two Buddhas who appear together in the jeweled stupa (*Lotus Sutra* XI), while its local deity, Hachiman, became a reincarnation of Shakyamuni Buddha.[33]

> The terms Buddhism, Taoism and Shinto might lead one to think of them as separate, but this would be incorrect, for the ritual and cultural reality of Kunisaki was essentially a combination of specific entities rather than of sects and doctrines, and was inscribed within certain discursive practices and ideological formulations whose relation to "Buddhism" and "Shinto" is not altogether clear.[34]

The *Lotus Sutra* is thus conceived of as itself a "sacred space," and the mountain which is assimilated to it becomes "the residence of a buddha or bodhisattva associated with a *kami*,"[35] a Buddha Land in this world, combining "indigenous and foreign conceptions of sacred space." The mountain thus represents the very principle of this world *within* this world. This is possible according to the *honji-suijaku* theory, which allowed the mountain ascetics to "read" natural phenomena as "signs" because all beings possess the Buddha nature. The "use" of the *Lotus Sutra* for the "protection of the state" (*chingo kokka*) is thereby enhanced, for the sacred nation (*shinkoku*), as the land of the *kami,* is the Pure Land in this world (*gense-jodo*), a ritual "sociocosm" whose *kami* hierarchy is the mirror of society.[36] Very early on, it seems, the Japanese assimilation of Chinese naturalism assumed fateful political overtones. It requires, in fact, considerable intellectual effort for Westerners to grasp that, traditionally, the Japanese never thought in terms of separate "religions" and "sects," some Buddhist, others Shinto. Rather, the Buddhas and Bodhisattvas *became* the *kami* of each particular place, inhabited the "mindscape" of the particular locality. This becomes more evident when we realize that the various shrines and temples formed "multiplexes" where worship, nourished from a variety of sources, was carried on as a seamless web of multifaceted ritual actions.[37]

The Meiji Restoration (1868) peremptorily installed Shinto as the national religion, bringing in its wake the widespread destruction of Buddhist temples and the prohibition of the Buddhist names that had traditionally been given to Shinto deities. For the first time, the "foreign" Buddhas and Bodhisattvas were forcibly separated from the "indigenous" *kami.* The Buddhist lineages, grown complacent as the custodians of social order under the Tokugawa military regime (*bakufu*), suddenly had to justify their existence, and the ways in which they did so make an unedifying story. In brief, unaware that Buddhism could have presented a "higher" or transcendent viewpoint from which to question it, they instinctively chose the way of nationalism, allying themselves conspicuously with Shinto and Confucianism in attacking Christianity and the West and acquiescing in the creation of State Shinto (*Kokka Shinto*) under the illusion that this artificial ethnocentric construct afforded them the breathing space of "religious freedom."[38]

Once started down this path, they found themselves constrained to give ideological legitimacy to such imperialistic ventures as the colonization of Hokkaido, proselytizing in China and Korea, the Sino-Japanese War (1894–95) and the Russo-Japanese War (1904–5). Prominent among those who provided such legitimation was the young D. T. Suzuki, whose teacher Shako Soen (1859–1919) had made a robust defense of Japanese aspirations before the World's Parliament of Religions (1893) and had rebuffed an invitation by Tolstoy to join him in condemning the Russo-Japanese War.[39] Suzuki saw no difficulty in mutual support of the state and religion, because outside interference in Japan's imperialistic undertakings had to be resisted in the name of all humanity; indeed, Japan's wars were acts of compassion towards the rest of Asia. Buddhist support for them was made to seem plausible by invoking the compassion of Amida in Shin devotion and Zen's ability to detach the act of killing from the individual's will.[40] Though there were small groups of Buddhists who resisted this overwhelming trend, these ideas helped to pave the way for the "nation-protecting" Imperial-Way Buddhism which saw the sacred nation as the great family of the Buddha portrayed in the *Lotus Sutra* and united under the emperor. From there it was a logical step to the Imperial-State Zen which invoked the *samurai* code of *Bushido*, the way of the warrior, as the essence of Japaneseness ennobled by Zen discipline.[41] Post-war apologies for these tortuous rationalizations of violence in the name of an ethnocentric ideology have been reluctantly forthcoming from some of the leading sects only in the late eighties and early nineties, though even then the Rinzai Zen master Yamada Mumon was not above portraying the war as Japan's self-sacrifice for the liberation of Asia.[42]

Two of the most influential of Japanese Buddhist lineages, Zen and Shingon, have been made responsible for the moral ambivalence of leading intellectuals before, during and after the Pacific War (known in Japan as the "Fifteen Years War" or the "Greater East Asian War"), but they have also given rise to searching reappraisals of the Buddhist relationship to ethics, the nation and the state. The position of the philosophers who were identified with the Zen-inspired Kyoto School, such as Nishida, Nishitani, Suzuki, Tanabe, Watsuji and Abe, was particularly difficult. Tanabe, having broken with Nishida in 1930, went through a period of intense personal conversion between 1941 and 1946, during which the "other-power" (*tariki*) of Amida became the religious source of his philosophical inspiration. The death and resurrection of the self through repentance (*zange*) was the centerpiece of his philosophy of "metanoetics."[43] Watsuji's ethnocentric essentialism lent plausibility to his sympathy for the Imperial Way, while Tan-abe's "logic of species" enabled him to show how the ethnic particularity of a people mediates the universality of the human to the individual human being. His personal crisis as the war neared its end consisted in his realization that this philosophy was unable to formulate a response to the racism and militarism of the regime.[44]

In an atmosphere of totalitarian repression and rigid thought control, these philosophers did make some efforts to intervene, e.g., Nishida's futile approaches in 1937–38 to his former students Prime Minister Prince Konoe Fumimaro and Education Minister Kido Koichi, who declared themselves too weak to stem the tide of militarism,[45] and some of them were involved in the much-misunderstood symposia on "Overcoming Modernity" (July 1942, under the auspices of the jour-nal *Literary World*) and "Japan and the Standpoint of World History" (November 1941, March 1942 and November 1942, for publication in the journal *Chuoko-ron*).[46] Part of Japanese Buddhism's Chinese heritage was the notion that the Empire was a manifestation of the Buddha realm, so that Buddha Law and Imperial Law were regarded as one.[47] It would seem that, although the Kyoto philosophers genuinely deplored the excesses of the Japanese Army and the Emperor cult — and said so in private communications — they shared the deeply ingrained notion that in being Japanese they were part of the "family" or "house-hold" of the emperor as the symbolic manifestation of Japan's "sacredness" as a nation. When Nishida spoke of the "place" (*basho*) of "absolute nothingness" and Tanabe of the "logic of species" they did not always necessarily recognize the overtones of legitimation of "cultural nationalism" in what they said, despite the fact that they were struggling to reinterpret the language of the Imperial Way in a "world historical" context. The tendency of Zen to take up a standpoint "beyond" truth and falsehood, good and evil, time and history, together with the conviction that Zen was not merely a sect but truth itself, only reinforced this ambivalence.[48]

It was therefore fatally easy to conclude, as Suzuki did, that Zen, as "religion itself," "has nothing to do with the state,"[49] and at the same time to propose Japan, the only Asian nation with a level of awareness capable of understanding the West, as the liberator of Asia from Western imperialism, a kind of anti-imperialist imperialism. This is particularly evident in Nishida, for whom "overcoming moder-nity" meant the creation of a "specifically Japanese modernity" deriving from the uniquely Japanese culture of "pure experience" prior to the distinction between subject and object.[50] It is the tragedy of these thinkers that, though they were groping for a truly cosmopolitan and pluralist international order in language at least as sophisticated as that of their Western counterparts, their immersion in the particularity of Japanese culture with its strong mythical and religious themes

imprisoned them in a "nativistic idealism."[51] So many Buddhist expressions —
"extinguishing the private self," "immanence of transcendence," "beyond subject
and object" — acquire sinister overtones in a discourse poisoned by the prevailing
ideology of "Japaneseness" (*Nihonjinron*). Though none of these thinkers joined
the militarists in a way comparable to Heidegger's becoming a Nazi, "it was one of
the principal virtues of Kyoto philosophy that made it most vulnerable to nationalism" in that they "aimed at an 'authentic' or 'existential' philosophizing."[52] It
was precisely their Zen philosophy, thoroughly assimilated to cultural assumptions
of Japanese uniqueness and superiority, that deprived them of a basis for criticism:
"The symmetrical negation of I and Thou leaves the individual with no ground
to stand on, neither towards other individuals nor vis-à-vis the state."[53] There
are obviously immense implications for religious particularism and universalism
in this, which can only be touched on here and to which we must return.

In such a context, the vehemence of the "Critical Buddhism" of Matsumoto
Shiro and Hakamaya Noriaki (the latter formerly) of the Soto-affiliated Komazawa
University in Tokyo as they search out the roots of nationalism sanctioned by religious "harmony" (*wa*) is understandable. They trace these pernicious doctrines
back to the teachings on "original enlightenment" (*hongaku shiso*) and the "seed"
of the Buddha-nature (*tathagatagarbha*) in all beings, which in eliminating discrimination between beings invalidate thought itself and with it critical analysis
and ethics.[54] In their view it was the failure of those Japanese who originally
brought Buddhism back from China to discriminate between the Indian original
and its Chinese distortions that prepared the ground for contemporary Japanese
Buddhism's ethical impotence and doctrinal vacuity. It has only recently been
confirmed that the immensely influential scripture *The Awakening of Mahayana
Faith*, the source of the doctrines of "original enlightenment" (*hongaku-shiso*) and
"innate Buddha nature" (*tathagatagarbha*, lit. "Seed of the Thus-Gone"), was not
Indian but Chinese. These teachings brought about a "substantialization" and
"universalization" of Buddhist thought, which allowed a total affirmation of the
mundane world and an uncritical assimilation of Shinto deities and practices
to Buddhism.[55] It is this that Matsumoto derides as *dhatu-vada*, a neo-Sanskrit
coinage indicating a new and inauthentic Buddhist "way" (*vada*) based on the
assumption of some underlying ontological "locus" (*dhatu*), which, in the eyes
of his colleague Hakamaya, gives rise to the moral and social failures of Japanese Buddhism through over-identification with "Japanism" (*Nihongaku*). It is
not without significance that Hakamaya himself sees a certain affinity between
his position and Cartesian rationalism as opposed to the romanticism of Vico.[56] As
Stone interprets him, Hakamaya wishes to claim that " 'Original enlightenment
thought' is no more than ancient Chinese 'topical' ideas of 'nature,' resurfacing in
a Buddhist context."[57] Not only that, but "the claim that 'all things, just as they

are, are Buddha' sacralizes the given social order and thus works to legitimate discrimination and other injustices."[58]

There is a certain purism, even puritanism, about the way the scalpel of abstraction is wielded by Critical Buddhists to cut through layer after layer of East Asian Buddhist tradition in the name of "true" or "original" Buddhism.[59] But in view of the challenge presented to Japanese Buddhism by Japan's recent history and present predicament, it is apparent that such critical discussion is urgently necessary. The ideal of "universal harmony" can have positive or negative effects according to its relationship with the transcendent principle from which it is derived.

> The Buddhist spirit of the non-self, expressed as "abandoning of the small ego and living in a larger self," became the ideology for the self-sacrificial "kamikaze" pilots and for the holy war. In identifying the large self with the emperor's will or the government's will, the value of harmony worked. The self-righteousness of a group is derived from the "identification" between the individual and its group in such a way that the "emptied" individual is filled with the will of the group.[60]

"Oneness" is not the same as "sameness": "A false sense of oneness tends to make the world equally uniform, losing the diversity of difference. Violence exists when sameness dominates over difference," whereas the "true, fundamental meaning of religion can be understood as truth-through-relation."[61] Such thinking contains the seeds of a genuinely Buddhist approach to social criticism and peace building.

3. In Search of an Ethic for Postmodernity

If one accepts the hypothesis that in receiving Buddhism from China Japan became the heir to an Axial civilization as described by Karl Jaspers, i.e., one in which the breakthrough to religious and philosophical transcendence occurred, then the developments we have reviewed become even more puzzling. The Japanese seem to have succeeded in re-converting the transcendent back into the immanent, accommodating its ethical and religious content to their own archaic myths and rituals while giving every appearance of becoming sincere Buddhist practitioners, even philosophical innovators. The paradox deepens if we accept that the de-Axializing of the Axial is the Axial act par excellence![62] It required great philosophical subtlety to "philosophize in the archaic," as has been said of Kukai,[63] entering fully into the complexities of Buddhist dialectic in the Perfection of Wisdom *sutras* and the Madhyamika philosophy as mediated by the Chinese, yet managing to find there an expanded interpretation of Japan's own primal traditions, which — unlike, say, those of ancient Greece — have remained intact to this day in folk culture and in the attenuated form of Shinto, its symbiosis with Buddhism notwithstanding. This continual return to the local, the particular, the phenomenal is one of the hallmarks of Japanese culture. As a result, it is not faced with the problem inherited by European culture of bridging the chasm between the transcendent and the mundane.[64]

The persecution of both Christians and Buddhists under the Tokugawa Shogunate (1600–1868) seems to have been motivated by the threat posed to this regime, at once feudal and absolutist, by the autonomy of these religious groups, an autonomy rooted in their transcendence of any given political arrangements, however sacralized.[65] The assimilation of Confucianism did not result in a distinct conception of "justiciable law" in Japan, and "[t]his absence was closely related to the tendency in Japanese society and culture to subsume ethics under the overall moral structure of the community."[66] Even prior to its self-imposed isolation under the Tokugawa regime, Japan had always refused to become part of any international network because it lacked any basis in universal conceptions of the world which it could have shared with other nations.

> Hence Japan's problem today, which may be a tragic bind: unable to change sociopolitically, without friends (unable to apologize) and perpetually awkward in its relations with other nations and cultures (because lacking the "bridge" of internalized universalistic principles).[67]

As isolationism intensified after the realization that Christianity would have provided just such a basis, the Confucian heritage was absorbed into Shinto, and Buddhism was marginalized.[68]

Like its Chinese ancestor Ch'an, Japanese Zen has survived these vicissitudes and has become one of the best-known forms of Buddhism in the West, though it is now being eclipsed by Tibetan lineages and questions are being asked about its ability to provide a this-worldly ethic. In Japan itself Pure Land or Shin Buddhism has by far the greatest following, no doubt because it is closer to the needs and aspirations of laypeople. But perhaps the most interesting religious phenomenon in modern Japan has been the rise of the "New Religions," especially *Soka-gakkai, Reiyu-kai* and *Rissho-kosei-kai,* inspired by Nichiren's appropriation of the *Lotus Sutra* in the thirteenth century (1222–82) as the supreme expression of Buddhist truth.[69] While it would be anachronistic to call Nichiren a nationalist, he was passionately concerned about justice and security in Japan, and he saw his country, the dwelling-place of the *kami* and the *bodhisattvas,* as predestined to save all beings and the entire world.[70] In the political turmoil and natural disasters of his own time he found evidence that he was living in the period of *mappo*, the final degeneration due to the waning of *dharma* (as portrayed in *LS* XIII, XIV). He divined in the apocalyptic vision of the *Lotus Sutra* a political eschatology which gave expression to his hope of purifying Japan from corruption and deceit, casting himself in the role of the Bodhisattva "Eminent Conduct" (*LS* XV, XXI, XXII), for whom opprobrium is predicted as the price of his fidelity.[71] *Soka-gakkai*, in particular, derives its mission to transform society directly from the spirit and writings of Nichiren, who found in the *Lotus Sutra* his legitimation for combating the Amida Buddhism of Honen and all those who show contempt for the *Sutra*.[72] *Rissho-kosei-kai*, by contrast, displays a spirit of tolerance and a concern for right relationships through personality development, and in recent years *Soka-gakkai* has evolved towards participation in interreligious dialogue abroad as its national political influence wanes. Many of these New Religions were founded by "ordinary" people of little education who knew poverty, illness and adversity and coped with them by a kind of instinctive return to the shamanistic traditions and ancestor veneration of Japan's ancient past.[73] Their success is an indication that they have helped millions to make sense of their lives in the traumatic past century of Japan's history.

The presence of the New Religions is also a reminder that, as "Japan Inc." struggles to make good the losses incurred in the Asia-wide financial collapse of 1997 and its current financial woes, the fundamental questions that remain unanswered are not straightforwardly economic:[74] Is forced, export-orientated economic growth fueled by construction projects and high technology developments with no demonstrable relevance to people's real needs — but with catastrophic effects on the environment — an attempt to fill a spiritual vacuum at the heart of Japanese culture? Is Japan's persistence in refusing to apologize and compensate for its war crimes, apart from some grudging concessions, evidence of a deep-seated attachment to precisely those aspects of its mythical past which legitimized the militaristic excesses of State Shinto? Is the manifest reluctance of mainstream politicians to fight free of their symbiosis with business and bureaucracy and embrace the opportunity for global ecological awareness and peacemaking offered by the 1947 constitution mere helplessness in the face of overwhelming Western pressure, or does it reveal a cynical disregard for the wishes of the Japanese people?[75] Where, in all this, is the point at which Japan's profoundly religious intellectual, aesthetic and moral heritage gains some purchase on its amoral infatuation with modernity?[76] Could it be that the transcendent perspective that would make this possible is no longer available to Japanese Buddhism after its centuries-long metamorphosis?

Though he did not actually predict the economic crisis which happened one year after his book appeared, Gavan McCormack's analysis of Japan's vulnerability is prophetic in that it suggests that the malaise is at root spiritual. He sees the country's single-minded dedication to meaningless growth as compensation for its inability to engage with a wider world.[77] "Not only is Japan's affluence deeply problematic, but it pulls the region around it toward social and ecological disaster."[78] McCormack points out that the public space for discussion of human rights and sexual equality has been constricted by the retention of the emperor system and the militaristic reinterpretation of the pacifist postwar constitution.[79] While in much of the rest of Asia "[t]he collapse of military-authoritarian regimes ... and the transformation of communist governments ... mean that spaces characteristic of 'civil society' begin to emerge and multiple voices to be expressed,"[80] in Japan he sees almost complete continuity between wartime and postwar political leadership, a profound rift between the "inner self" of traditional imperial identity and the "outer self" of the Western-style success story.[81]

> During the postwar, high-growth decades, Japan withdrew from international space into political, moral and psychological isolationism in the privatized spaces of high growth.[82]

The fact that it thereby became a model and a magnet for the rest of Asia does nothing to remove the suspicion that Japan's new ideology of "Asianness" is "tactics rather than strategy, and rhetoric rather than substance."[83] Now that Japan's interlocking political and economic structures are in chronic crisis, it is hard to see how an alternative perspective could be found.

McCormack's hardheaded "secular" analysis, using the aftermath of the 1995 Kobe earthquake as a paradigm of fundamental inadequacies and drawn largely from Japanese sources, thus cannot avoid touching on deeper dimensions of Japan's political and economic problems. Referring to the thought of Mushakoji Kinhide, admittedly "a lonely voice," he indicates the possibility of countering the "Confucian, rational, bureaucratic hierarchy" by drawing on the values of Daoism as "a postmodern alternative ideology stressing self-organization and ecological symbiosis," the "anarchic, destabilizing, and decentralizing creative chaos that flows from the Daoist tradition."[84] This suggests that public debate about how the "sacred sphere" and the "public sphere" interact has scarcely begun in a postwar Japan preoccupied with economic success. It also raises once more the questions about particularism and universalism debated by the Kyoto philosophers during the Pacific War. Is the Japanese religion of "Japaneseness" too inward-looking to be of relevance elsewhere, or could it, if critically leavened by traditions of explicit transcendence such as Daoism, Buddhism and Christianity, yield insights and values that would enhance the "global ethos" which is beginning to be envisaged as the setting for a truly universal ethic? Or are even these so-called "world religions" too culturally particular to have any influence on what has been called the first truly universal religion, "the religion of the market" with economics as its "theology" and its twin ideologies of consumerism and violence?[85] Japan, as so often, is a special case. Whereas other Asian leaders can embrace Confucianism, however hypocritically, as the guarantor of so-called "Asian values," "Confucianism, which...is central to the Southeast Asian construction of the new Asian identity, is commonly perceived as an unassimilated foreign ideology in Japan."[86] Whence, then, is the needed moral and spiritual orientation to be drawn?

The case has been made that Buddhism gained acceptance in Japan on the condition of becoming "this-worldly," of legitimizing the very desires it originally transcended and acquiescing in people's wish to be "saved" through devotional practice. The outcome of the encounter between Buddhism and Shinto was not the transcendence, but the absolutizing of the phenomenal order and the acceptance of the dualism between pure and impure. There thus emerged a specifically Japanese Buddhism in which "in many cases the universal tradition was abandoned in favor of a concern with the concrete world of the Japanese in a Japanese state."[87] Paradoxically, this tendency was intensified by Shinran's assertion that "*Even* those who do good can be saved; *how much more* those who do evil!." The implication is that nature itself is impure.[88] The Japanese understanding of nature (*jinen*, the "self-originating"), which lacks the concept of a transcendent creator or an absolute distinction between gods, souls and inanimate beings, allows scope for both an asceticism and an aestheticizing of nature reminiscent of the monks of Celtic Christianity. But the accusation still stands that the much-vaunted Japanese "love of nature" is artificial and detached from real-life problems such as the devastation of the environment and the export of pollution, discrimination against the socially outcast *Burakumin* and disregard of the indigenous *Ainu*.[89] In short, original Buddhism with its robust ethic of intention and desire and its careful analysis of the transitoriness of natural phenomena has been aestheticized to the point of inarticulateness and ineffectiveness and at the same time secularized by progressive association with the institutions of the state. The Meiji edict of April 1872 "allowed monks under state law to eat meat, to marry, to grow hair, to take on a family name, and not to wear robes except at services." This

> codification of a secularized lifestyle for the monk coupled with the revival of the emperor system and development of State Shinto were fundamental in desacralizing Buddhism and pushing it to the margins of society [as a result of which] monks began to lose their monopoly over the sacred realm.[90]

As a result, temples have become a hereditary family-run funeral industry whose cumulative turnover is among the largest in the Japanese economy, though today they have to compete with secular funeral homes for this lucrative business. As if Japanese Buddhism did not have enough problems to contend with in its difficult passage through modernity, its traditional lineages and temple priests are becoming increasingly marginal in Japanese society.[91]

What, then, does "transcendence" mean in Buddhism? Why has the Japanese attempt to grasp Buddhist transcendence philosophically and live it existentially not enabled this ancient culture to develop the ethical principles needed for effective intervention in the political process? Is the "immanence of transcendence" in Japanese culture somehow inimical to the emergence of individuality and the enhancement of the private sphere? Is the immanence of Buddhism in the aesthetic "sacred space," the "mindscape" and "landscape" of the Japanese people with their highly localized culture, necessarily fatal to its integrity as a foreign, "universalist" religion? Is the "public space" of critical discussion, the pluralism of viewpoints and arguments that constitute "public opinion" in an "open" society on the Western democratic model, necessarily inhibited within the "sacred space" created by Japanese religion, to which Buddhism has become so thoroughly assimilated? It will be seen that certain aspects of these questions intersect with those raised by our study of the interaction of Christianity with Aboriginal and Melanesian religion, whereas others lead us in quite new directions.

Chapter Four

DEVELOPMENT
WITHOUT VIOLENCE?

The Rebirth of Ethics in Thai Buddhism

In the Buddhist countries of Southeast Asia it is Theravada Buddhism that has brought forth innovative critiques of economic exploitation, initiatives to prevent ecological destruction and novel ways of working for peace, achievements which have largely eluded its Japanese Mahayana counterpart. Why is this? In a country like Thailand Buddhism is so comprehensively indigenized that there would appear to be little scope for criticism or innovation, yet it is precisely here that the "engaged Buddhism" revived by Thich Nhat Hanh in war-torn Vietnam has become a social ferment alongside more "evangelical" middle-class movements of Buddhist renewal. On the other hand, there is an element of dogmatic intolerance in Thai Buddhism, which equally deserves scrutiny. A closer study of the Buddhist component in the complex structure of Thai culture and society promises to enhance our understanding of how elements of transcendence can be present in an entirely "this-worldly" religious context in such a way as to reactivate a dormant social ethic in the face of rapid modernization and political instability. I shall do this by looking at the role of Buddhism in traditional village religion (section 1) and in the political history of Thailand (section 2) before going on to investigate its resources for an ethic of non-violent development (section 3).

1. The Symbiosis of
Theravada Buddhism and Thai Culture

Present-day Thailand, whose traditional name was Siam,[1] is an extremely complex patchwork of predominantly Tai-speaking ethnic groups from the surrounding region, many of which were the channels for introducing different kinds of Buddhism at different historical periods. As much of this history has come down to us in the form of legend, it is difficult to reconstruct. Following Tambiah, I have therefore opted for a synchronic rather than a diachronic account of Thai Buddhism, for "the anthropological study of the present can illuminate the past":

> ... the structural relations of hierarchy, opposition, complementarity and linkage between Buddhism and the spirit cults arranged in one single field in contemporary life can therefore give insights into the historical processes by which Buddhism came to terms with indigenous religion in its march outwards from India.[2]

Our concern is thus with the ways in which the spirit cults of Thai village religion encountered the great Buddhist tradition.[3] A village in the far northeast of Thailand such as the one studied by Tambiah, though it is on the one hand a closed world far from the centers of civil and monastic power, exists nevertheless at the outer rim of what Tambiah calls the "galactic polity" of traditional Thailand.[4] Its religious life revolves around the interaction between "this world" (*laukika*) and "other world" (*lokottara*), the latter connoting more precisely the "hypercosmical" dimension signified by Buddhist *nirvana* and not merely the realms of rebirth, the various heavens and the spirits, whether benevolent (*thewada*, i.e., the Hindu-Buddhist *devata*) or harmful (referred to by the indigenous Thai term *phii*).[5] Whatever has to do with death, especially when it is violent or untimely, is the province of the Buddhist monks, for death means the departure of the *winjan* (from Pali *viññana*, "consciousness"), whereas illnesses and psychic disorders concern the *khwan* (Thai for "spirit essence") and are the concern of indigenous mediums and healers.[6] Village ceremonial is largely preoccupied with gaining merit (*bun*) and avoiding demerit (*baab*), though always for practical ends; though these terms are derived from Buddhist doctrine, village rituals are by no means "other-worldly" but are intended to have empirical results.[7]

There is however a clear demarcation between rites of life intensification (*sukhwan*) including those for marriage, pregnancy, enterprise, reintegration and illness, which are overseen by an elder called the *paahm* (derived from *brahman*), and the mortuary rites (*winjan*), which are the province of the monks.[8] Indeed, "In no other rite of passage — excepting ordination for monkhood — is Buddhism so directly concerned with a human event," whereas the *phii* cult of malevolent spirits is "spatially and conceptually separated from the *wat* and Buddhist ritual."[9] In all these cases Tambiah discovers a paradox which refutes the prevalent assumption that in dealing with this separation we are dealing with the "other world" vs. "this world," "religion" vs. "magic,"[10] "the paradox that the actual words recited deal with the great acts of renunciation of the world by the Buddha, but the grace transferred by virtue of their recitation is an affirmation of this world."[11] The words thus become the medium of a ritual exchange between monk and laity by which "the monk as mediator and specialist can transfer Buddha's conquest of the dangers inherent in human existence, transmuting it into prosperity and mental states free of pain and charged with merit," though not without "ethical effort and right intention."[12] The potency of the ritual recitations (*paritta*), then, "paradoxically derives from the mild non-violent ethical merit of the Buddha and his disciples."[13] This is indeed a paradox, for to a considerable extent the village rituals represent the polar opposite of Buddhist teaching, yet Buddhism has been able to accommodate them in a synthesis in which they appear as the "primary" level of religious experience upon which the "secondary" level of transcendence depends.[14] The relationship between immanence and transcendence is thus harmonized by being hierarchialized, thus making possible the harmony between indigenous and Buddhist practices that characterizes the Thai religious scene.

Other village ceremonies, too, involve structured reciprocities between Buddhist supra-local perspectives and local needs. A whole cycle of ceremonies based on the *wat* accompanies the agricultural year, the most elaborate of which is *Bun Phraawes*, "the grandest merit-making ceremony in the village."[15] This involves not only homage to the *thewada* or "divine angels" but an invitation to Phraa Uppakrut, the water spirit (or *naga* in traditional Buddhist cosmology) who inhabits the nearby swamp. The importance of water in a rice-growing economy needs no comment, but the significance of the stories which interpret these rites seems to lie in the taming of this natural element so that "the ritual successfully recruits the power of the *Naga* to protect human society and Buddhism"; thus Uppakrut "is incorporated into Buddhism," exemplifying "the universalizing aspects of Buddhism, its attempt to bring nature under man's metaphysical control."[16]

> There are complex levels of communication between village tradition and the grand tradition, a complexity at least showing, rather than a *separateness* between them, a *mutual reinforcement* and *illumination*. The anthropological perspective as it focuses on contemporary village behavior and traditions demonstrates more than this: the *contextualization* of literary and artistic themes and forms of a grand past may be in humbler form, but importantly not as a dead past but as a living reality; one also sees the elaboration and expansion of meaning of these themes as they are closely woven into the texture of contemporary social life and interests.[17]

The extraordinary "rocket festival" of *Bunbangfai,* in Tambiah's view, "portrays a 'necessary' linkage between Buddhism and the guardian spirit cult."[18] Again, "the Buddhist sequence is separated from the guardian spirit cult propitiation; yet they are complementary and supplementary."[19] The myth associating the calling of the spirit essence of rice, *sukhwan khaw,* straightforwardly postulates: "Lord Buddha and rice were born at the same time. Rice came along with religion.... When one eats rice... one can wish to enter *nirvana*, to possess an excellent *winjan* (soul), to be reborn as Phraa Pachek Pothiyan (Pacceka Buddha)...."[20] Tambiah succeeds in presenting village religion as one complex religious field in which the Buddhist rites, focused on the *winjan* and aiming, through the agency of the monks, to afford the whole community the opportunity to make merit, are part of a single ritual complex which also includes the rites of malevolent spirits (*phii*), the cult of guardian spirits through mediums and intermediaries, and the *sukhwan* or life-orientated rites of passage in which the village *paahm* invokes the "divine angels" (*thewada*).[21] "The great tradition," he concludes, "is a major component of village religion and what is unique to a village is truly residual."[22] Yet tension remains between the "great" and "little" traditions:

> The traditional peasants of South and Southeast Asia live in a single (*samsaric*) universe which is still populated by pre-Buddhist gods and local spirits of the earth. For them the Buddha is less the "thus-gone" (*tathagata*) than one who really "lives" in the higher spheres. For despite the instruction of the monks not to "pray" to the Buddha and to ask for favors, this is exactly what the country people do.[23]

Thai Buddhism is thus an unresolved but harmonious amalgam of universal and particular, transcendence and immanence.

2. The Political Context of Religious Resurgence in Thailand

As Tambiah reminds us in his magisterial study, the *chakravartin* or "wheel-turner" of classical Buddhism was both World Conqueror and World Renouncer, the two being seen as ultimately equivalent. The historical Gautama Shakyamuni, though destined for the former role, chose the latter and became the Buddha; about two centuries after his *parinirvana*, the Emperor Asoka, grandson of Chandragupta Maurya, having become a World Conqueror through bloody conflict, styled himself a World Renouncer after his "conversion" to the *Buddha-dhamma*. The profound ambivalence between the two roles neatly epitomizes our theme of transcendence and violence: the way of transcendence, of the monk who renounces everything for the sake of final liberation, does not lead to the summit of political power, which in ancient times was normally reached by the path of violence; yet the Asokan ideal of the enlightened ruler who repents of violence and henceforth wages "*dhamma* war" by instilling morality into his subjects remained determinative for all subsequent Buddhist monarchs of south and southeast Asia.[24]

The Theravada countries are thus founded on the complementarity between *anacakra,* or royal power, and *buddhacakra,* "the spiritual power of the *Sangha* deriving from its inner discipline and the vocation of the monks," although "at the very apex of society there was a fusion of politics and religion, spiritual and secular power, to a degree perhaps unknown in India."[25] There the morality of *dharma,* embodied in the *brahman,* was superior to the exercise of power (*artha*) by the *ksatriya* caste, and both stood above the economic domain (*kama*). The *rajadharma,* the duties of a king according to his station (classically set forth by Kautilya, the minister of Asoka's grandfather Chandragupta, in his *Arthasastra* or treatise on statecraft) was considered subordinate to the accomplishment of the *dharmaraja,* the king who ruled according to the *Buddhadharma.* But this ideal was fused with that of the *devaraja,* the "divine king" of classical India, whose worldly power was sustained by the rituals of Brahmin priests. The Buddhist variation on this theme was to regard the king as both *chakravartin* and *bodhisattva,* a quasi-divine being whose power was ennobled by his links with the *sangha,* the Buddhist monastic community. The ideal Buddhist king thus saw it as his duty to intervene and reform the *sangha* if he deemed it necessary, as happened at various times in Sri Lanka and Thailand. This conception can still be seen at work in leaders as recent and diverse as U Nu in Burma, Bandaranaike in Sri Lanka and Pridi Phanomyong in Thailand, each of whom saw himself as a Buddhist socialist in pursuit of a social utopia inspired by *dhamma.*[26] Tambiah traces this ideal right back to the canonical *Aggañña Sutta* (*DN* 27), in which the gradual decline of morality is countered by the election from among the first humans of a ruler who unites within himself social contract and charisma.[27] Even in post-revolutionary Thailand, prime ministers and coup leaders alike secure legitimacy by seeking the royal assent, which in fact amounts to the approbation of the *sangha,* for the state and Buddhist hierarchies are symmetrical and the king stands at the apex of the ritual complex of what Tambiah calls the "theatre state."[28] Unlike classical Hinduism, Buddhism accepts the polity and legal system of the state in which it finds itself rather than enforcing its own, always provided that the independence of the *sangha* is guaranteed, yet in a country like Thailand national consciousness and Buddhist piety have become fused.[29] It is in this context of the Indian *devaraja* in the role of the Buddhist *dharmaraja* that the status of the Thai king has to be understood.

In the case of Thailand, both Indian (Hindu and Buddhist) and Chinese (Taoist and Confucian) cultural influences are present and the military has traditionally taken the initiative in holding the country together. The Tai-speaking peoples who make up 85–90 percent of present-day Thailand trace their origins to southern China. They must have been migrating south into what was to become Siam for many centuries before they began to establish their own principalities from about

the ninth century C.E., though the kingdom of Sukhothai (thirteenth–fifteenth
centuries) marks their initial domination of their Mon-Khmer and Tibeto-Burman
predecessors. The Mon, having come from southern Burma, had already adopted
Theravada Buddhism under Singhalese influence, leaving numerous Buddhist
monuments in their kingdom of Dvaravati (third–seventh centuries) in the central Menam valley. "Khmer culture had been heavily influenced by Sanskritic
brahmanical forms, especially Saivism and, to a lesser extent, Vaishnavism. Apart
from this, Khmer civilization had by the eighth century also been affected by
Mahayana Buddhism through the Srivijaya and Sailendra dynasties of Sumatra."[30]
These "Indianized Kingdoms of Southeast Asia" (Coedès) "left behind them cultural imprints which became the legacy and heritage of their successors" even
after their political influence waned.[31]

The Thai, whose forbears in Yunnan may have been influenced by Chinese
Buddhism, must also have been affected by the Theravada convictions of their
Burmese neighbors and their Mon masters. If the displacing of the Mon by the
kingdom of Lan Na with its capital Chiengmai (1296) heralded a new era, the
establishment soon afterwards of the kingdom of Sukhothai further south brought
with it the definitive adoption of Singhalese Pali Buddhism, which was however
by no means free of Hindu and Mahayana influences. The same goes for the Thai
kingdom of Ayudhya, founded even further to the south in 1350.[32] There followed
centuries of struggle against Burmese aggression from the west and Laotian and
Cambodian ambitions to the east, culminating in the unification of Siam under
a single monarchy. Under the somewhat elitist King Mongkut (Rama IV, 1851–
68, who had been a monk for twenty-seven years before ascending the throne),
King Chulalongkorn (Rama V, 1868–1910) and King Wachirawut (Rama VI,
1910–25), an era of wise and enlightened reform policies opened the way to modernization while avoiding colonization, though paradoxically it was these reforms
that paved the way for a revolution by members of the military and the civil
service in 1932. In the modern period the monarchy has had to make painful
compromises with an ambitious military, the invading Japanese and the forces
of capitalism.[33] Thailand thus retained its monarchy (albeit a constitutional one
since King Prajadhipok, Rama VII, was deposed in 1932), which traditionally
played a key role in the modernization of the country and the preservation of
its independence.[34] The present King Bhumipol intervened to rein in ambitious
generals as recently as 1992.

The continuing moral authority of the monarchy is intimately bound up with
its patronage of the Buddhist *sangha*. In this modernized yet profoundly traditional setting the rise of a prosperous middle class with its optimistic, bourgeois
Buddhism has led to clashes of interest with both the educated military elite and
the monarchist Buddhist aristocracy.[35]

In a sense, democracy, development, and many other concepts associated with modernism do not exist as independent notions in Thai intellectual life but rather assume significance by being refracted through the meaning- and value-giving medium of Buddhist doctrine.[36]

The stock Western vocabulary of "liberal," "progressive," "traditionalist" and "conservative," therefore, is liable to mislead us, for none of these concepts really applies, for instance, to the feminist philosopher Chatsumarn Kabilsingh (now ordained a *bhikkhuni* as the Ven. Dhammananda), the lay social critic Sulak Sivar-aksa or the ecological and development monks of rural Thailand, whom we shall meet in the next section.[37]

Many of the most radical developments in modern Thai Buddhism may be traced back to Bhikkhu Buddhadasa (Phra Phutthatat), founder of the Suan Mokh forest monastery in southern Thailand.[38] Dissatisfied with the traditional training he received, he formulated what he called "dhammic socialism" (*dham- mika sanghaniyama*), though his thought is firmly based in meditative practice (including Zen) and the Pali canon, and its implications are moral rather than political.[39] He prefers to follow "the traditional pragmatic Buddhist approach to political structures . . . that the system of government, whether decentralized and democratic or centralized and authoritarian, is irrelevant provided that the political leaders are moral."[40] Buddhadasa's contribution is both spiritual and intellectual in the tradition of Mongkut (the modernizing King Rama IV). He tries to draw his people's attention away from exclusive concentration on canoni- cal studies and temple rituals to the basics of Buddhist practice, which "is designed to teach us how things really are."[41] His polemics against the "tumor" of rites and ceremonies are based on the conviction "that *nirvana* is something that may be attained at any time or place . . . just as soon as desire has been completely extin- guished."[42] Though what he calls the "relative" truth attaching to doctrines and folk beliefs has its importance for social life, only the traditional Buddhist way leads to insight into "deep hidden truth": for this, "one must be directly concerned with bodily action, speech and thought."[43] The anti-establishment implications of Buddhadasa's rationalization of Buddhism are of interest to those "who use his ideas and interpretations to justify their criticisms of the establishment and of political authoritarianism," thus "providing a potential theoretical base for actual development . . . by offering a Buddhist justification for the overthrow of the traditional social structure."[44]

One of those who has learned from Buddhadasa is the lay Buddhist social critic Sulak Sivaraksa, who ever since his return in 1962 from nine years spent studying and working in Britain has tirelessly propagated what he calls "radical conservatism": Siam (he refuses to use the hybrid and racist "Thai-land" imposed by the dictator Phibul and debased by the militarist Sarit) can only achieve true development by adapting its cultural and religious traditions to meet the challenges of both capitalism and communism.[45] He has been equally indefatigable in his criticisms of successive Thai governments. His bookshop and publishing business in Soi Santi Pap were ransacked and burned by government troops in 1976 during a crackdown on dissidents, turning Sulak's absence abroad into enforced exile. In 1984 he was jailed on trumped-up charges of *lèse majesté* after a series of critical interviews was published under the title *Unmasking Thai Society.*[46] He was again in exile from September 1991 to December 1992 after narrowly escaping arrest as a result of a talk to students at Thammasat University in Bangkok, in which he reminded them of the need to defend what was left of their democratic constitution, set the monarchy free from its suffocating immunity from criticism, reactivate Buddhism as a social force and expose the hypocrisy of the army which is ruthlessly exploiting the nation.[47] Sulak is an ideologue of neither the right nor the left, yet his political influence has been considerable. His aim, pursued unerringly through the founding editorship of the *Social Science Review* and the chairmanship of organizations such as the Asian Cultural Forum on Development and the Spirit in Education Movement, is to foster responsible development at the "rice roots" of Thai society in the hope of stemming the tide of what he calls the "think-big" strategy of development which is devastating the social and cultural life of his country.[48]

At a different point on the spectrum of protest, movements such as Phra Potirak's Santi Asok and the Wat Thammakay center take a more indirect approach.[49] Phra Potirak broke with the official *sangha* in order to establish his austere version of Theravada Buddhism, providing among other provocations a spiritual home for Major-General Chamlong Srimuang, the reformist governor of Bangkok and opponent of General Suchinda Kraprayoon during the 1991 coup. For social critics such as Sulak Sivaraksa and Prawase Wasi, Santi Asok is "symptom, not sickness,"[50] which seems to imply that, though its intentions are above reproach, it does not come to grips with the causes of the social ills it wishes to change. Santi Asok also attracts criticism from conservative monks such as Anan Senakhan on account of its non-conformism, and in 1989 Potirak was defrocked and his organization was expelled by the Supreme Sangha Council.[51] Potirak's social criticism is less analytical but more puritanical than Sulak's, castigating the social and moral ills of modern society. His personal asceticism and the public example of Chamlong Srimuang constitute a highly unorthodox attempt to adapt Buddhist ethics to an urban environment.[52]

Wat Thammakay on the outskirts of Bangkok presents itself as a reassertion of traditional Buddhism and it is much more acceptable to the classical arbiters of power in both the *sangha* and the army establishment than Santi Asok, but in effect it represents an attempt to turn back the clock and recreate what Tambiah called the "galactic polity" of a nation with a royal monastery at its center.[53] Built on a thousand-acre estate reclaimed from local farmers, dominated by a modernistic temple and equipped with modern technology and amenities, Wat Thammakay draws on an extensive meditation training called *Dhammadayada* ("*dhamma*-heir") for lay people, including government personnel and army officers. It stresses the traditions of asceticism (*dhutanga*) and absorption (*samadhi*) rather than the insight meditation (*vipassana*) favored by other contemporary teachers, and the orientation is quite explicitly towards career success. The atmosphere reminded me of nothing so much as an evangelical bible camp.[54] Participants meditate for up to nine hours a day and live in the open with only a sunshade and a mosquito net. After a month's preliminary training mass "ordinations" of up to a thousand candidates precede another month of temporary monkhood. If Wat Thammakay could be characterized as an attempt to create an "evangelical" civil religion for modern Thailand, the "exclusivist" Santi Asok invokes the ancient tradition of non-conformist forest monks, while Buddhadasa laid the foundations for an "ecumenical" Buddhism.[55]

Admirable as such initiatives may be, they tend to shore up precisely those social structures that produce the moral shortcomings they try to alleviate. "Through 'strategies of compromise, ambiguity, and silence' similar to those adopted by Buddhist sects in Japan, establishment Buddhism in Thailand has proven to be a 'passive enabler' of capitalist development."[56] The irony is that the Four Noble Truths, far from sanctioning anybody's status quo, are an incomparable diagnostic tool for unmasking the illusions not just of the individual, but of society. As such they are deployed with considerable effect by Sulak Sivaraksa and increasingly by Western Buddhists such as David Loy and Ken Jones.[57] There is thus every reason to expect that the resurgence of Buddhist social ethics in Thailand may have an important contribution to make to the ethics of economic development and ecological integrity in the wider context of globalization.

3. Towards a Buddhist Ethic of Development

Among the most striking manifestations of socially engaged Buddhism in Asia are the "development monks" of Thailand, some of whom I was privileged to visit in 1991. Seeing the state of dependence and impoverishment, both spiritual and material, to which villagers in the poorer parts of Thailand had been reduced by crassly inappropriate "development,"[58] these very traditional abbots of rural monasteries — their number is estimated at over two hundred — have each found original solutions to the problem of helping the people effectively whilst remaining true to their monastic calling. In almost every case, their starting point has been the reintegration of the *sangha* into the lay community, which meant overcoming the villagers' antipathy to outside interference and recovering traditions of self-help and mutual enrichment. These monks have shown great ingenuity in adapting local ceremonies, especially those involving generous giving (*dana*), as occasions of merit making. In this way, such untraditional activities as buffalo banks and savings schemes have become acceptable because imbued with recognizable meaning.[59] The monks' manifest love of nature and their solicitude for the well-being of animals accord equally well with the people's belief in spirits (*phii*).[60] Phra Prachak in northeast Thailand even went to the length of ordaining trees to save them from loggers.[61]

When I visited Acharn Sanong at Wat Ku Samuan, about forty kilometers from the Khmer ruins at Phimai, I noticed a portrait of Buddhadasa behind his desk. After the evening chanting of *dhamma* he led his novices in intensive meditation. Buddhadasa's maxim, "Working is practicing Dhamma,"[62] is fundamental to these monks' attempts to bring development work and spiritual growth into harmony. Development, of course, means human and ecological development, and the monks' economic initiatives such as training schemes for young married couples and experiments with alternative crops are strictly subordinate to this principle. Though none of these monks could be described as overtly political, some have experienced government harassment, because what they are doing is the antithesis of the "big development" espoused by successive Western-orientated regimes. In the words of Seri Phongphit, a Roman Catholic layman who has made a sympathetic study of eight development monks, their endeavors "have injected the original ideal with a new spirit so that the alternative model of development has become Buddhist," giving traditionally acceptable meaning to slogans such as "Dhammic socialism," "Buddhist economics" and "Buddhist agriculture."[63] This is of course a delicate operation, for the introduction of alien concepts such as "entrepreneurship" and "development" into traditional rural contexts can be extremely disorientating: "In their transformed world villagers often find that their economic actions no longer reflect an implicit ethos."[64]

> Although the cultural transformation that has taken place within Thai-Lao villages has not undermined the basic premises of the Buddhist world view, it has challenged the sheer givenness of the ethos based on those premises. No longer does social life flow naturally from an implicit practical morality. Instead, villagers today often find themselves constrained to make conscious moral choices about which of several potential courses of action they might follow.[65]

This implies the need for "a new practical morality, albeit one that is still recognizably Buddhist."[66]

Phongphit sees the key to the monks' success in the *parami* (perfections) displayed by them and recognized by the people, beginning with *dana* (generosity), including *viriya* (energy) and *adhittana* (resoluteness), and culminating in *metta* (loving kindness) and *upekkha* (equanimity). These perfections are "'personal' but not 'individual'"; they transcend the personal to embrace a "social dimension, which extends from human beings to the universe," thus realizing the ideal of *anatta* and *suññata* (emptiness of self). There is, then, a definite basis in Theravada Buddhist doctrine for the new southeast Asian initiatives in economics, ecology and peacemaking.[67]

It has often been remarked that the texts preserved in the Pali canon present the Buddha — as befits a scion of the *ksatriya* or ruling class — as conversant with the political issues and social questions of his day and personally acquainted not only with priests and ascetics but with leading businessmen and rulers.[68] The Noble Eightfold Path includes not only "right action" but "right livelihood," the way of moderation in economic activity, which explicitly prohibits trade in weapons, human beings, flesh, liquor, poisons, drugs and narcotics while encouraging participation in agriculture, industry and government. The many stories of the origins of society are etiologies of power, which is redefined for the *sangha* thus:

> Here, a monk, by the destruction of the corruptions, enters into and abides in that corruptionless liberation of heart and liberation by wisdom which he has attained, in this very life, by his own super-knowledge and realization. That is power for a monk. (*DN* 26,28)

"In this very life": there is no suggestion here of escapism or abdication of responsibility. In the *Cakkavatti-Sihanada Sutta* (*DN* 26) a "wheel-turning monarch" who neglects to give property to the needy finds that theft becomes widespread and is not deterred by capital punishment, thereby reducing the life span of human beings to such an extent that they eventually take stock of themselves and revert to a wholesome way of life, thus preparing the ground for the coming of the Buddha Metteyya (*Maitreya*).[69] In the *Aggañña Sutta* (*DN* 27) the Buddha almost playfully tells a story of light-filled beings who become corrupted by desire for material pleasures until the differentiation of the sexes and the urge to accumulate property make it necessary to elect a *Maha-Sammata* or "People's Choice" to rule them. As in many other cases (see *MN* 84, 93) the setting of this story is Brahmin criticism of the Buddhist *sangha's* disregard of caste, but there are others, such as the *Kutadanta Sutta* (*DN* 5), in which the just and generous distribution of wealth in society is expounded as the true meaning of sacrifice. Buddhism, by repudiating the sacrificial system of the Brahmins, internalized sacrifice by transforming it into the ethical ideal which rejects all violence, though as we have seen it still had to deal with the problem of legitimating political power based on violent conquest. The *sangha* represents a kind of parallel social order which not only prescinds even from "legitimate" violence but, unlike the Christian monks under St. Benedict's motto *laborare est orare*, participates only indirectly in economic activity.[70]

It is made quite explicit in the *Mahaparinibbana Sutta* (*DN* 16,1,1–6) that the political advice given to the Vajjians when they were under threat from King Ajatasattu may be transposed to the *sangha*: the monks, like the northeast Indian republics from which the Buddha himself came, should "hold regular and frequent assemblies," "carry on their business in harmony," "proceed according to what has been authorized," "salute the elders of long standing," "not fall prey to desires," remain "devoted to forest lodgings" and "preserve their personal mindfulness," if they wish their "counter-society" to survive as a standing rebuke to the power politics of the expansionist and militaristic kingdoms of the time. Far from being passive and negative in their attitude to life, a monk or nun deploys skill akin to that of a carpenter and "generates resolution, strives, puts forth energy, stretches forth and exerts his [her] mind" (*MN* 78). But the theme of all this striving, whether social or individual, is non-violence: "Therefore do not kill or cause to kill," exhorts the *Dhammapada* (129–30), adding that "no amount of penance can help a person whose mind is not purified" (141).

> Conquest breeds hatred, for the conquered live in sorrow. Let us be neither conqueror nor conquered, and live in peace and joy. (201)

The Buddha vigorously refutes the accusation that he is a "suppressor of life" (*MN* 75), but the discourses often connect incentives to violence, which is described with the realism born of experience, with "worldly pursuits" (e.g., *MN* 13, 18, 21).

It is therefore not surprising that contemporary Buddhists, whether Bhikkhu Buddhadasa in Thailand[71] or Joanna Macy in America,[72] refer to these texts as the earliest recorded instances in which collective government by consensus and the just distribution of wealth are proposed as the basis of social harmony, insisting that their teachings are just as relevant today as they have been throughout history. The Buddhist way means practice in the present, not escape into a timeless realm removed from the transitoriness (*anicca*) and unsatisfactoriness (*dukkha*) of human existence. Buddhist practice, starting with the individual but radiating love and compassion (*metta-karuna*) to all living beings, is meant to make a difference to the world, to involve the meditator in the long-drawn-out drama of existence in time.

As we have seen, the Noble Eightfold Path offers a therapy in the form of practical steps towards deliverance from the bondage of hatred (*dosa*), greed (*lobha*)
and delusion (*moha*).[73] The fifth stage of the path, "right livelihood" (*samma-
ajiva*), directly addresses economic activity.[74] Buddhadasa's "Dhammic socialism"
has been reformulated by Santikaro Bhikkhu as an "Elevenfold Social Path" containing the elements of an alternative political and economic order.[75] Buddhadasa
thinks of *dhamma* not as the literal meaning of canonical texts, but as the fundamental order of things (*dhammajati*, "born of nature"). In this sense he speaks of
behavior which conforms to the "norm" (*pakati*), i.e., nature, including morality
(*sila*) as the guide for social life.[76] He refers to the uniquely Buddhist teaching of
the arising of all things in mutual dependence (*paticcasamuppada*), above all the
concept of interdependence or reciprocal conditionality (*idapaccayata*) implied
therein, which suggests that Buddhism as such and indeed the whole world are
intrinsically "socialist."[77] The community of monks (*sangha*) established a system
of social discipline (*vinaya*, the monastic rule), which led to a just distribution of
wealth and the necessities of life. Buddhism thus deserves to be called a "community of self-limitation" (*sanghaniyama*). This is the conception that underlies
Buddhadasa's "Dhammic socialism" (*dhammasanghaniyama*).[78]

In Buddhadasa's view such a community is more conformed to the "norm"
of *dhamma* than Western liberalism, with its individualistic preference for the
entrepreneur, or Marxism, with its authoritarian option for the workers, for both
are dualistic. The *dhamma* community, on the other hand, makes no distinction
between "social" and "spiritual" and is therefore intrinsically democratic, although
it differs significantly from Western ideas of democracy in that here freedom
is not diminished by self-seeking (*kilesa*), but brings about loving kindness and
compassion (*metta-karuna*).[79] Democracy, thus interpreted, is a moral rather than
a political matter.[80]

It is not so much unjust distribution in itself as the inability to be content
with little that is the basic cause of social conflicts. The prosperous person who
conforms to Buddhist principles is called in Thai a "benefactor" (*rong than*), but
a Western-style rich person who grabs everything for himself is a "profiteer" (*nai
thun*).[81] This is the point at which the two most characteristic concepts of Buddhism come into play: "no-self" (*anatta*), which prescinds from any relationship
to a substantial "I" continuing in time, and "emptiness" (*suññata*), the absence of
self or substance in all things and constituents of reality (*dhammadhatu*). Buddhadasa creatively captured these concepts in a new and easily understood Thai
expression: *cit-wong*, "empty mind," with the connotation "let go."[82]

Buddhadasa was a moral exemplar and the teacher of a practice, not a political
philosopher in the Western sense, and the published versions of his oral instruction may seem idealistic and moralizing. We can easily miss the integration of

the moral and the natural in such a way that the overcoming of evil happens of its own accord, "naturally," not because it is "good."[83] The principles that determine his thought are in a very profound sense "ecological." Swearer summarizes them as:

1. The well being of the whole world and all life

2. Self-limitation (*niyama*) together with generosity (*dana*)

3. Benevolent love (*metta*) and the capacity for compassion (*karuna*).[84]

The importance of this approach lies in its being the first truly alternative conception of economy and society to be developed within the Theravada tradition. Its effects, as we have seen, are considerable, extending from the "development monks" of rural Thailand, with their ecological concerns and their ministry to AIDS victims, to Asian and Western intellectuals who are striving to formulate a Buddhist basis for a humane and ecological economy.

But have such ideas any hope of being realized in an increasingly globalized — which, for the present, means Westernized — international market? Their strength lies in their not being reactionary but in the best sense traditional. Recent research is shedding new light on the historical relationship between Buddhism and economic activity.[85] Buddhist laypeople (*upasaka/upasika*) of all periods have obtained "merit," i.e., good *karma* for future lives, by contributing generously towards the well being of the *sangha*. The point of this practice is to make it possible for the monks to pursue their own individual salvation. The monastic ideal, however — unlike that of Christian monasticism — consists not in poverty, but in obtaining and using wealth in a way that conforms to *dhamma*. Those seeking merit (*kamma*) and those striving for final release (*nibbana*) make up a single social whole, into whose ethic the highest attainments of the meditators are integrated.[86]

Monastic wealth only became a problem in traditional Buddhism when it was wrongly used; the remedy was not punishment, but discipline, for the monastic community as such was not primarily concerned with poverty but with equality. The danger of this arrangement was that the monasteries tended to receive the gifts of the laity in proportion to their reputation for spiritual attainment, to the point where their accumulated wealth led to self-enrichment and corruption, despite all precautionary measures. Though Buddhist tradition contains innumerable stories of kings who donated the state itself and merchants who made over their entire fortunes to the Order, thereby securing for themselves enormous karmic benefits, this was done in such a way as not to interfere with the economic life of the state and thus did not entail actual economic redistribution. On the contrary, the massive accumulation of wealth by the monasteries in the form of land and precious artifacts which they did *not* redistribute was often the cause of their persecution by the state, though the *sangha's* own ideal remained that cases of abuse were best corrected not by punishment, but by more just distribution of goods.[87] "Landed wealth thus serves as the mediating vehicle by which the *sangha* and the state share political power and moral legitimacy," although kings can refuse monks the gift of land and monks can refuse kings the opportunity to gain merit by refusing to accept their donations ("inverting the alms bowl," *patta-nikkujjana*): "In each case the connection is broken by denying the exchange relationship."[88]

The traditional attitude to wealth was thus basically positive, though always on the understanding that there was no attachment to it. "A true Buddhist lay person not only seeks wealth lawfully and spends it for the good, but also enjoys spiritual freedom, not being attached to it, infatuated with or enslaved by that wealth. At this point the mundane and the transmundane intersect."[89] *Dhamma*, as cosmic truth and moral norm, formed the basis of this relationship, binding the cosmic and social orders together into one, such that the accumulation of wealth merely for its own sake was a transgression against this order. Even though the work ethic and the entrepreneurial spirit are still somewhat alien to traditional Buddhist societies, they have a basic sense of economic justice which derives directly from *dhamma*.[90] Buddhist economic ethics takes as its point of departure not distribution, but the defiling of the mind, whose antidote is the renunciation of greed. This holds for all, monks and laity alike, for although their ways of life are radically different they are both based on the same moral code (*sila*) and the same cosmic-social order (*dhamma*). In every way they depend on each other.

This gives rise to the further question of the applicability of this ethic of economics to other cultures with different cosmologies: is it universalizable? Its inherent rationality tends to be pragmatic and praxis-oriented; it has never been made explicit in a theory of economics; "the problematic relationship between the possession of wealth and further dhammic activity has never been fully resolved."[91] Indeed, "the Theravadins appear to exhibit nothing comparable to the western theological and philosophical traditions' cogitation and controversy over distributive justice and intense perplexity over the plight of the poor. There is, apparently, no similar Theravadin literature on distributive problems, nor is it the poor as such who are for the Theravadins the primary objects of beneficence."[92] As an ethic it remains closely tied to "religious" values, which in itself raises problems for an "autonomous" ethic on the Western model. But the social consensus on which this ethic is based continues to exist, despite the individualism fostered by King Mongkut's modernizing reforms,[93] and as such it offers a solid basis for an ethics of economics with very different priorities from those of Western growth-oriented economics.[94] Robin Lovin suggests that "despite the apparent similarities between Buddhist and Christian monasticism, an important distinction emerges, for Christian monasticism has an eschatological understanding of social evil that leads to a strategy of social *transformation,* whereas the Theravada tradition suggests that social evils require social *purification.*"[95] If it is true that "there is no Buddhist social ethic, if one means a single, normative form of society that all Buddhists . . . recognize as applicable in all ages," it is equally true that "by these criteria Christianity has none either."[96] Nevertheless

> Each [the *dhamma* and the Good News of the Kingdom of God] has inspired in its hearers a continuous concern for the moral state of the whole society, and each message has created a community that is neither completely mystical nor completely materialistic. Each community understands itself as having a distinct responsibility toward the wider society, yet each insists that the truth it has heard transcends the truths that happen to work in the present social setting.[97]

If this interpretation is correct, then Theravada Buddhism, too, is able to translate a transcendent vision into practical social and political morality.

Not only in the diachronic perspective of development through time, but even in the synchronic perspective we have adopted here, tensions nonetheless remain in the Buddhist conception of a just polity and economy as exemplified in the case of Thailand. Indeed, Tambiah concludes that

> canonical and postcanonical doctrines, the commentaries and the verbalizations of the believers, the structures embedded in their myths and rites, the pattern of their actions — which together reveal the coupling of Buddhism and the polity — are ridden with dialectical tensions, paradoxes, and ambiguities. . . .[98]

Though the gap between monk and laity has been significantly narrowed with the encouragement of monastic teachers such as Buddhadasa, "the antithetical role of the monk . . . as world renouncer and pursuer of transcendental ends" who at the same time "receives gifts and sustenance from laymen with no obligation to make a return" remains ambiguous, for "on the other hand the monk has an obligation to be a 'field of merit' and to reciprocate and give spiritual and humanitarian services to the laymen."[99] Whereas Burma and Sri Lanka, perhaps because each was repeatedly engaged in independence struggles, have seen the emergence of "political monks" at different times, in Thailand these have been suppressed; nevertheless, traditional rulers and present-day politicians in Burma and Thailand have regarded close association with the *sangha* or even a period in the monkhood as a boost to their political status, reversing the ancient pattern whereby rulers expiated the violence necessary to gain power by subsequently embracing a life of piety. These are all attempts to find the "elusive balance" between "morality and politics, *ahimsa* and force."[100] Even the saintly forest-dwelling monks, who characteristically took up their abode on cosmologically significant sacred mountains, gave rise to millennial movements in Burma and Thailand.[101]

Theravada Buddhism in its Thai incarnation thus leaves us with unresolved questions about the immanence of religious ideals in social and political practice and the relationship between transcendence and violence. If political power necessarily involves making compromises with the use of "legitimate" violence, how can Buddhism identify itself with any political order? Is the monastic core of Buddhism similarly compromised even by indirect participation in economic activity and non-violent "development"? Does Buddhism have a unique contribution to make towards an ecological ethic, or are its ecological sympathies the result of an illicit synthesis with indigenous cultures? Is the Buddhist ethos intrinsically otherworldly, so that both Theravada and Mahayana approaches to questions of social and ecological ethics are in the end responses to purely extraneous demands rather than expressions of an ethic which flows directly from Buddhist spiritual practice? Is the idealization of the rural community — itself the result of the process of modernization — compatible either with the monastic community of the *sangha* or the entirely new patterns of urban community life? It is now time to take up these and other questions arising from our empirical studies in a broader context of reflection.

Part III

STRANGE
ENCOUNTERS

Prologue

Unable to fulfill my original hope of continuing my studies in an Asian country, I arrived in Rome towards the end of 1967, still reeling from the impact of brief stopovers in Hong Kong and Delhi, my first ever experiences of the Asia-Pacific world outside Australia. It was the high point of the anti-Vietnam war protest movement and the student revolt. I spent the famous summer of 1968 in London as Paul VI's encyclical *Humanae Vitae* rocked the Catholic Church and the hopes raised by the Prague Spring were abruptly crushed by Dubcek's removal from power. Two of the most powerful institutions of the twentieth century, Catholicism and Communism, had reacted decisively against the forces of change which seemed to be breaking out everywhere. This was all the more dramatic in that the Second Vatican Council and "socialism with a human face" had seemed to offer the prospect of renewal and even convergence.

To move on to Germany in 1969 was to enter a cultural context almost as strange to a naive Australian as any Asian country would have been. With a shock I realized that this democracy was barely a quarter of a century old, and was prone to conceal its insecurity by proclaiming its superiority over the "other Germany" *drüben*, across the border that had already been turned into a minefield after the erection of the Berlin wall. FRG vs. GDR: it was like rival shopkeepers facing one another across the street. Living in the awareness of this historically palpable dialectic was my political awakening. The atmosphere was fraught with tension between radical Marxism and Enlightenment liberalism, even in the Faculty of Catholic Theology at the University of Münster, where Christians for Socialism scoffed at German idealism's aspiration to freedom and neither faction took much notice of the few remaining dogmatic conservatives and neo-Thomists.

Kritik set the intellectual standard, whether Marxist *Praxis* or liberal *Freiheit* was under discussion. The new ecumenicity, it seemed, that was going to replace the fragmented unity of discredited European Christianity, was that of *Vernunft*; we were to look to reason for the source of the new ethic that would underwrite the construction of a truly universal human community.

The voices of political theologians in Germany and liberation theologians in Latin America, some of whom were studying in Münster with Johann Baptist Metz, rejected this vision as ideologically biased in favor of the West, and my sympathies lay with them. Christianity, if it recovered its original biblical impulse, could insist on the "eschatological proviso," the relativizing of all human endeavor within the transcendent horizon of God's absolute future,[1] and on the "option for the poor" which gave theological priority to the voices of the victims of injustice. For my part, I became more and more aware that perspectives offered by the great religious traditions of Asia were being left out of this equation and that the future of Christian theology lay in the coming dialogue of religions, which was going to present the greatest opportunity for theological creativity in my lifetime. Yet in the German theological milieu of the seventies this was still a sideline — today at least it has advanced to become a threat!

A visit to Sri Lanka in 1979 as the guest of the Jesuit liberation theologian Aloysius Pieris at his Tulana dialogue center brought Buddhism into focus as the most profound challenge of all: a challenge to the universalistic pretensions of European rationality and to the moral and religious superiority proclaimed by Christianity, both of which seemed hopelessly compromised by their alliances with colonialism and economic injustice.[2] Buddhism, in contrast, seemed to rebuke Christianity by its tolerance, its pacifism, its awareness of nature and the purity of its transcendence, while at the same time appearing eminently rational. Where was the question of truth in all this? I had been brought up on the Thomistic axiom *ens et verum convertuntur*: truth is one, and it is the truth of being itself. Was Buddhism, which itself knows theories of two truths, conventional and transcendent, the product of a different rationality? If so, are we going to need some kind of meta-language in which the meta-dialogue about ultimate presuppositions can be conducted? I realized that one would need to be equally at home in Asian and European philosophical traditions to do justice to this need, and here I reached the limits of my possibilities at that time.[3]

As we now try to do justice to our empirical studies of Christian and Buddhist encounters with cultures that were utterly alien to the European and Indian presuppositions these traditions brought with them to the Pacific and East Asia, these questions become acute. The satisfaction of being able to deal with them at last, however inadequately, is correspondingly great. Though I find it impossible to take all that is offered under the banners of "postmodernism" and "deconstruction" equally seriously, there is no doubt that we have entered a period of profound historical transition — what it will eventually be called is of secondary importance — and that this is manifested in a crisis of European self-confidence, whether in the ethical problems posed by scientific advance, the status of rationality itself, or the authoritativeness and credibility of Christian teaching. For one with a truly ecumenical — or, if you like, "catholic" — perspective, this is a time of unsuspected opportunity and high intellectual excitement. The possibilities that are opening up, though rooted in ancient traditions, are new precisely because they arise out of the global encounter of these traditions. It only remains to make of them what we can. If this perspective seems vaguely humanist or merely religious, it is because we as yet lack a category that would unite the contributions of "Buddhology" and "Christology" in an integrated approach to both understanding and *convivencia*. But as Ninian Smart is reported to have said with characteristic wit, if a thing's worth doing it's worth doing badly. So let us begin.

Chapter Five

TRANSCENDING DIFFERENCE

*Parameters, Strategies
and Outcomes of the Encounters*

The Japanese philosopher Watsuji Tetsuro, reading Heidegger's *Sein und Zeit* in Berlin in 1927, asked himself "why, if he [Heidegger] gave so much weight to temporality *(Zeitlichkeit)* as a *subjective* structure of existence, he did not at the same time allow spatiality *(Räumlichkeit)* to be an equally primordial existential structure." Not that Heidegger ignores the spatial; his sympathy with German Romanticism's ideal of "living nature" made him intensely aware of the natural world. But his central preoccupation with time shows that the influence of classical Western philosophy was stronger, and this Watsuji saw as a limitation, "for temporality without spatiality is not really temporality." Heidegger understands time as the individual's time, and existence *(Dasein)*, understood from this perspective alone, remains abstract. The full historicity of human existence is disclosed only when geographic and climatic space is taken into account.[1]

Watsuji's observations as his journey to Europe took him through the climatic zones of the China Sea, the Arabian Peninsula and the Mediterranean, though occasionally eccentric, are remarkable for their precision and insight. Today we would have to accuse him of "essentialism" for the way he deduces different peoples' national characters from the climates of the monsoon, the desert and the meadow environments, yet his reflections on his own Japanese culture after his return provide an interesting starting point for our own reflections on the encounters we have studied historically. Watsuji was struck by the contrast between the small size of Japanese houses and the immense significance of the "house" in the sense of the household *(ie)*,[2] in whose relationships the space "between" is characterized by "a fusion of sad and tender love with combative selflessness" and is thus "a between without distance *(distanzloses Zwischen)*."[3] This is reflected in the disposition of the Japanese house itself as living space, with only the suggestion of dividing doors and walls yet clearly demarcated from the street and the city "outside," unlike the European apartment, which needs the street, the restaurant and the park to compensate for its box-like rooms. "Entering or leaving a room in Europe is thus equal in significance to entering or leaving a 'house' in Japan."[4] The garden hedge in Japan, marking the polarity between domestic privacy and the public sphere of the city-state, plays the same role as the city wall in Europe, now expanded to become the nation-state with its clearly defined borders.[5] It is thus not surprising that the political in Japan has something of the family about it, so that the single word *matsurigoto* (from *matsuri*, "festival") can encompass both "holding a feast" and "administration and politics."[6] The *Tenno* represented the whole, including its religious dimension, in a way the pope never could, and "the people's sense of belonging to this whole was the source of all values."[7]

If modern Western philosophy and theology, taking their cue from Heidegger, have emphasized the temporality of existence, there have been many — albeit obscure — thinkers who have emphasized its spatiality.[8] There is in fact an astonishing number of thinkers from a variety of disciplines who have taken as their starting point our need to orientate ourselves in space. The mystical tradition knows U-, S- and O-shaped movements linking "above" and "below"; other binary dimensions are left/right, behind/before, inside/outside, coming to be/passing away.[9] In their attempts to conceptualize the transcendent, thinkers as diverse as Plotinus, Eckhart and the mystics of the Kabbala have tried to formulate the "fourth dimension" beyond conventional space-time.

Space and time thus make up one set of parameters within which the encounter of religious traditions can be mapped conceptually. Other such sets which have played a part in our analysis are immanence and transcendence, especially in relation to Buddhism's mode of presence in Japan and Thailand; biocosmic and metacosmic religion, illustrated particularly by the contrast between Christian theism and Pacific cultures, whether Aboriginal or Melanesian; and the primary and secondary symbolizations of experience which allow us to formulate such distinctions. At this stage of our enquiry it will be useful to make these parameters more explicit with a view to understanding better the dynamics of the encounters (section 1). We shall then look at the strategies employed by the religious traditions concerned in order to cope with the shock of difference (section 2). The next step will be to articulate the outcomes of such interreligious encounters in the new context of globalization (section 3). This will prepare the ground for the argument of chapter 6 that it is such strategies for transcending difference, discovered in the encounters of cultural and religious traditions, that disclose the potential of Buddhist, Christian and "primal" traditions for resolving conflict by transcending difference and thus hold out the hope of learning how to overcome violence.

1. Parameters of the Encounters

Difference implies dualism: the separate existence of the Other immediately raises the question — at least for the Western, subject-centered consciousness — of why it is "outside," "over against" the Self, not in every respect the Same, which in turn gives rise to the primordial question of responsibility: how is Self to react to the realization that the Other is irretrievably "beyond" Sameness and is unavailable for assimilation to one's own identity-with-oneself?[10] Is this the signal of a transcendence that relativizes difference, or a threat that triggers the impulse to react violently?

These are spatial metaphors, but difference has a temporal dimension as well: is there such a thing as continuity through time? How is this affected by change? Is development on an upward or downward course? Am I now the individual I confront in memory? Do traditions sustain an identity over time? These lines of thought are radically undercut when dualism itself is denied, as happens at high points of both Buddhist and Christian reflection and is being attempted again in certain forms of postmodernist deconstruction today. What then happens to difference? Can it replace identity as the governing paradigm of philosophy? Does this not amount to its being dismissed as illusory? Or may it be granted a qualified reality at a "first level" of conventional truth, to be superseded at the "second level" once reflection or realization opens the way to transcendence? Does transcendence, as the capacity to recognize successively more inclusive contexts pointing to an horizon that is at once completely undetermined and completely comprehensive, hold the key to overcoming attachment to the interests and identities that motivate violence? Picking up again the line of thought suggested in the Introduction (section 1), we need to look more closely at the parameters within which transcendence is thematized, for these too can be significantly different across cultures.

1(a). Sacred Space

On a visit to *Uluru* (Ayers Rock) and *Kata Tjuta* (The Olgas) in central Australia some years ago I could not help comparing the experience to the overwhelming impression of sacred space evoked by the great cathedrals of Europe or the imposing Buddhist temples of Asia.[11] Why do we respond intuitively to these "spaces," the one sculpted by nature, the other crafted by human hands, as "sacred"? On our way to Ayers Rock, our tour guide gave equal weight to the Aboriginal dreaming story of a battle between the python people and the black snake people which tells those who share the myth what the rock "is," and the European account in terms of height and circumference and subterranean strata emerging to be weathered by wind and rain. In the case of the cathedral, it is still sufficiently part of

Western culture for most Europeans to be able to decipher the signals of transcendence, encoded in every architectural detail, which tell us what a cathedral
"is"; Asians are familiar with the significance of temples in a similar way. In these
two vastly different forms, the natural and the constructed, particular spaces are
marked off as sacred, and in each case this act is as much social as physical. Paus-
ing to say grace before a meal, withdrawing to meditate, donning ritual dress —
in these and in many other ways social space is created for those meanings which
transcend everyday perceptions yet without which reality and society as "wholes"
do not make sense.[12]

As we saw in chapter 1, it has taken a long time to realize that in Aboriginal
Australia we are dealing with what Tony Swain calls a "locative" view of the
world, an "ontology of place" in which every topographical feature is the mark
of an "Abiding Event" performed by ancestral beings in places entirely permeated
by eternity, the "everywhen" of what has inadequately been called the Dreaming.
The fact that this ontology, when translated into Western languages, gives the
impression of being overwhelmingly static and impervious to change or development, should not deflect us from the realization that Aboriginal people, inasmuch
as this can be reconstructed from records that are all post-contact, were constantly
reinventing and rethinking every aspect of their lives — but in a context in which
no aspect of their world-construction was detached from place. The singularity
of each culture group's reality, however, was at the same time pan-Aboriginal
in that it shared a symbolic structure or syntax which made it communicable
to others along the "songlines" or dreaming tracks that traversed the continent.
The Aborigines' problem with Christianity was that it resisted location; it insisted
on another kind of transcendence altogether, one that presupposed time as the
arena in which a connected chain of events moved out from an initial point in
space-time through which it was connected to infinite time, eternity. But Christian transcendence could not *become* Aboriginal localities in the sense of *places*
which gave birth to new life and received the dead. The Aborigines' (ultimately
unsuccessful) countermove was to posit a supplementary ontology of limitless
Space in which to "locate" the Christian God. This allowed dis-placed people to
maintain ceremony outside country and to return to a sky-realm no matter where
they died: the "locative" worldview had become "U-topian" (not bound to place).

This reflection gives us a further clue as to why Buddhism, which is replete
with spatial imagery such as the Pure Lands and the immense Buddha-realms
illuminated by the *Lotus Sutra,* eventually reached an accommodation with East
Asian cultures such as those of China and Japan, as we saw in chapter 3. Its
tendency to associate its lineages and cults with sacred mountains in China, for
example, was one of its chief attractions for the Japanese, who regarded their
entire territory as a sacred place issuing directly from the gods.[13] Even the Zen

and Nichiren lineages founded places of cult and pilgrimage, and the Pure Land movements transposed the sacred place into a transcendent space in which the Buddha nature was fully manifest. But in most other cases the various Buddhist schools only became "translatable" into truly Japanese terms by becoming fused with localized cults, even to the point of identifying the *kami* of the place with particular *bodhisattvas*. With the medieval assimilation of Buddhism to the sacred space of the Japanese sociocosmic entity went an almost total instrumentalization by the imperial lineage, the aristocratic families and individual Shoguns in order to sanction and sanctify the institutions of government. The combinatory genius that created the shrine-temple "multiplexes" defined the terms of Japanese religiosity for a thousand years. The tenacity of this synthesis was evident in the effort needed to prize Buddhism apart from the shrines when they were redefined as exclusively "Shinto" once Buddhism had been declared an unwanted "foreign" religion in the Meiji era.

Though the various Buddhist divisions (*nikayas*) in Thailand became unified through a centralized administration under the control of the state, in chapter 4 we saw that at village level the presence of the *sangha* is justified by the monks' access to spirit realms which extend beyond those of local deities and thus assist at the inevitable transition through sickness and death. Once again the symbolic structure is spatial, but it is worked out largely at the level of primary symbolization without attempting to create world-transcending sacred spaces. In both cases, Japan and Thailand, Buddhism, itself conceived in predominantly spatial terms, simply found a niche in the existing primal religious culture, which it then leavened and enhanced by remaining immanent within it while maintaining a certain distance which was its signal, however faint, of an abiding transcendence.

But what does "transcendence" mean in Buddhism? Surely no Buddhist culture has tried to grasp it philosophically and live it existentially with more tenacity than the Japanese, yet what characterizes this culture is the almost total immanence of Buddhism in the "aesthetic space" of the sacred, the "mindscape" of the Japanese as manifested in the landscape of their highly localized religion. This seems to have affected the integrity of Buddhism as a universal but foreign religion. It served to unify the Japanese nation, but it seems to have proved incapable of deriving ethical judgments critical of the existing order from principles which could be formulated in the public space of the political arena. On the other hand, as the legitimating role of Buddhism in Thailand shows, political power involves compromises with "legitimate" violence, and although monastic Buddhism has found ways to keep itself apart from the quest for power, it has allowed itself to become identified with a quasi-sacral monarchy and a religious bureaucracy to an extent which makes even the most tentative criticism of economic and political processes, such as fostering non-violent and ecologically sound "development," susceptible to charges of *lèse majesté*. Both the Mahayana in Japan and the Theravada in Thailand seem to have entered into such an intimate relationship with indigenous cultures that the transcendence they represent is rendered not only religiously inauthentic but ethically and politically impotent.

1(b). Sacred Time

Not only modern physics but the history of religions have taught us the futility of trying to separate space and time. In Jewish tradition memory and promise are one with rootedness in the land, but displacement from the land and the eventual destruction of the cult center, the Temple at Jerusalem, stimulated the prodigious effort of remembrance and anticipation recorded in the Biblical narrative (in a way that is not dissimilar to the Aboriginal extension of an ontology of place into one of transcendent Space under the impact of invasion, which brought with it the necessity of *remembering* the injustice of displacement from the land and *re-locating* the sources of identity and hope). This narrative, often quasi-historical in its tenacious retention of detail, is framed between protology and eschatology, the accounts of the First Things and the Last. The Christian continuation of this story, including its proclaimed culmination in the Christ Event, completely detaches it from place in the sense that, though the story is precisely located within both geographical and chronological parameters, the celebration of its memory is in principle repeatable and ubiquitous; its everywhen is everywhere.

The route traveled by indigenous Australians from an ontology of space into historical time may be a two-way street which could lead "us" — the Westerners represented by the invading whites — back to a lost immediacy with the Self and the Earth, our repressed Archaic Other. The quality of our relationship to the alien Other is a moral test of the relationship to the Infinite symbolized in our religion and conceptualized in our theology. Are "horizontal" social and interpersonal relationships only possible, in the end, because of the "vertical" relationships implicit in the human openness to transcendence, which become explicit in the teachings of the religions? Where the difference is as great as that between European Christians and Aboriginal Australians, it must be asked whether we — the former — can travel this route back to the chthonic Self without illegitimate appropriation, cognitive violence and the colonization of culture. Or is the difference so great after all? The better we understand Aboriginal religion, the more we feel compelled to question our own dualistic understanding of the relationship between transcendence and immanence. How different is the transcendence so lately disclosed to us and so patently present in the contemplative side of Aboriginal culture — expressed in the concept of *dadirri* and celebrated in the ritual enactment of the Dreaming — from that found in Christian faith and Asian traditions?[14] Aboriginal spirituality seems to embody a transcendence that does not seek expression in relationships of domination, intolerance and aggression. Is this simply due to a limited awareness of alternatives and a lack of technical means of domination, or is it transferable to systems of belief at present characterized by an absolutism which projects their dualism onto all who are different?

The cultures of the Pacific Islands bear a certain affinity to those of Aboriginal Australia with regard to their rootedness in land, though in their case the context is that of ensuring fertility and the production of abundant wealth by the process of ritual exchange. The advent of the Christian story with its idea of transcendence in terms of time — God's absolute future — was thus an epoch-making disruption which radically threatened the prevailing worldview of a stable community consisting of the spirits of the living, the dead and the natural world, as we studied in the case of Melanesia in chapter 2. In this case, the locus of transcendence was these relationships themselves, ritually renewed in ceremonies of exchange. The Christian account of reality, on which ultimate salvation was said to depend, not only forced the memory back to precise points in far-distant time but opened up the prospect of an as yet undetermined future which would be the culmination of the entire scheme of creation and salvation. This teleological vision necessitated a complete reorientation of the existing Melanesian patterns of exchange on which the stability of the entire sociocosmic order depended. The enormous tension thus set up was one of the main causes of the cargo cults, which were collective attempts to redefine the terms on which *gutpela sindaun*, the "good life" of communal prosperity — symbolized by "cargo," the good things of modernity in their fullness — could be attained in some definitive and transcendent sense. But the new order also suggested that responsibilities extended beyond clan barriers to include reconciliation with former enemies and the inclusion of strangers in the circle of obligation, to say nothing of altruistic love and the necessity to protect the natural environment from the ravages of economic exploitation. At the root of this reorientation are reciprocal attempts at hetero-interpretation: indigenous appropriation of the Christian notion of "redemptive sacrifice" on the one hand, and Christian accommodation to the pragmatism institutionalized in Melanesian patterns of exchange on the other. On each side, over and above this, there remains the deeper question of retributive violence, which in Melanesian eyes may seem to be embodied in the Christian story of redemption by Christ's substitutionary sacrifice, at least in its Western version.

The full extent of this imposition of a Christian eschatological scheme of things on the "biocosmic" religion of physical life implicit in Melanesian cultures remains to be seen; it has undoubtedly obscured profound indigenous insights into the human relationship with nature and effective ways of maintaining community which may yet prove crucial to the creation of a genuinely Pacific Christianity, though for a long time they were overlooked by European Christians. The element of transcendence in Christian faith undoubtedly contributed — for a time — to containing and transforming the violence endemic in Melanesian patterns of retribution, without always recognizing that this was a structured violence with its own inbuilt restraints, and without always admitting that Christianity itself had been associated with the violence of invasion, coercion and exploitation. The Melanesians produced their own version of an eschatological future in the form of the cargo cults as attempts to mediate between myth and modernity. The resulting "cargoist mentality" still determines economic and political activity to a considerable extent, not excepting the Westernized commercial and parliamentary sectors, despite the considerable influence of the Christian churches.

1(c). Dualism: The Transcendence of Immanence

Christianity in its various European cultural incarnations achieved a striking, not to say overwhelming formulation of transcendence in its conception of God as absolute Being (*ipsum esse*, "the pure act of existing itself," in the words of St. Thomas Aquinas). Unlike Buddhism, however, Christianity did not originate in a philosophical milieu but had to re-interpret the Jewish story of salvation in the terminology of Greek philosophy. Christian theology is thus character-ized by a kind of structural dualism which continues to generate tension even in the medieval synthesis. True, the dual acts of creation-in-view-of-redemption and redemption-for-the-sake-of-creation form a single plan of salvation revealed in Christ, and using both Aristotelian and Platonic concepts the human being is conceived as the unity of form-as-act and matter-as-potency. The human as enfleshed spirit tends towards participation in divine Being, a participation ulti-mately made possible by God's Spirit, the communication of the divine life itself. This powerful theistic vision survived the reification of its metaphysics in late scholasticism, the vigorous criticism by the Reformers of its too optimistic view of corrupted human nature, and Karl Barth's rejection of the doctrine of anal-ogy on which it is based. In its affirmation of the divine transcendence, if not in its metaphysical orientation and philosophic details, it remained fundamental to the conceptualization of the Christian God which may be found in the preach-ing of missionaries of all denominations during the great Catholic and Protestant mission eras in the Asia-Pacific region.[15] Yet this magnificent conception of God as absolute Being sits uneasily with the biblical story of God's dealings with a covenanted people throughout the vicissitudes of history; it has proved vulner-able to the philosophical critiques of modernity; and it seems, on the face of it, utterly incompatible with the Buddhist anti-ontology of absolute Nothingness.[16]

Whilst carrying all before it in the mission fields, especially those of Africa and the Pacific, this Christian theism was exposed to drastic criticism in the course of the European Enlightenment and was successfully resisted by most countries whose civilizations had been shaped by Buddhism. The target of these critiques was the dualism which the medieval synthesis was unable to overcome and which seemed unacceptable to both European and Buddhist philosophers, albeit for different reasons. A chain of criticism beginning with Descartes, Hume and Kant and inherited by Nietzsche, Foucault and Derrida radically questions the human mind's capacity to make a judgment about the independent existence of God, going on to question not only the possibility of God's existence but the subjective authenticity of aspiring to any kind of "higher meaning," and ending with the deconstruction of the human subject itself as a fully autonomous originator of cognitive and volitional acts — thereby unwittingly falling into line with the age-old, pre-Christian Buddhist critique of the notion of an independently existing self.

This is a curious state of affairs for the Christian tradition, which bequeathed to the West such fundamental concepts as "person," "character," "individual," "subject" and "conscience."[17] These, as we have seen, played a crucial part in the mission strategies that reshaped the development of Asian and Pacific cultures. Christian theism held out the prospect of a truly radical transcendence which relativized every single alternative object of human aspiration and desire except this one unique Being who created them all and who was revealed in Christ as the source of inexhaustible and forgiving love. But it also raised the question of the internal consistency of such a conception: is God as Being-itself nevertheless *a* being, though unique among beings, or does the very concept of Being-itself entail a radical critique of the Western notion of being such as that initiated by Heidegger? In popular preaching and practice, the *idea* of God as Being was only acceptable anyway on the grounds of faith supported by divine grace. This may help to explain the resistance of various forms of "primal" and "sapiential" religion to the intellectual demands of Christian theism. Where Land, Life and Community are supreme *religious* values, where wisdom consists in bringing one's life into harmony with the rhythms and balance of the cosmos itself, is this Christian construct not only subversive but superfluous? And is it not simply incomprehensible in the Buddhist intellectual context of *sunyata*, the absolute emptiness at the heart of all reality, whether this includes the individual self, the universal Buddha-nature or even *nirvana* itself?[18]

The test of the Christian conception comes not so much in the form of philosophy as of ethics. If nothing but this divinely revealed vision, of the world and human beings as created out of nothing by pure love and subject to a covenant of ultimate reconciliation, suffices to overcome once and for all the enmity that leads to violence and all the evil in the human heart, then it must be acknowledged as the disclosure of a transcendence that gives the "good life" and "right conduct" an ultimate sanction. As an instrument for removing any conceivable grounds or rationalizations for violent conflict this appears unsurpassed and it has indeed served this function many times over in Pacific Islands contexts. At the same time its inherent meliorism, its tendency to legitimize religious superiority and spiritual self-righteousness, especially when these are identified with ethnic particularity and ideological certainty, has immeasurably intensified the motives for conflict and the exercise of violence. Can this ambivalence be traced to the dualistic structure of a transcendence conceived in a dialectic tension with immanence? Or is a certain dualism indispensable as the basis for moral discrimination and hence as a structural principle of ethics? These questions are relevant to our attempt to conceptualize transcendence as a practical path to the transformation of conflicts.

1(d) Non-Dualism: The Immanence of Transcendence

Before Buddhism became established in China it had already radicalized the Buddha's "middle way" in the Madhyamika philosophy systematized by Nagarjuna in the second century C.E. The teaching on "no-self" (*anatman*), what we might call the deconstruction of the notion of an autonomous subject by showing that any alleged constituent of the self is in reality "not-self," implied "no-substance" in any area of reality, including language and ideas. True to the Buddha's teaching of not entertaining "views" (*ditthi*) or theories of the world, the object of this teaching was not to offer an alternative ontology but to destroy any basis for attachment by dismantling the last vestiges of dualism in the individual's knowing and willing in the world. This non-dualism encompasses both being and nothingness. Thus neither theism nor nihilism could have been options for the Chinese Mahayanists (though in the early stages of their assimilation of Buddhism the "Dark Learning" of the Taoists seemed to provide the matrix for mutual understanding as the Taoist paradoxes were matched point for point with the Buddhist dialectic; for more detail see Appendix II). Thus was forged a powerful surgical instrument for stripping away the layers of self-deceit and illusion which in the state of "normality" protect us from the realization of the emptiness at the heart of existence. It is also an equally powerful diagnostic tool for what we would call the critique of ideologies, including those of modernity, the ever more frenetic "immortality projects" of consumerism and technology. The irony is that it is in Japan, where the Zen lineages made the most radical attempts to translate transcendence-as-emptiness into practice, that Buddhism became so thoroughly assimilated to every aspect of the culture. Here, too, an uneasy synthesis resulted in that the principles of what could have become a Buddhist ethic of transcendence were evacuated of meaning, allowing the worship of technology and its products to triumph completely. In Thailand, by a contrast that can only be described as paradoxical, at least pockets of Buddhist-inspired resistance have emerged despite the ravages of capitalist-driven "development."

The other side of the coin of *sunyata*, absolute emptiness, is absolute identification with everything, absolute fullness. In this respect *sunyata* takes the metaphor of space to its absolute limits. In doing so, however, it seems to lose touch entirely with the dimension of time, eliminating the role of historical memory because prescinding from the identities it shapes. May we transcend our historicity to this extent? Is there not a non-dualistic way of participating in existence in space-time? And is absolute truth, once realized, so remote from experienced reality that we need to posit, as the Buddhist philosophers did, a conventional truth (*samvrtisatya*) in order to refer to the exigencies of ordinary life, whereas the transcendent dimension, unattainable and ineffable in itself, belongs to another order of truth altogether (*paramarthasatya*)?[19]

To the Chinese, Indian Buddhism must have seemed profoundly dualistic, and their puzzlement at the efforts of dialecticians such as Nagarjuna to resolve this dualism logically must have been huge. The two-truths theory might well have suggested to them that Buddhist non-dualism is the most spectacular dualism of all. The medieval Christian philosopher-theologians had always insisted on the transcendental unity of being, truth, goodness and beauty (*ens et verum, bonum, pulchrum convertuntur*), which is present, though only imperfectly and analogically, in every aspect of created being. Buddhists would say that this construction does not succeed in overcoming dualism. According to the Kyoto School Zen philosopher Masao Abe, non-dualism is the contrary of neither monism nor dualism, but represents a "positionless position"; the "ground" of pluralism is therefore itself "positionless."[20] The standpoint "beyond" good and evil, discrimination and non-discrimination, if it is indeed that of Absolute Emptiness, does not eliminate these alternatives but grasps each in its "suchness" (*tathata*), seeing good and evil as they *really* are and making an ultimate *affirmation*.[21] Time, in this perspective, is neither linear nor circular and has neither beginning nor end, which leads to problems with the notion of history. "Time becomes 'history' when the factor of spatiality (Worldhood, *Weltlichkeit*) is added to it. History comes to have meaning when time is understood to be irreversible and each moment has an unrepeatable uniqueness or once-and-for-all nature (*Einmalichkeit* [sic])."[22] In the light of wisdom, "everything and everyone is realized in its suchness and time is overcome," while in the light of compassion, "time is religiously significant and essential," for "*Sunyata* turns itself into *vow* and into *act* through its self-emptying." If this yields a Buddhist view of history, however, it is a non-eschatological and non-teleological one.[23] The way back from radical non-dualism to radical engagement thus remains problematic, for in transcending identity and history non-dualism seems to carry us beyond good and evil and to make morality itself impossible. Yet this Buddhist perspective leaves us with what is perhaps the most radical artic-ulation of transcendence ever achieved: the inconceivable resolution beyond life and death, Self and Other, Being and Nothingness.

2. Strategies of the Encounters

Some reflection on how religious cultures have coped with the "strange encoun-ters" which form the subject of this book may help to clarify, however sketchily, *why* conflict so often arises in such first-contact situations and *how* it can be transcended.[24] Acknowledging the Other, welcoming the Stranger and reconcil-ing the Enemy might be said to represent three stages of such encounters whose moral demands may be plotted on a scale of increasing difficulty. As each stage is reached, the spiritual resources of the individuals concerned and their religious traditions are tested accordingly.

2(a). Repression

European Christians arriving direct from Britain at the end of the eighteenth century in what was then called New Holland — the "Great South Land" that was to become Australia — were quite patently unprepared for what they found, and they reacted in a variety of ways. As we saw in chapter 1, they were confronted with difference, both human and geographical, so extreme that relatively few of them were able to regain their moral bearings after the initial shock of discovery. There were those who perspicaciously made the adjustment that allowed them to gain a partial understanding of the Aboriginal peoples they encountered, even to the extent of learning their languages and beginning to respect them in their otherness. For most, however, the moral gap was too great to bridge and they either refused to acknowledge that these creatures were human at all or, if they did go so far, assumed that the Aborigines' evident inferiority predestined them to swift extinction in the face of a superior civilization.

There were processes at work here which I think can best be described as anal-ogous to the mechanisms of repression and projection known to psychoanalysis. The spectacle of the Aborigines, so completely integrated into this alien natural environment, evinced a kind of primitive terror in these white Christians, so much so that they refused to credit the Indigenes with full humanity lest they them-selves be forced to scrutinize the fragility and artificiality of their own beliefs and principles. They therefore repressed this dawning awareness in something akin to the clinical sense, thereby setting up a field of tension which forced the unac-knowledged reality to the surface of consciousness again in the form of distorted symbols — the Aborigines as embodiments of evil and the land as an existential threat — which seemed to them eminently reasonable and morally justifiable, but which were in fact the symptoms of a moral and cognitive failure. Their unacknowledged fear of the Stranger reappeared as hostility and aggression directed as much against the land itself as against its incomprehensible inhabitants.

The wholesale destruction of forests, the overgrazing of grasslands, the refusal to learn from the Aboriginal inhabitants, and above all the violent retaliation for real or imagined aggression on the side of the Indigenes may be traceable to such a mechanism of repression. For the Aborigines, the Land was Life itself; for the settlers, it was the Enemy. The settlers' deep sense of inadequacy and illegitimacy was projected onto the country and its indigenous inhabitants in the form of genocidal violence, then of forced assimilation policies, and finally of institutionalized social deprivation — and all this, until very recently, with the active cooperation and moral sanction of Christians and their churches. Another way of putting this is to say that the European Christian "Self" was incapable of finding space in its collective sense of identity and its social consensus about meaning for this archaic, chthonic Other which in reality was a powerful embodiment and symbolic evocation of humanity in close symbiosis with nature, something the Europeans were not prepared to accept. In this way these Christians did not only physical but cognitive violence to a social and religious world which remained almost entirely closed to them.

2(b). Ritualization

The Aborigines, meanwhile, were reacting in their own way, not only by physical resistance against overwhelming odds but by reconstructing their mythic thought world, as they had already done when confronted with Melanesian neighbors and Indonesian visitors in the far north. Just as Captain Cook's ship, the *Endeavor,* appeared in cave paintings dedicated to the ancestor spirits or Dreaming heroes, the new reality of white invasion eventually found its place in Dreaming stories and their re-enactment in ritual. The sky gods, who seem quite un-Aboriginal when seen against the background of what anthropology takes to have been traditional beliefs, make ritual sense in that they provide more transcendent contexts for elaborating the new meanings suggested by white conquest.

In the Pacific Islands, especially in Melanesia, the necessary mythico-ritual adjustments had more freedom to develop among peoples who, being always in the majority, were more readily able to resist and reinterpret the advent of the whites with their Christian message of salvation. Recognizing the Europeans' technical superiority in warfare, the Islanders could enlist their support against traditional enemies in return for concessions in the form of (the use, not ownership of) land, timber, plantations, women and in some cases positions of influence, which happened extensively in Micronesia and Polynesia. Or they could take a more radical stance, recasting their own myths of dispossession, which anticipated the return of more cunning and intelligent ancestors (sometimes depicted as white) bearing superior cultural techniques. They could thus nurture the ambition of being able to offer the whites some equivalent of the benefits they saw the whites enjoying in order to secure these for themselves. They did this by experimenting with collective rites of initiation which would unlock the ritual secrets of the whites' superiority. Once again, in the context of almost total mutual misunderstanding and much wasted energy on both sides, the Melanesians in particular nevertheless coped with difference by vigorously readjusting to the new reality and trying to force it into the mould of their magical worldview.

I am unable to say whether processes of repression and projection were also at work here, but at the least this was an expression of clan-group ethnocentrism which could only ward off the threat posed by the Otherness of the Stranger by trying to steal the strangers' secrets and outdo them in the production of "cargo." Though this project was doomed to failure in the face of what in the nineteenth century were already global cultural forces, it represents a powerful strategy of intercultural appropriation.

2(c). Absorption

The case of Buddhism's gradual permeation of northeast and southeast Asia gives evidence of yet other strategies for dealing with cultural and religious difference. Let us be under no misapprehension about *how* different these Indian schools of Buddhism were from the East Asian civilizations into which they percolated, not primarily with missionary or colonizing intent but largely as a by-product of commercial contacts. Indian culture from ancient times has been primarily interested in the universal, the transcendent unity of things, which meant that "one's individual self is ultimately nondual with other selves"[25] and neither the state nor the nation was sacralized.[26] In China the focus was on the particular, and "for the Japanese the phenomenal world may be said to *be* the absolute"; as a result, "In China the extended family functioned as a small state; in Japan the state was one big family."[27]

"The religious goal of Taoism and Ch'an is not to experience another realm but to become aware of the true nature of this one"; in Japan, the sacred is *in* this world, not distinct from it, so that for Shinto, "death is simply impurity." "Instead of understanding this world as a *samsara* to be fled, 'everyday mind' is enlightenment in Chinese Ch'an."[28] Syncretism came naturally to the Chinese, who simply put the baffling Indian doctrines in a hierarchical order rather than investigate their inner logic, while Shinto, lacking doctrine altogether, allowed Buddhism no scope for developing universal principles or an independent position from which to criticize state policies and institutions.[29] This meant that there was no sense of a "categorical imperative" or "ethical universalism" because there was no transcendental truth in which to ground them. Transcendence "as higher realm, as ethical universal, and as critical perspective on the given"[30] was thus eliminated in the course of Buddhism's Chinese and Japanese transformations. It is thus not so much that the Indian Buddhists were taken aback — which they surely were — by the daunting task of "converting" the pragmatic Chinese, Koreans, Japanese, Vietnamese and Thais to their demanding doctrines, as that these ancient peoples felt challenged by the strangeness of a religion which insisted on such doctrines and drew from them the consequence that Buddhism must keep its own monastic institutions separate from those of the state.

This process can perhaps best be described as mutual assimilation or absorption, a kind of osmosis which reached its apogee in Japan, where Buddhism was only ever tolerated as an enhancement of the divine nation (*shinkoku*) and acquiesced in this role. So we find indigenous *kami* and introduced *bodhisattvas* merging into shared identities in numerous local shrines and sacred places whose very topography becomes charged with Buddhist meaning in ways that are at times reminiscent of the "locative ontology" of Aboriginal Australia. Buddhist ritual and doctrine thus come to be almost entirely determined by the religious needs of the people and the exigencies of the state.

In Thailand, by contrast, we find less an osmosis than a symbiosis, an assimilation of Buddhism with its sacred scriptures and celibate monks into the ritual and magic of "primal" village religion while preserving a certain distance, a place apart. Despite the integration of the monastic system into the state apparatus and the all-pervading ritualism, a core of integrity remains, which produces instances of resolute opposition to the destruction wrought by so-called development, something that seems less evident in Japan, where Buddhist transcendence has become entirely immanent in the sacredness of the nation. Has difference, in these cases, been dealt with or denied? Will the psychological mechanism of repression yet wreak its revenge? Or is this merely a Western cavil, premised on the cult of the ego, which has little or no application in Asia?

2(d). Institutionalization

To conclude this rapid survey it may be worthwhile to mention a way of dealing with difference which, though it originated outside the Asia-Pacific region, determines virtually every society there in one way or another, even if only as what is rejected: the institutionalized pluralism of Western liberal democracies. As a political system derived from the philosophies of the Enlightenment and the European and American revolutions, pluralism emphasizes not hierarchy — as in the caste system of India and other parts of south Asia — but equality; not harmony — as in virtually all Asian social philosophies and Pacific lifestyles — but competition; not hereditary privilege but just distribution; and, crucially, no one political ideology or religious doctrine is to be given precedence over any other, except for the almost purely formal liberal philosophy underlying the whole.[31] In a democracy one can be against just about everything — except democracy. This political system, which obviously has profound implications for culture and religion, is now under severe strain, not only in the West but in the Asia-Pacific as well, as evidenced by the Asia-wide economic crisis of 1997 — in reality a crisis of political leadership.

Designed to neutralize the endemic Christian sectarianism of post-Reformation Europe and to allow the free exchange of political and scientific ideas, pluralist democracy reaches its limits when cultural groups to whom its liberal presuppositions are alien refuse to be assimilated to it. If home-grown European ideologies such as fascism and communism could be put down militarily or outmaneuvered economically, Islam remains recalcitrant and numerous other ethnic groups, deposited on Europe's shores by the reverse flow of post-colonial immigration, prefer to cling to familiar cultural and religious identities rather than to play the game of open competition from a position of disadvantage.[32] The strains imposed by "multiculturalism" upon Pacific societies such as those of Australia and New Zealand well illustrate the inherent contradictions of liberal democracy in the face of significant ethnic diversity, as do the emergence of communalism in India and Sri Lanka, the successive coups by ethnic Fijians against resident Indians once these obtain political power, the creakings of the Chinese Confucian-Communist monolith as economic liberalization becomes imperative, the threatened disintegration of the Javanese Indonesian empire and many other stresses and strains as countries throughout the region try to maintain the facade of democracy while pursuing indigenous agendas. The balance of conflict and consensus is difficult to maintain once extreme cultural differences remove the common basis of understanding and the minimalist framework of values it presupposes.

Running through all these strategies for dealing with difference is a dialectic of Same and Other, of Self and Stranger, of Own and Enemy which marks one of the main points of intersection of culture, politics and religion. If this dialectic is not mastered, whether psychologically or socially, tensions result which find expression in various forms of repression and avoidance and can easily lead to violent conflict. Most conceptual models for dealing with such conflict and its causes have strongly Western and ultimately Christian presuppositions which may not easily be shared by cultures such as those of the Asia-Pacific region. We therefore need to look again, and more deeply, at these cultures' own presuppositions for dealing with difference and transcending violence, in order to see if they contain an ethical and spiritual potential which may prove capable of engaging with the global philosophical order which the West, in the context of global dominance, has put in place. This we shall do in the next chapter. But first we should reflect in a more general way on the dynamics of these processes of cultural accommodation in the new global multicultural environment.

3. Outcomes of the Encounters

The processes of accommodation and appropriation, of indigenization and contextualization that we have studied bring with them, as we have seen, either compromises with the particularities of indigenous cultures or their refusal.[33] The response depends on the ways in which universalist traditions conceptualize and operationalize transcendence or, reciprocally, how localized traditions transpose transcendence into immanence. We characterized this in general terms as the superimposition of "metacosmic" or world-transcending religious traditions on the "biocosmic" or life-related traditions of "primal" religious cultures. Just as universalist religions like Christianity and Buddhism represent a profound challenge to the ethnocentricity and localization of primal religions, so the latter contain an implicit critique of the absolutist pretensions of metacosmic religions to final revelation, definitive salvation and ultimate truth. There is a dialectic here which we have noticed but must now explore.

In the new context created by global communication and trade, systems of knowledge and authority that purport to legislate for the "whole" lack credibility, for the emerging global system knows only functionally differentiated subsystems, none of which exhaustively defines it.[34] Even the self-proclaimed universal religions, in this perspective, are in fact territorial, socio-cultural particularisms whose inability to communicate with one another is a danger to world order.[35] From the point of view of systems theory, the solution to this is the "elimination of structures that negate functional differentiation,"[36] i.e., which are unable to demonstrate their contribution to the maintenance of the "whole," defined, in the case of the religions, in terms of their very transcendence. The consequence for the culture groups which have traditionally been the bearers of religious messages is that no *one* of them can any longer presume to thematize the whole, but all must be recontextualized in the much more complex society-of-societies whose tendency is to become global.[37] This not only brings about the relativizing of any cultural particularities which might lay claim to absolute significance, it opens up for the religions the new role of subsystems in global society, which is "greater" than any of them yet lacks the means to define itself unless these are supplied by the religions with their symbolizations of transcendence.[38]

From this systems theory point of view, religion shares with morality the disadvantage of being wedded to the particular and the communal. Morality, in the sense of universalizable *Moral* as distinct from localized *Sitten* (customs and

habits), is becoming less binding as its normative force is weakened by the eleva-
tion of individual choice to become the sole point of reference for ethics. This no
doubt represents a certain liberation from the constricting controls of life in small,
tightly knit villages and communities, but providing — let alone enforcing —
moral norms for a global community is a task that still lies before us.[39] Religion's
primary function of pointing to transcendence is what makes the thematization
of reality as a whole possible, but only to the extent that transcendence can be
grasped as, or in terms of, immanence. The binding force of moral norms in particular situations is an example. But for this to happen the religions must thematize
transcendence in mutually complementary ways, despite the particularity of the
various terms — symbols and myths with local as well as universal reference —
in which they do so. The concept of transcendence cannot even be formulated
unless in terms defined by the immanence of religious traditions in the phenomenal worlds of different cultures; this also applies to rationality, the capacity for
transcendence intrinsic to reason itself. The very diversity of such expressions
of transcendence, however, could leaven the implicit totalitarianism of global
economics and politics, science and technology as rational projects. No such sub-
system, not even science, philosophy or art, can truly represent the whole.[40] But
this only holds good on condition that the internal dynamic of such diversity
remains peaceful.

The characteristic abstractness of this functionalist approach makes it difficult
to close the gap between theory and experience, norms and history, but it does
provide a framework for reflection on the dilemma of basing identity on a relationship to land as "place" in the newly emerging post-modern world of virtual spaces.
The seductive fascination of "real virtuality"[41] must not divert our attention from
the capacity for transcendence encoded in the myths and stories of land-based
primal traditions, which corresponds to a continuing human need to belong to a
place, for identity mediated by historical narrative. Even on the magnified scale
of Buddhism's relationship to India, Christianity's to the Mediterranean or Islam's
to Arabia, the particularity and locality of cultural identity remains a constant.
The challenge of inculturation in the context of globalization is to realize — in
both senses of the word: to grasp and to make real — that this particularity of
place must not become a barrier to communication and a cause of conflict. The
struggles of Aboriginal Australians, Melanesians and other Pacific Islanders, of
the Thais and the Japanese and their own indigenous minorities, among many
others, to avoid self-isolation in the new global context because of their religious
attachments to land and localized cultures are not incidental but paradigmatic.

The localization of transcendence achieved by primal traditions takes the
absolutist sting out of the transcendence proclaimed by their universalist counterparts, though the particularism of place brings with it the danger of confining

identity to ethnicity and making it impossible for ethnic groups to look beyond their local horizons to a wider, more "catholic" cosmopolitanism. The Pacific and Asian inculturations of Christianity and Buddhism thus remain problematic. Their "secondary symbolizations" of transcendence sit uneasily with the various indigenous modes of "primary symbolization" drawn from the continuance of life in the world of phenomena. Yet without the mediation of primal traditions neither the "samsarization" of Buddhist transcendence nor the "incarnation" of Christian transcendence could have taken practical forms. Primal traditions, orientated to the celebration and continuation of life in particular places, are the idiom of the poor everywhere, offering as they do the prospect of articulating the meaning of suffering and death and satisfying people's need for consolation and hope. We must bear this in mind as we now proceed to reflect on how the failures of the past may yet lay the foundation for cooperation in the future.

Chapter Six

TRANSCENDING VIOLENCE

Dialogue as the Practice of Non-Violence

If the end of the Cold War and the purported "triumph" of capitalism over communism are regarded as the outcome of the contest between the two "master ideologies" of the twentieth century, the world is facing new patterns of conflict and must find new strategies for dealing with them. One influential proposal has been that the principal source of conflict in the new century will be the "clash of civilizations," the rivalry of the great religiously inspired civilizational blocs along whose "fault lines" conflict is most likely to break out.[1] In the same context the father of peace research, Johan Galtung, has suggested that the "religious cosmologies" that give rise to fundamentally different economic and political systems also hold out the promise of producing strategies for peacemaking if their archaic symbolisms could be transposed into a vision of dialogue and collaboration in the postmodern era.[2] These could plausibly be characterized as "realist" and "idealist" accounts of the role religions could play in peacemaking. The political calculus of international relations insists that more diversity means more conflict potential; the inevitable multiculturalism of global society may not be reproduced in individual national polities without grave risk of violence. The religious riposte says that we need an ethic of survival, which only the religions can provide by learning to overcome their differences in dialogue.[3]

The studies undertaken in this book suggest that neither response to the new global situation does full justice to the peacemaking potential of the religions. Despite the lamentable failures of both Christianity and Buddhism to come to terms with cultures alien to their original forms of inculturation, each has retained the capacity to transcend difference and thereby to overcome the violence that is so often sparked off by the encounter with the Stranger. The cultures they encountered, for their part, also showed evidence of non-violent strategies for assimilating difference without identity loss. Where this has happened it has been the liberative, non-violent *praxis* of non-conflictual communication that has made possible the *Konvivenz* of wider, more inclusive communities in which the "otherness" of the Stranger is accepted and respected.[4] But how can this be achieved more widely, given the histories of hostility, alienation and misunderstanding we have seen? It is our task in this final chapter, based on the preliminary reflections in the previous one, to work towards an answer to this question, taking account of the declared doctrines and the actual behavior of Christians and Buddhists in their encounters with Pacific and Asian cultures. First I shall offer some more abstract considerations of what is involved, morally and intellectually, in intercultural encounters between religions (section 1). Having looked at the respective Pacific and Asian inculturations of Christianity and Buddhism, we know that these relationships have in many cases been chronicles of failure, but we shall ask what can be learned from such failures and whether the acknowledgment of failure can itself play a part in interreligious communication. Then we shall look at the transformations that are called for in each tradition if they are to deal with the reality of one another's presence and the collaborative task awaiting them as the world becomes one and community becomes global (section 2).

1. The Dialectics of Dialogue

One of the greatest challenges faced by any culture is the degree of difference it is prepared to tolerate, the limits it sets on the dialectic of sameness and otherness, both in its own internal development and in its encounters with others.[5] It has been proposed that the primordial social act of forming a community and asserting its distinctive identity is the primordial act of violence;

> that imagining identity as an act of distinguishing and separating from others, of boundary making and line drawing, is the most frequent and fundamental act of violence we commit. Violence is not only what we do to the Other. It is prior to that. Violence is the very construction of the Other.... Ironically, the Outsider is believed to threaten the boundaries that are drawn to exclude him, the boundaries his very existence maintains.[6]

The problem is discussed by anthropologists and philosophers under the heading "ethnocentrism" in the context of an alleged opposition between "relativism" and "universalism."[7] When cultural and religious diversity is really experienced with a minimum of avoidance and repression we perceive the contingency of our own socially constructed worlds; we realize that the strangers are indeed aliens whose ways may not even be able to be compared with ours if we restrict ourselves to our own analytical categories. The more we "know" about the others, the less accessible their culture seems to be, and if we are Europeans we find ourselves asking whether the very idea of trying to find a place for their strangeness in our own context may not itself be a cultural peculiarity which "they" do not share.[8]

Yet though anthropology may need to practice "descriptive relativism," the quandaries surrounding human rights remind us that cognitive and ethical relativism are self-defeating because self-contradictory.[9] The universal validity of truth, including religious truth, some participants in the discussion believe, must be taken as axiomatic if it is indeed "truth" we are speaking about, otherwise there is no ultimate basis for shared knowledge or mutual understanding.[10] Are there "cultural universals," then, and if so in what do they consist? Wimmer proposes that the apparent incompatibility between the rational criteria of intentional action and the norms imposed by different cultures can be resolved if "in place of the oversocialized individual we put the strategically acting human being."[11] The rationality of the individual's actions is self-reflexive and for that very reason pragmatic, in that always and everywhere — not just in Europe! — it is able to question given norms and negotiate new meanings by making "cultural compromises."[12] Precisely this is the universal:

> What binds all human beings together and makes it possible for them to set the cultural landscape in motion and to move within it themselves is the capacity to find a compromise between meaning and use. This I should like to call the pragmatics of cultural production.[13]

Although "the ethnocentric perspective can not ultimately be overcome," something like a "global cultural compromise" is conceivable "through an alliance of cosmopolitans."[14] This means that universality is not given *a priori*, nor may it be imposed on others by those who imagine that they already possess it. Rather, it must be "elaborated cooperatively," because it lies precisely "in the interaction, in listening and dialogue, in what one negotiates with others," yielding the "paradox of a plurality of universalizations (*einer Universalisierung im Plural*)."[15] It follows that ethical complementarity need not imply ethical relativism. There is also almost always the chance that cultures will "overlap" sufficiently to make initial understanding possible, despite cultural differences and incompatible media of expression (literary/oral, conceptual/mythical). Difference may no longer be equated with inferiority as the obverse of European intellectual superiority: "It may come as a surprise to Europe that Europe has now become decipherable."[16] The Western assumption that science and rationality are exclusively European preserves is being superseded. The transcendence implicit in the assertion of truth and the violence implicit in the assertion of identity may yet be reconcilable in theory, as indeed they must be in practice.

1(a). The Analogia Relationis *in Interreligious Encounters*

Religious traditions, however, pose special problems of their own. Those such as Buddhism and Christianity, which implicitly or explicitly make universal claims based on a central enlightenment or revelation, have a tendency to consider themselves in possession of definitive truth, on which the well being of all and the salvation of the world depend. This saving truth tends to be embodied in institutions — scriptures, rituals, practices, authorities — whose ultimate sanction transcends all processes of development and dialogue because it comes from within, beyond, above and is therefore *prior* to the interactions out of which history is made. Truth as the *outcome* of such interactions with those whose traditions are radically different seems unthinkable. This intrinsic certainty of salvific truth is therefore projected onto others as a relationship with inferiors. The religiously Other is so construed that its image confirms the conviction of the religious Self's superiority. The primal traditions have their own more ethnocentric versions of this attitude. The known Other (e.g., a neighboring people) and the unknown Stranger (e.g., invading colonizers) are marked out, simply in virtue of their being different, as the Enemy of one's Own. Their destruction is justified because their very difference seems to threaten one's own group, in terms of whose well being the "good" is defined. Such attitudes, of course, are by no means restricted to tribal peoples. As a hermeneutics for the dialogue of religions, in any case, neither absolutist nor ethnocentric viewpoints are appropriate.

From the ethical point of view, on the other hand, religious traditions generally regard hospitality offered to the Stranger as a profoundly religious gesture. Religion could even be defined as the capacity to create space for *the* Other, the absolute Stranger who is nevertheless closer than one's own Self: God, or the equivalent symbol of the transcendent in the non-theistic religions (Advaita-Vedanta, Theravada Buddhism, many primal traditions). In many different ways the religious person is continually encouraged to make space for the Stranger, to transform the unfamiliar into "family."[17] Seen in this light, dialogue becomes an eminently religious act; in Christian terms, it celebrates the sacrament of the Stranger. The pragmatic presuppositions of all communication — intelligibility, truth, sincerity, appropriateness — thus become the preconditions of all theology. We arrive at the position of an "intersubjective universalism" which arises out of communicative practice. No one dialogue partner's assumptions about meaning and truth may be imposed on the others in advance. This extends to understandings of reason itself: we may need to acknowledge that other people's systems of meaning constitute an "other-rationality" whose compatibility with our own is not immediately obvious.[18] We are thus confronted with an unsettling dissymmetry: in the realm of *gnosis*, the religions assume their own superiority based on the certainty that they possess definitive truth; in that of *ethos*, however, they defer to the prior demand of the Other as Stranger, in extreme cases even as Enemy, to be treated with respect and love. Disparities such as the Vatican's inflexibility in matters of doctrinal and moral orthodoxy alongside its impressive advocacy of social justice and human rights, or Mahayana Buddhism's discipline of transcendence coupled with its apparent indifference to moral issues in the public sphere, become explicable if this is better understood.[19]

This amounts to a disparity between ideology and charity. It may be possible to resolve it if we compare the mutual understanding which ideally takes place in the encounter of religious traditions, and which should result in a shared ethical practice, with a mysterious phenomenon which we nevertheless take for granted in our everyday lives: our knowledge of other persons. The other human being is at one and the same time absolutely the Same — inasmuch as we are members of the one species — and, as a person and therefore an autonomous center of cognition and volition, absolutely Other. Indeed, it is the knowledge of the Other as an "I" that can know and will that first sets in train the process of my own self-awareness. In a phenomenological perspective it is from this knowledge, which is only possible in the presence of the Other, that my own — already retrospective — awareness of being embodied in a world correlative to my knowing Self arises. Yet in another, equally important way the presence of the Other has an epistemological priority over the awareness of Self. In being enjoined to respond, to acknowledge, to make the fundamental option to embrace, not exclude; to cherish, not harm; to read in the face of the Other, as Emmanuel Levinas has memorably expressed it, the primordial command "Thou shalt not kill," I take the very first step into consciousness.

In the order of knowledge, ontology has priority: in attributing existence to the Other I realize that I have already indirectly affirmed the existence of the Self and its world; but in the order of responsibility, the priority of ethics is absolute: the Self as the originator of moral acts does not arise unless the summons disclosed in the face of the Other is responded to.[20] There is something incommensurable between the uniqueness of this absolute Stranger, the other Self, no matter how familiar — whether through intensive love or long acquaintance — and one's own uniqueness as a conscious Self; though disclosed in the face and therefore knowable, the other person is transcendent, incomparable and inassimilable. No amount of personal, cultural or biological compatibility can cancel out the absolute strangeness of the other human being, yet to become aware of him or her is to experience a categorical imperative: I can and must find space in my own Self into which to welcome this Stranger, not in proportion to his or her similarity but precisely because of an unfathomable dissimilarity which can never be reduced to a shared identity.[21]

There is possibly a basis here for understanding how knowledge of the religiously Other comes about when we enter the cognitive and experiential world of an unfamiliar faith community. In moving from individual micro-encounters to the social patterns of macro-encounters we are of course setting up an *analogia relationis* in order to clarify our understanding of what happens when traditions meet as Strangers. But in speaking about encounters of cultural and religious communities we often use the language of interpersonal relationships analogously. The *analogia relationis* simply systematizes this usage while making us aware of possible distortions. If we accept this usage, we see that, in the case of most really existing faith communities, the exact opposite of the relational structure outlined above usually applies: each one's own beliefs and practices are presented as unique and superior to all others, and with all means at its disposal each tradition tries to convince religious Others of this or at least to assimilate them conceptually to a particular classificatory scheme, thereby short-circuiting the ethical potential of the encounter. According to the *analogia relationis*, such an approach is simply unethical and unworthy of religion.[22] By analogy with the unfathomable human Self, which cannot be derived from any set of social or historical conditions and nevertheless discloses itself in the face of this particular socialized and culturally determined individual, the autonomous center of a faith community, which cannot be derived from any historical or social process, presents itself through the social media of an historically determined tradition with its unmistakably particular scriptures, rites, languages and structures in such a way that its absolute claim to acknowledgment shines forth from its institutional "face."

This claim, inasmuch as it stems from a genuine and undistorted religious impulse, holds good *precisely to the extent* that beliefs and practices that are recognized as "religious" *differ from our own*.[23] It need no more imply a fusion of religious identities, however, than an interpersonal relationship demands that two personalities become one; here the primordial violence of identity-construction can and must be transcended as relationships form the matrix of meaning and truth. What it does demand is *unconditional respect for the unfamiliar faith* and an effort to understand it. The other religious tradition (in diachronic perspective) or community (in synchronic), being recognized in its irreducible Otherness, becomes *by reason of this very Otherness* — and not because of some Sameness which we purport to discover in it or project onto it — something we *can and should* relate to. The paradox of identity is that we achieve this, not by *assimilating* Other to Self, thereby imposing Sameness, nor by repudiating Self, but by *expanding Self to become more fully Self* by accepting Otherness. The understanding that transcends difference and precludes violence thus becomes possible, but only in Levinas's sense, i.e., to the extent that the ethical has precedence over the cognitive, justice over truth.[24]

According to the *analogia relationis*, the other tradition's alien religious "personality" challenges us to respond to it in the encounter itself. This does away with the misconception that, for example, it is Islam itself and not its alien inculturations that is "the problem" for the Christian West.[25] On the contrary, precisely here, in the other tradition's central assertion of its Otherness, lies the ethical basis for relations between religious traditions. Unless this challenge is accepted and mastered, any purported "understanding" of the Other remains merely tactical and must be suspected of ideological manipulation. The opportunity to grow in faith through such relationships is then lost. And this is indeed what happens in most actual relationships between religions. Theological (or equivalent) reflection or the findings of comparative religion are insufficient in themselves to raise these relationships to the ethical level necessary for real understanding; this impulse must come from within the tradition, from its lived spirituality. Without wishing to indulge in moral rigorism, which would be a new kind of exclusivism, we can still say: *the spirituality of a religion may be measured by the ethical quality of its relationships with other religions.*

Complementing this spirituality is the attitude the religions and their representatives share — or otherwise — to human suffering, especially if unjustly inflicted, and to the suffering of the earth and its creatures, which thereby becomes not just a topic, but a hermeneutical criterion of dialogue: it is not *religious* dialogue if it is not narrating, interpreting and contextualizing the universal experience of suffering as its point of access to the culturally diverse ways of symbolizing transcendence. In Christian terms: there is a direct relationship between truth and love; to be indifferent to the sufferings of the poor is to be atheistic.[26]

The relation between religion and violence — not always a popular topic for interreligious conversations — is closely bound up with this hermeneutic of dialogue. Religion has the potential to prohibit and prevent violence, even towards animals and all living creatures (as in the ancient Indian ethic of *ahimsa*, "being unwilling to harm"). But religion is also able to supply legitimations of violence which appear to issue from a transcendent authority and thus command absolute obedience. Such abuses show from another angle how dialogue must aim at nothing less than a global nonviolent way of life and must manifest this incipiently in the participants' relationships with one another; they also suggest that dialogue — in the form of long-drawn-out historical interactions — is the matrix within which religion itself emerges.[27] Peace thus becomes, not just the topic, but the medium of interreligious communication itself. In this way, perhaps, peace between the religions really can become the precondition of peace between peoples.[28] Whether such an "ontology of peace" can ultimately prevail over the omnipresent "ontology of violence" is, of course, the pre-eminent religious question. It is continually complicated by the widely differing presuppositions upon which the various religious traditions base their accounts of suffering, their symbolizations of transcendence and their strategies for dealing with the stranger-creating potential of difference.

1(b). *The* Analogia Relationis *in Transcultural Contexts*

While the *analogia relationis* may be helpful in confronting Western Christians with the full implications of their own tradition now that theology is starting to come to grips with the dialogue of religions, its limitations become apparent when we learn from that dialogue that by no means all traditions construct the dialectic of Same and Other, Self and Stranger, Own and Enemy the way Christians and Westerners do. Concepts such as "person," "conscience," "subject" and "consciousness" evolved as Greek and Latin Christianity struggled to express the Jewish heritage in universal terms, to recontextualize the story of a personal God who acts in history to choose a particular people and thus intervenes directly in the drama of human salvation. Against this background the analogy between the encounter of persons and the encounter of religions has a certain plausibility. But — quite apart from the warning issued by Cantwell Smith forty years ago about speaking in terms of discrete "religions"[29] — what if these historical, philosophical and psychological parameters are absent? What if the presuppositions upon which "we" — Western Christians — enter into communication with "them" — religious Strangers — are either incomprehensible or unacceptable to them? If they are unable to communicate their presuppositions to us and we cannot make ours intelligible to them, the well-known phenomena of mutual incomprehension, such as the "cargo cults" of Melanesia or Japan's total closure to the outside world, are likely to result. We should look more closely at alternative constructions of the Self before returning to the question of Christian and Buddhist responsibility in interreligious encounter.

We have seen, for instance, that Aboriginal Australians conceive the self in terms of a locative ontology in which self-identity is achieved by participation in the abiding events of the time-beyond-time known, however inadequately, as the Dreaming. At the very least this shows that the individual's progression through historical time is not the only way of coming to terms with the embodiment of the self. We have also learnt that the construction of the self in Melanesia proceeds in the course of an immediate physical relationship to nature mediated by community belonging. Here the "person" has no one single name, but a complex of names deriving from various roles. "Thus the Melanesian person does not proceed solely from the affective structure of the individual, nor from society, nor from thought, mythical or otherwise, but manifests itself through all of these, it has need of all in order to be borne along; it is participative . . . 'the to-him/her' ('*le lui*')."[30] The theoretical problems — not to mention the psychological traumas — involved in detaching the person, thus conceived, from its social-natural, anthropomorphic-cosmomorphic, "mythic" matrix become apparent.

An even more radical alternative to the Western way of constructing the Self is the Buddhist deconstruction of the illusion of substantial existence continuous through time, the doctrine of "not-self" (*anatta*). Though something similar is hinted at in the empiricist analyses of philosophers like David Hume and psychologists like William James, the Theravada doctrine is much more comprehensive, in that it proceeds directly from the fundamental Buddhist philosophy of the mutually determined co-origination of all things (*paticcasamuppada*). In a kind of inverted mirror-image of the ontological-existential Western theories outlined above, the Buddhists argued that, if independent substantiality (*svabhava*) must be denied of all constituents of reality whatsoever ("All states are without self," *sabbe dhamma anatta*, *Dhammapada* 279), there are no grounds for supposing that the knowing "I" is any exception. In what is reputed to be his Second Sermon, the Buddha took his disciples through all the constituents of the Self: body, feeling, perception, the habitual tendencies and consciousness, showing them why they must say of each: "This is not mine, this am I not, this is not my self" (*Mahavagga* I,6; *SN* III,66; *MN* III,19). What the Buddha was proposing was not, however, another philosophical doctrine, this time denying the existence of what most philosophies affirm, but what has been well called "a strategy in 'mental culture'" (*bhavana*).[31] As summarized centuries later by the great medieval commentator Buddhaghosa:

> No doer of the deeds is found;
> No one who ever reaps their fruits:
> Just bare phenomena roll on —
> This view alone is right and true.
> (*Visuddhimagga*, XIX)

The Mahayanists radicalized the doctrine still further, culminating in Nagarjuna's dialectic of absolute emptiness (*sunyata*) which includes in its de-essentialization its own analytical categories and *nirvana* itself. The distinction between the truth of conventional language (*samvrtisatya*), in which even the enlightened talk in terms of existing persons, and the language of ultimate truth (*paramarthasatya*), in which the doctrine of not-self is expressed,[32] as well as the concept of emptiness itself (*suññata*), are already present in the Pali texts. The influential Thai Buddhist thinker Bhikkhu Buddhadasa can thus make the non-self doctrine, interpreted in terms of ultimate emptiness, the centerpiece of his teachings about non-attachment and social compassion, as we saw in chapter 4,[33] and the Western Buddhist David Loy can develop the theme of "lack" as the root of the "immortality projects" continually devised by post-Renaissance Western civilization (and its Eastern clients!) to stave off the realization: " 'I' am not real."[34] Ethics, on this view, belongs to the realm of conventional, not ultimate truth, and thus does not participate in transcendence: "There is no continuous path from ethics to Emptiness."[35] Yet "ultimate truth can express itself only in the mundane world"; indeed, "Nagarjuna says, '[t]he ultimate truth is not taught apart from practical behavior.'"[36] Placed in the context of the immanence of *nirvana* in *samsara* and the Bodhisattva's "return" from the threshold of *nirvana* in order to alleviate the sufferings of unenlightened existence in *samsara*, this shows that Buddhist and Christian ethics are different, though "it is of course not the case that Buddhism is less ethical than Christianity."[37] But the relationship between love and justice in Christianity does not exactly parallel that of wisdom and compassion in Buddhism.

By overcoming the dualisms that generate the dilemmas continually faced by Western philosophy (how does the subject know the object? how does existence realize its essence?), radical non-dualism shows how the abandonment of subject-based projects of infinity-construction results in our identification with absolutely everything, the realization of absolute interdependence which makes the autonomous Self superfluous. Absolute nothingness thus becomes absolute fullness and offers a paradoxical answer to the riddle of death and existential *Angst*. The Western presuppositions of the dialectic of Same and Other, Self and Stranger, Own and Enemy, quite apart from their having been at the root of continual crises in European epistemology, are not necessarily shared by some of Christianity's most interesting prospective dialogue partners.

Our reflections on ethnocentrism therefore need to be developed in a kind of trans-cultural "meta-dialogue" as we proceed with the interreligious encounter itself.[38] The "primal" construction of the self as "biocosmic," in relation to a body which is itself an integral part of the natural world, gives rise to ways of dealing with the strangeness of other cultures which are radically different from those available to universalist traditions with their abstract concepts and powers of generalization. Buddhism radically deconstructs the very notion of a subsistent Self continuous through time, and indeed of identifiable substance in any dimension of reality. The otherness of the Stranger is thereby not so much transcended as disallowed along with the reality of one's own imagined Self. The relationship between transcendence and immanence is then not so much dialectical as identical: like *nirvana* and *samsara*, they are convertible without remainder. What is the conflict-transcending potential of such strategies in spiritual practice and religious philosophy? And how do they relate to the dominant religious conceptions and political ideologies of the Asia-Pacific and the West? The outlines of an answer are beginning to emerge: Buddhism, Christianity and primal traditions have radically different ways of symbolizing transcendence, yet each can be understood by the others as being engaged in this task to the extent that their modes of communication are marked by mutual respect and the disavowal of violence. In this, however, they have all signally failed at different times, and it is in facing these failures together that they can help one another to discover the deepest roots of transcendence in their traditions. Transcendence, at bottom, is a practical-ethical, not a theoretical-intellectual affair. Such, as least, is our hypothesis. We are now ready to submit it to further testing.

1(c) The Acknowledgment of Failure as a Basis for Dialogue

Our study has focused, perhaps one-sidedly, on cases where transcendence was not achieved in practice and which therefore, according to our hypothesis, resulted in violence. The transcendence we have been talking about all along is not only cognitive but moral: it transforms situations by liberating the parties to conflict from the misguided commitments and loyalties that fuel violence. Interreligious relationships that avoid this topic would have to be characterized as underdeveloped and immature, whereas the acknowledgment of failure, one's own and others', could be a fruitful medium of communication within the dialogue itself. Strictly speaking, we have been considering *moral* failures by the various traditions in the face of far-reaching challenges: in the Christian case, by the encounter with the completely alien, archaic civilizations of Australia and Melanesia; in the Buddhist, by the confrontation with the indigenous cultures of Thailand and Japan; and in the latter, by a high-technology, information-driven civilization without apparent relation to their own or the universalist traditions. Our question is twofold: whether such *moral* failures have *spiritual* origins and whether they are influenced by *doctrinal* expression; whether, for instance, in the Christian case nineteenth-century doctrine and ecclesiology had lost touch with ethics, and in the Buddhist, whether spiritual practice has become detached from the spheres of ethics and politics. Some kind of resolution of this disparity between doctrine and ethics, already touched on above, is necessary if we are to demonstrate that religious conceptions of transcendence could engender and nurture practical steps towards overcoming violence.

This need is all the more urgent in that a "global ethic" based on interreligious cooperation and understanding is increasingly regarded as imperative, yet it is hard to see how it can happen unless the religious traditions demonstrate their credibility in the ways in which they relate to one another.[39] Identifying compatible doctrines is one thing, but the problems of relating those doctrines to the ethical demands of politics and technology might also be comparable, and this could provide the basis for a truly committed conversation between Buddhism and Christianity (assuming that primal traditions do not normally possess "doctrines" in this sense). If they were seen to be dealing in a mature way with one another's failures, their credibility as conflict mediators and peacemakers would be immeasurably enhanced. This would involve, on the Buddhist side, coming to terms with the inescapability of historical responsibility, and on the Christian, learning how to go about deconstructing absolutism by exposing its epistemological inconsistency and ethical unacceptability.[40] It is immediately apparent that each can give decisive help to the other in identifying and overcoming their respective failings.

In the course of such a "dialogue by the back door" there might be unsuspected mutual enrichment. It has struck me, for example, that there are unexplored similarities between the Aboriginal "ontology of place" with its notion of "sacred space" and the localization of Buddhism in the sacred sites of Japanese religion, or between the ways in which Christians tried to understand the Rainbow Serpent of Aboriginal mythology, which characteristically inhabits water holes, and the Buddhist assimilation of the water-dwelling *Naga* or serpent spirit in Thai village Buddhism. Development initiatives in rural Thailand could be seen to have certain affinities with their counterparts in rural Melanesia to the extent that both are based on the implementation of traditional beliefs and values in the modern economic context, just as the role of the lay Buddhist social critic Sulak Sivaraksa in Thailand has much in common with that of the lay Catholic philosopher-politician Bernard Narokobi in Papua New Guinea. On the way to becoming one of the most multicultural nations on earth Australia is still struggling to overcome deeply ingrained racist rejection of Asians, just as Japan is now being challenged to accept its indigenous and immigrant peoples. Christian attempts to redress the wrongs done to Aboriginal people have contributed greatly to the process of reconciliation; an exchange of experiences in moving beyond the infamous "White Australia Policy" and the ideology of "Japaneseness" (*nihonjin-ron*) could be instructive for both Christians and Buddhists. Profoundly different as they are, the ways in which European Christianity and Asian Buddhism have related to the state surely provide much material for comparative evaluation.

The Japanese attempt to establish a Greater East Asia Co-prosperity Sphere by force during World War II has been superseded by intensive economic and cultural relationships throughout the Asia-Pacific, which many in the region see as economic imperialism. The Christian ethic of social justice and the Buddhist critique of consumerist capitalism have much to contribute to a more humanly and ecologically responsible approach to economic "development."[41] But this harvest can only be reaped if each tradition, in company with many others, is honest about its failings and is not afraid to look for the presuppositions of these failings in some of its own most basic doctrines. Is not such a daunting task best carried out together? And would not this open up the way to a humbler acknowledgment and a more adequate grasp of what the "primal" religious traditions have to offer in striking a balance between the absoluteness of transcendence and the relativities of cultural identity and community life? The proposed "global ethic," it would seem, is still some way from achieving this balance. In conclusion I offer a somewhat fuller sketch of what might be involved in reaching such an accommodation.

2. Failures of Transcendence
and Their Transformation

The failures of the religions, whether large or small, universal or local, transcendent or immanent, to prevent their various encounters with the "otherness" of those who are religiously and culturally different from leading to violence, suggest that all must change and change radically in the new global situation of religious interrelationships now taking shape. Christianity's failure to circumvent the violence used against Aboriginal people in Australia and to channel the social disruption caused by its introduction into Melanesia; Buddhism's failure to find an answer to rampant maldevelopment in Thailand and nationalistic militarism in Japan; the primal traditions' failures to adapt to the new social contexts and political structures of modernity — these are only some examples of the religious ferment stimulated by the new reality of globalization as the era of modernity nears its end.

This implies not only the necessity of change but also the challenge of mastering the techniques of peaceful change. Such change has to be mutual, brought about in each tradition by its encounters with others. This will only work if such encounters are themselves exemplars of non-violent communication. But change is not merely a reaction to external stimuli. It must come from within, from a rediscovery and re-appropriation of each tradition's sources of inspiration, authority and practice. This was always the intention of the liberation theologians of Latin America and the socially engaged Buddhists of southeast Asia, though they are often given little credit for it within their own traditions. The primal traditions, lacking written sources and philosophical frameworks and bound to the particularities of land and locality, are perhaps more vulnerable to identity loss in this situation. But precisely because their sources of meaning and continuity are so deeply rooted in the natural rhythms and mythical symbolism of the earth they have an irreplaceable contribution to make to the global dialogue.[42]

We shall look first in this concluding section at the doctrinal crises sparked off in contemporary Christianity (section 2(a)) and Buddhism (section 2(b)) by the conscious confrontation, not only with one another, but with their inadequacies and failures both in past intercultural encounters and in the transition to post-modernity, suggesting that this very realization could form the basis for a new, mutually communicable account of their basic beliefs that would be *ipso facto* peace-promoting. I shall also attempt to show in conclusion that all such dialogue will only be truly "earthed" and rooted in people's lives if the great task of reconciling transcendent and immanent is not regarded as a purely doctrinal one, but as a practice to be learned in dialogue with the primary stories and rituals of "people's religion" everywhere.

2(a). Christianity's Christological Crisis

I have summed up the reasons for Christianity's failures in the Pacific under the heading "idealism." We have seen that this involves a certain characteristic abstractness, even dualism, which prevented many Christian missionaries, despite their morally impeccable motivations, from engaging with the realities of the unfamiliar and the unexpected in the culture groups they confronted. In particular, as we saw in Part I, a theistic, at times even deistic concept of God lent credence to the conviction that Christian moral precepts were supported by doctrinal propositions that were indubitably and universally true. These were then imposed willy-nilly on peoples to whom they were utterly alien. It was this framework of idealism in the sense of the *a priori* certainty of abstract propositions, shared by most of the Christian traditions despite their sectarian controversies, that allowed Christian doctrine to become the ideology of forcible adaptation, assimilation, at times even exploitation and near-extermination of Pacific peoples and their cultures. Churches thus found themselves the instruments and accomplices of domination.

At the core of the Christian belief system are the doctrines articulated under the heading "Christology." In Christology the blessing and the curse of European Christianity's Greek heritage become manifest: it is a blessing because in the early Christian centuries what Christians believed needed to be fixed in agreed statements which could give coherence to the church's faith in an age of rival cults and worldviews, not unlike our own; but it is also a curse to the extent that the questions of that age are no longer ours, and the terminology derived from its philosophical presuppositions has either become meaningless or has shifted in meaning so much as to become useless.[43] Among the theologies devised to meet this situation, it would seem that, while the minimalism of John Hick is ultimately self-defeating because based on rational premises which owe nothing to revelation, the reinvigorated Christology so impressively developed by Karl Rahner is unable to deal convincingly with the problems raised by pluralism and dialogue, despite Gavin D'Costa's able defense of it.[44] Traditional Christology seems irreformable and non-negotiable in the new context of interreligious encounter, it has difficulty coming to terms with the agendas of the various liberation theologies, and it falters entirely when we realize the futility of finding some kind of Christological "meaning" in the *Shoah* or the destruction of indigenous cultures. Traditional Christology, in short, is in crisis.[45]

This "Chalcedonian Christology," as I shall call it after the ecumenical council at which it was definitively formulated in 451, does not leave Christians much room for maneuver. The dogma defined at Chalcedon seemed to solve the problems over which the church had agonized at the previous councils of Nicaea (325), Constantinople (381) and Ephesus (431), but these problems were extremely context-specific and the terminology used to express them now appears correspondingly remote. Indeed, some of these councils (Ephesus, Chalcedon) were called by emperors who needed an ideology to unify the empire after the demise of Roman religion. The earliest attempts to state the relationship between Jesus and God had wavered between docetism — Jesus' humanity is only an appearance — and adoptionism — Jesus' divinity is subordinate to that of the Father. This was not felt to be a problem until the Alexandrian presbyter Arius stated baldly that the divine Word made manifest in Jesus was a demi-god on the neo-Platonic model, mediating between the divine and the human but fully equivalent to neither. The council of Nicaea (325) proclaimed that the Son incarnate in Jesus is "of one substance" (*homoousios*) with the Father, but it remained unclear what the word *ousia* (essence? being? substance?) actually meant.

Chalcedon's great achievement is to have clarified and made explicit some of the main themes of the New Testament narratives about Jesus; its great limitation is that it obliterates the pluralism of New Testament Christologies by settling upon one conceptual solution which, to us, seems like no solution at all: that Jesus must be understood as two natures, human and divine, united in the second person of the trinity. Guided by the *Tome of Leo* (a letter addressed by the then pope, Leo I, to patriarch Flavian of Constantinople in 449), the council steered a path between the *logos-anthropos* Christology of the school of Antioch, which tried to show how the human and divine natures are united in the man Jesus in such a way as to affirm his full humanity, and the *logos-sarx* Christology emanating from Alexandria, which in insisting on one single subject tended to absorb Christ's human nature entirely into the divine (monophysitism, "one nature"). The Antiochenes saw the divine Word uniting itself with the man Jesus, endowed with a human soul, as its "temple"; the Alexandrians insisted that the divine Word assumed the "flesh" of human nature, which seemed to leave no room for Jesus' intellect, will and capacity to suffer. The solutions advanced by Nestorius, who proposed a union of the two natures (*ousiai*) in the one person (*prosopon*) without being able to say precisely how they are united, and the monophysite Eutyches, who said that Jesus' nature was exclusively divine, were rejected as heretical.[46]

The Chalcedonian "definition" of Jesus Christ as "perfect in divinity and perfect in humanity, the same truly God and truly man composed of rational soul and body, the same one in being (*homoousios*) with the Father as to the divinity and one in being with us as to the humanity ... without confusion or change, without division or separation" manages to incorporate all the strengths of the various solutions in an harmonious balance and remains the normative core of all properly Christian discourse.[47] Yet the enormous effort expended in order to give a metaphysical account of what Christ *is* tends to leave unsatisfied those whose main question is what Christ as prophet and savior *does* in order to bring about cosmic, social and personal liberation and fulfillment.

Because of the prominent role played by philosophical concepts, especially *ousia* ("nature," though in a sense which has little in common with the way the word is used today) and *hypostasis* (literally "substance" but used as an equivalent of *prosopon*, "person," whose modern connotations — "personality," "autonomous subject," "self-identity" — had not yet emerged), the Christological articles now appear to contain a universalist and essentialist ontology of the human and the divine whose presuppositions are, to say the least, suspect. Indeed, the meanings of "nature" and "person" as used today have virtually been reversed: we mean by the one what the Fathers meant by the other.[48] It is incomprehensible to us how divine "nature" and human "nature," as we understand the term "nature," could come together, as if they were objective realities, in the one person Jesus, just as it is impossible to think of God in terms of three individual "persons" in the modern sense of the term. The whole concept of "incarnation" as a three-stage process of divine pre-existence, human indwelling and final exaltation seems mythical, and to take it literally is to invite the accusation of fundamentalism. The simple statement, "Jesus is God," seems to be anything but simple, to be in fact unutterable: we are no longer able to assign a meaning to the copula "is," though we can begin to make sense of Jesus as the "image," "parable," "symbol" or "presence" of God.[49]

To continue thinking of Christ *only* in the traditional way is like sticking to the examples in a grammar book instead of *using* a language freely and creatively after having assimilated the rule systems of its "generative grammar." This, in fact, is just what we observe the New Testament authors doing. Biblical scholarship has shown that the New Testament contains a wide spectrum of incipient Christologies, only one of which — the "descending" Christology most clearly evident in John's gospel — has remained dominant in the doctrine of incarnation.[50] The Chalcedonian Christology is itself an instance of the kind of inculturation through encounter with otherness which we have been studying throughout this book, yet in Christianity's contemporary encounters with primal traditions and with Buddhism it is in danger of becoming an insuperable barrier to mutual understanding. This is not simply a matter of its "truth," as conservative theologians and fundamentalist Christians would have us believe; the problem is its inadequacy, after centuries during which it was subjected to scarcely any doctrinal development, to express those facets of the New Testament's pluriform narratives about Jesus

which need explication today in the light of historical experience and the intellectual realignments of post-modernism.[51] Liberation theology, feminist theology
and ecological theology have shown in sometimes complementary, sometimes
antagonistic ways that there is scope for prophetic, wisdom and Spirit Christologies which allow us to thematize the religious insights characteristic of our own
time and context.[52] As a rule, however, these new pluralistic Christologies have
shown little interest in doctrinal innovation, which is just what the new situation
of interreligious dialogue seems to call for.[53]

Theological reflection on the Holocaust of European Jews in the *Shoah,* often
in close dialogue with Jewish religious thinkers, and the theological ferment in
what has been called the "Third Church" of the world outside the West have led
to the formulation of what I shall call "Covenant Christologies" which point in
quite new directions and offer to complement, if not supersede, the traditional
doctrinal formulations.[54] Instead of dwelling on the precise interrelationship of the
divine and human "natures" in Christ considered as a pre-existing "being" whose
ontology can be formulated *a priori,* these Christologies see Jesus, in thoroughly
biblical terms, as God's continually renewed covenant with *all* the suffering and
all the poor, including and especially the forgotten and unrequited, symbolized by
God's continuing fidelity to the people of Israel. Jesus is not only the *logos* of divine
nature but equally the *dabar* or efficacious Word of God's promise, to which the
appropriate response is not speculation but commitment.[55] As the risen Christ this
Jesus is the symbol or medium of God's presence in fulfillment of God's ancient
promises to Israel. Jesus embodies the divine "nature" in the sense that through his
suffering and death God is present and active in history, keeping alive a collective
memory of God's absolute future. History, no matter how blighted by violence
and suffering, is thus grasped as what the New Testament calls the coming of
the "Reign of God," which is the all-pervading theme of Jesus' preaching and the
fulfillment of his prayer "Thy kingdom come, Thy will be done, on earth as it is
in heaven" (Mt 6:10). Its point of reference transcends history yet promises the
final realization of God's justice in the midst of it, among all the ambiguities and
inadequacies of human actions and structures, despite the Crusades, despite the
Inquisition, despite the *Shoah,* despite the church's complicity in colonialism.[56]
To this extent it is a powerful symbol of the immanence of transcendence.

It is pointless and unfair to speculate what the Christian missionaries might
have done with such a Christology if they had had access to it; indeed, its emergence is due in no small part to the legacy of their misconceptions and mistakes.
In the context of God's fundamental option for the poor made present and efficacious in Jesus, the emphasis shifts from the ontic to the relational, from theory to
praxis, from doctrine to life.[57] As symbolized and made present in Jesus, God can
now be conceived as suffering, dying, self-emptying in solidarity with the victims

of injustice.[58] To be faithful to this God is to be "like Jesus." God is thus conceived from the "history-side" of divine transcendence and pre-existence, not as a "supreme being" which happened to co-inhabit a human being for the span of Jesus' lifetime, but as the teleology of Jesus' dramatic story as it unfolded in his consciousness and prayer.

Though it can only be sketched here, Covenant Christology offers a way of taking up the Christian struggle with violence and injustice throughout history in continuity with the numberless victims who, in the eyes of those who share this hope, find their exemplar in Jesus' own martyrdom. His death on a cross can now be understood, not so much as the definitive sacrifice which "pays the price" for human redemption and in a certain sense short-circuits history (as we saw in the discussion at the end of chapter 2), but as God's own solidarity with the suffering of the entire creation. On the other hand, the concept of covenant carries connotations which are less useful in cultural contexts characterized by pluralism and tolerance.[59] In the ancient world, covenants were exacted by the powerful from the weak and were enforced by violence, and the corresponding imagery informs the Biblical accounts.[60] Covenants were meant to reinforce identities that were exclusive and jealously defended. Covenant language represents a return from Greek abstraction to Hebrew historicity, and the narrative form derived from the story of God's dealings with Israel brings with it an inevitable particularity.[61] But this is a price every contextual theology has to pay, just as the Chalcedonian one did. As Pieris pregnantly expresses the resulting re-orientation: *"Love is God's own Self as well as God's own Word to us* [and] *God's Word to us is Jesus both eliciting and embodying our love for God and neighbor."*[62]

2(b). Buddhism's Buddhological Crisis

We have already noted that the reign of the Maurya emperor Asoka exercised a formative influence on Buddhism not unlike that of the emperor Constantine at a similar stage in Christianity's development. There is a tendency to think of Buddhism as being somehow "above" history, but in fact it determined the course of history and legitimated political structures.[63] Buddhist-Christian dialogue has been largely concerned with the history of ideas and psychological experiences; Buddhism's very distinctive ways of engaging with history and the state have seldom been addressed.[64] The "Asoka paradigm" of the relationship between the Buddhist religion and the state saw a clear demarcation between the "Two Wheels of Dhamma" which allowed the worldly ruler to work in concert with the monastic hierarchy. This model became determinative for the southern Buddhism of the Theravada countries and remains so to this day.[65] Under Asoka, for the first time, a society and a polity came into being which could in some sense be called

"Buddhist." The "second wheel" of king, state and morality moved in a kind of pre-established harmony with the "first wheel" of Buddha, *dhamma* and *sangha*.[66]

Under Asoka's grandfather Chandragupta Maurya the first minister Kautilya, the Indian Macchiavelli, had devised in his *Arthasastra* a theory of statecraft which legitimized the use of cunning and violence in order to acquire and maintain power. In the Buddhist order of things, the king exercised worldly domination over the village populace through his bureaucratic apparatus of state, but this was complemented by the order of justice and final liberation embodied in the *sangha* right down to the village monks. The tension between the transcendent reference of the *dhamma* and the political power and even violence it legitimated, however, remained.[67] In the Theravada tradition preserved by the monks Asoka becomes a benevolent *dharmaraja* who (in this, again, a precursor of Constantine) calls the Third Council to restore the unity of the *sangha,* though the chronicles are careful to note that this is actually achieved by the monk Moggaliputta.[68] The Asoka paradigm in this idealized form gave legitimacy to the Mahavihara model of divinely sanctioned kingship in Sri Lanka, which can still be detected undergirding the Buddhist-inspired Singhalese nationalism of today. The scholastic rationalism on which it is based, however, as von Brück and Lai rightly note, does not lend itself to opening up a transcendent perspective, for:

> It lacks poetic imagination. In its internal consistency Theravada intellectualism is still impressive even today, but it is only with great difficulty that it can assimilate stimuli from outside or build bridges to other ways of thinking. And it has long ago moved away from its experiential basis in meditation (which probably resided with the forest monks). Modern academic Theravada thinking (which continues the tradition of the educated urban monks) is alien to the rural population as well. But because in the Theravada countries today (with the exception of Thailand) Buddhist kingship, the *samgharaja* and the network of temples controlled by a single Nikaya has disappeared, Theravada philosophy is in the process of losing its sociological basis.[69]

The relationship between king and Buddha, state and religion is thus anything but clear in the new contexts created by the democratization of traditional "Buddhocratic" polities.

There is another, equally powerful paradigm of this relationship which we might call the "Kaniska paradigm" after the so-called "second Asoka," the northwest Indian Kusan emperor Kaniska who ruled around 100 C.E. in the kingdom of Gandhara (Kashmir) and is said to have called the Fourth Council. Its outcome is supposed to have been a compromise between conservatives and progressives about the proper scope of the monastic rule. It is unclear whether or in what sense

Kaniska was Buddhist at all; coins show him receiving the kingship from the Buddha or from Shiva, more in the manner of Zoroastrian deities and certainly not in conformity with the strict distinction made by the Theravadins between the worldly and the transcendent realms.[70] Whatever the veracity of these legends, there emerges a quite different, hieratic model of transcendentally legitimated royal power, a "high Buddhology" as the ideology of a "high regology."[71] The king is now regarded as "divine" *by birth*. The result is a hierarchy of power reminiscent of the Caesaropapism of the Byzantine church with its vertical structure of God-Christ-emperor-people: Under the supremacy of the Buddha stand the "four heavenly kings" whose power comes to the emperor's aid in time of war. He, the "king of kings," is regarded as the future Buddha Maitreya, and stands above the royal priest and prophet who in turn has authority over the monastic hierarchy, to which the people are subordinate. Outside this system, significantly, there remained the self-authenticating forest monks who eventually gave rise to the Mahayana; within it, in a way uncannily reminiscent of the "high Christology" of Chalcedon, the Pure Land tradition found its place as a message of redemption for the whole of suffering humanity.[72]

In the Kaniska paradigm the Two Wheels of Dharma tend to, and in some historical cases actually have, become one. The king as Bodhisattva "from below" becomes the Bodhisattva "from above" or is identified with Maitreya, the future Buddha, or with Amitabha. In southern China the monks felt constrained to resist this total incorporation of the *sangha* and the *dhamma* into the state ideology.[73] Those who resisted most effectively, however, were the forest monks, though the development that led from their secluded quest for the "higher perfection" (*paramita*) to the Mahayana movement was long and is imperfectly understood. From the time of Asoka their forebears were known as *pratyekabuddhas* who achieve enlightenment outside the *sangha*, an implicit critique even then of the latter's acceptance of state patronage. The monk Subhuti comes to symbolize this movement, which nurtured the *Prajñaparamita* or "Perfection of Wisdom" tradition out of which the specifically Mahayana teachings on emptiness grew.[74]

The Mahayana, at once "protestant" and "catholic," manifests an inclusiveness whose integrative power inevitably led to a philosophical break with the Theravada. This new, non-conformist Buddhism draws on what von Brück and Lai call a "narrative Buddhology," rich in stories, legends and revelations, which they suggest can be compared under certain respects to the "narrative Christology" underlying today's liberation theologies.[75] But the emergence of totalitarian ideologies in China and Japan coincided with the development of a kind of "Trinitarian Buddhology" based on the equivalence of *samsara, nirvana* and the ultimate realization of *sunyata* (for the historical background see Appendix II). T'ien-t'ai, with its three-in-one (*san-i*) of being, emptiness and the mean that integrates them, developed this thinking further, and Hua-yen turned it into an "onto-logical totalism" of One and All, consciousness and absolute, symbolized in the cosmic sun-Buddha Vairocana. If T'ien-t'ai purported to transcend (in Christian terms, "docetically") even the historical appearance of Sakyamuni, Hua-yen points beyond time itself. We have seen the influence such teachings had in Japan, though it was the more skeptical Zen and the more life-orientated Pure Land that survived the savage persecution of 845 C.E. in China and largely determined northern Buddhism's future form.[76]

Buddhism, which has its own subtle but no less emphatic forms of meliorism, also faces its own "Buddhological" crisis as it becomes aware of the ways in which its history in east and southeast Asia has modulated Buddhist teaching to the point of distortion in order to harmonize with the various institutional forms of political power. Intrinsically peaceable as Buddhism has always been, such accommodations with feudalism and imperialism have laid it open to at least indirectly sanctioning violence, either in the name of the state or in defense of Buddhism's own privileges. In the course of these historical transitions the influence of lay Buddhists and forest meditators on the institutionalized monastic life of the *sangha* eventually exerted such influence on the tradition that conceptions of the Buddha began to undergo radical change. In the course of this process both the absolute emptiness (*sunyata*) at the heart of the Buddhist analysis of reality and the person of the Buddha himself were "ontologized" to become a kind of equivalent of the Vedic "absolute" of pre-Buddhist India (the identification of *atman-brahman,* whose existence the historical Buddha Sakyamuni had resolutely refused either to affirm or deny).[77]

A "systematic Buddhology" was worked out in which the realm of "every-day truth" (*samvrtisatya*) was distinguished from the realm of "absolute truth" (*paramarthasatya* to which only the enlightened have access. This amounts to a distinction between the Dharma "as manifested" and the Dharma "in itself."[78] At the level of absolute truth one knows not only of an "earthly Buddha-body" (*nirmanakaya*) and the "body of bliss" (*sambhogakaya*) in which the Buddha of the Mahayana Sutras appears, but also of the utterly transcendent "Dharma body" (*dharmakaya*) which makes the Buddha in the enjoyment of *nirvana* identical with the cosmic reality of ultimate emptiness.[79] This, in effect, is a theory of revelation. In Christian terms it is both incarnational and docetic. There are "seeds of the Thus-Gone" (*Tathagatgarba*) in every last constituent of reality; the Buddha-nature is universal. But the "appearance" of the Buddha in history and to the meditator is only a "skilful means" (*upaya*) designed to communi-cate the all-important truth of *dharma.* This truth is ultimately inconceivable; any possible manifestation of it is necessarily unreal. We, however, who cannot take up the standpoint of Absolute Reality, must attempt to express the ulti-mate by using the penultimate, even if the result is always ambiguous. Zen, at least according to its founding legend, rejected scriptures altogether and relied only on the transmission of enlightenment from patriarch to patriarch, i.e., on the attested experience of absolute emptiness (*sunyata*). Pure Land, by contrast, made the *Sutras* themselves into objects of devotion, and its adherents look to the Buddhas-to-be (*Bodhisattvas* such as Avalokitesvara/Kannon) or transcendent Buddhas (Amitabha, Maitreya) for assistance in realizing the Pure Mind as they negotiate the struggles and temptations of life. In Japan these two streams came to be known as "own-power" (*jiriki*) and "other-power" (*tariki*).[80]

The philosophy of Tanabe Hajime, inspired by the "other-power" of Shin Buddhism and developed in an intensive dialogue with Christianity and German philosophy (Kant, Hegel, Heidegger), is an example of an attempt to retrieve the Buddhist ethic of non-violence as Buddhism underwent one of its greatest tests in wartime Japan. Tanabe's "logic of species" tries to make the historical link between transcendence and action without having recourse to a separately existing One or a pre-existing Being. Rather than assigning the standpoint of Absolute Nothingness to Nishida's indeterminate "place" (*basho*), Tanabe assimilates the Absolute to the universality of the genus. In the classical syllogism, the universal is mediated to the historically existing individual by the intermediacy of the species.[81] The world, in Ozaki's phrase, thus becomes "the active presence of eternity" thanks to the "absolute mediation" which transforms transcendence into an "actual reality" that is necessarily historical.[82] Thanks to this absolute mediation, Nothingness is acted out as an ethical way of being in history (Nothingness-*qua*-Love); the Absolute returns (*genso*) to the relative, the eternal is mediated to the present. "Actuality forms the content of the mutual identities of the self and the others, transcendence and immanence in history."[83] There is no unmediated precursor to this absolute mediation, which is nevertheless fully immanent in the irreversibility of time and the asymmetry of history.

The primordial Nothingness is in no sense a substance or source, as Nishida, perhaps unconsciously influenced by the Taoist antecedents of Japanese Zen, tended to believe. In accordance with the authentic Buddhist teaching on emptiness, transcendence and immanence are mutually inclusive.[84] In Tanabe's "other-power" there thus remains an element of "own-power"; in this he differs significantly from his master Shinran (he is, after all, a philosopher rather than a believer).[85] There is, however, something absolutist about this philosophy, reminiscent of its Hegelian antecedents, which leads one to wonder whether Tanabe's wartime crisis did not contain an element of self-delusion analogous to Heidegger's Nazi sympathies.[86] Yet the resulting reconception of philosophy as "metanoetics," the intellectual conversion or death-and-resurrection of the self arising from the historical realization of "repentance and restitution" (*zange*), has undoubted moral power.[87]

This story of doctrinal development is no less bound up with historical vicissitudes and political entanglements than is its Christian counterpart. It shows Buddhism reaping the rewards of its various accommodations to the use of state power and violence just as Christianity did. As a result, each tradition not only shaped a civilization but was profoundly affected in its own internal structures and doctrinal self-understanding. Where does this heritage leave contemporary Buddhism in the Asia-Pacific? The Theravada, while thoroughly integrated to the point of total assimilation into the societies in which it is predominant, and somewhat hampered by a philosophical tradition that has become sterile and uncritical, has had to face the full brunt of military takeovers (Burma, Thailand), economic exploitation (Thailand, Sri Lanka), massive influxes of refugees from regional wars (Thailand), and militarized ethnic conflict (Sri Lanka). It has not only coped as well as might be expected of any beleaguered religious tradition but has brought forth fresh approaches to peacemaking and social criticism from its own Buddhist sources. The Mahayana, fragmented into many scarcely compatible lineages and largely unsuccessful in its attempts to co-opt the state, has allowed itself to be instrumentalized for nation-building in the past and now conforms to the predominant ideologies of material progress. The integration of Taoism in China, Shamanism in Korea and Shinto in Japan into Buddhist doctrine and practice has favored particularistic interpretations which have not been proof against advocating or even embracing violence in the name of territorial integrity, ethnic identity and imperial expansion. Yet Buddhism, in whatever form, has always contained an implicit universalist ethic which is integral to its "performative philosophy" of liberation from transience and desire.[88]

Both Christianity and Buddhism, we conclude, face major doctrinal reorientations as a direct result of their encounters with one another and with the "primal" religious traditions of the Pacific and Asian cultures within which their missionary expansion took place. It remains to ask whether these very encounters, in particular the impact of indigenous cultures on the introduced "universalist" traditions, could mediate the future relationships between Buddhism, Christianity and primal religion in such a way that they could each be re-empowered to take the ethical stances demanded of them. The non-dualism of absolute transcendence, we have found, tends to lead in practice to total immanence within cultural forms and political systems, whereas the eschatological anticipation of God's absolute future, at the price of a dualistic tension between "already" and "not yet," unleashes an historical dynamic. Can Christology and Buddhology be re-conceived in order to give effective contemporary expression to their potential to build peace?

Christian theology, using concepts borrowed from Greek philosophy, is premised on an ontology which allows God to be conceived as absolute Being and

Christ as the fusion of this divine nature with a human nature understood in essentialist terms. The resulting theo-ontology, though able to be expressed in the clear-cut propositions of dogmas and creeds, remains "ontic," even "positivistic" in its orientation to Being, of which God, in the end, is regarded as a unique instance. Such theology tends to identify deviations from its own norms as heresies, and it has difficulty acknowledging the moral integrity and spiritual autonomy of the religious Other. Alternative perspectives such as the priority of ethics over ontology (Emmanuel Levinas), of Love over Being (Jean-Luc Marion), of covenant over dogma (Aloysius Pieris) suggest entirely new ways of getting at the uniqueness of Christ and the decisiveness of faith without prejudice to the reality of other religious worlds.

Buddhism, which from the beginning opted for praxis over doctrine and (in the idealized version of Zen tradition) even repudiated the scriptures and the humanity of the Buddha, prescinds from ontology and transcends ethics, even where it symbolizes the ultimate goal as the Pure Land and the divine assistance necessary to reach it as the Bodhisattva or transcendent Buddha. The danger remains, however, of "ontologizing" emptiness itself, of regarding Absolute Nothingness as Absolute Reality. In accommodating itself to different political systems and cultural contexts, Buddhism in its various Asian forms — with the exception of some characteristically modern developments — has shown neither inclination nor ability to resist cultural disintegration, economic injustice or political extremism. Faced with the ethical dilemmas posed by imperialistic militarism, economic rationalism and global technology, Buddhism finds itself unable to articulate the response of practical reason because, with the exception of rather transparent apologetics, it has forfeited conceptual expression and rational discourse.

The primal and sapiential traditions encountered by both Buddhism and Christianity as they expanded into the Asia-Pacific region generally either lack altogether or have only approximations to universalizable doctrines or ethics. Their religious worlds remain particularistic, entirely immanent within the archaic mythic-ritual complex in a wide variety of forms. Yet without some kind of inculturation into these neither Christianity nor Buddhism could be mediated culturally or exist socially in the Asia-Pacific. The universalism of these faiths makes the indigenous cultures more widely communicable, but the faiths themselves are "earthed" by these cultures in ways that may be historically obscure or doctrinally questionable, yet are surely indispensable if human beings in their life situations (*Lebenswelten*) are to articulate the transcendence immanent within their traditions and achieve global consciousness. This suggests a complementarity without prejudice to the autonomy of each tradition, whether metacosmic or biocosmic in scope. In conclusion, I shall attempt a brief outline of what such complementarity could look like and what it could achieve.

Conclusion

BEYOND VIOLENCE?

*The Deconstruction of Absolutism
and the Completion of Religion*

It is illusory to think that "Buddhism" and "Christianity," taken as some kind of organic, homogeneous wholes, can dialogue in the abstract by comparing and correlating doctrines. Each of these broad traditions as we know them today has emerged from involvements with history, politics and culture such as those we have studied, and latterly from involvements with each other that are already having mutually transformative effects. They are emerging into a new, shared context, not of their making, which results from the dynamic of new, a-religious transcendence implicit in the rise of science and the explosion of technology. This has created the unprecedented phenomenon of globalization, though only the members of educated elites with access to information technology are equipped to grasp its implications at present. In this new situation all the religious traditions have to face past failures, present inadequacies and future possibilities together.

For Buddhism and Christianity in particular, our researches have shown that they need to re-learn how to relate to the primal reality of our common human "earth-soul," the repressed "archaic other," our forgotten rootedness in the whole of nature. Thanks to the survival and resilience of "primal" traditions the world over, this is now being rediscovered by Western and Eastern Christians and by various Buddhist traditions as an integral part of being human. Perhaps it is true to say that Buddhism has remained more closely in touch with this level of consciousness than Christianity. But of both it can be said that the mediation of "biocosmic" religion is necessary if "metacosmic" religion is to become historical and embrace the human in all its dimensions. Indeed, the "biocosmic" religions of immanence might be said to be the indispensable medium for the cultural embodiment and historical reality of the "metacosmic" religions of transcendence. This mediation, as we have seen, can take many forms and can be subject to inadequacies, even pathologies. Both Buddhism and Christianity, as highly elaborated doctrines of transcendence, need to come to terms with immanence and the ways in which

148

they have allowed themselves to become embodied in it. "Immanence," in this context, may be understood as the immediacy of transcendence in the "soul-life" of everyday experience as the religious person copes with the transience and joy of existence and struggles with the guilt of moral failure. Rootedness in the life and rhythms of the earth from which we all spring is an integral part of this primal awareness; transcending the limitations of locality and ethnicity is the corresponding challenge to primal traditions. If each such process of transformation can be accomplished with minimal loss of particular identity coupled with a gain in universality, the religious traditions we have been considering, and others like them, may be in a position to enter the new, post-modern period of increasing globalization with the prospect of contributing to the ethical consensus of an emerging non-violent global society.

The abstract problem of relating transcendence and immanence, which has emerged as the dominant theme throughout our attempts to understand the historical situations we have studied, must be conceived not only in "vertical" terms — God "descending" to the human state and "ascending" to heavenly exaltation; the historical Shakyamuni being transformed into an eternal Dharma-body mediated by the quasi-divine "body of bliss" (*sambhogakaya*) — but also "horizontally," as the ability, inherited from the religious traditions, to withstand the shock of otherness with its implicit threat of violence and ethnocentrism. More awareness of the primal traditions may help to wean adherents of universalist religions from the absolutism to which doctrines of transcendence can give rise; a more explicit awareness of transcendence might make the experience preserved in primal traditions more easily communicable to one another, to the universalist religions and to the world of scientific and economic rationalism. The "meliority principle," the conviction of uniqueness and superiority based on divine revelation or the exclusive possession of higher truth, which is integral to the self-understandings of all the "higher" religions, far from providing a firm basis for such relationships, in the end makes them impossible, because their purported universality is in fact *someone's* particularity projected onto all. All the religions are having great difficulty in grasping that the time when this may have been conceivable has passed. The primal traditions, for their part, face the temptation to withdraw into the isolation of traditional identities based on land and ethnicity; their task is to articulate the transcendence encrypted in their myths and rituals in such a way that it becomes accessible to people of widely differing cultural backgrounds. In both types of religious awareness, whether transcendence or immanence predominates, there lurks the danger of deriving a justification for violence from the assumption of uniqueness and superiority. Can each also devise practical ways of effectively overcoming violence?[1] That is the religious question in a nutshell as we enter a new century and a new era, whose beginning may have been marked by the atrocities of 11 September 2001 and the ensuing "war on terrorism."

We may speak of a dialectic of *rootedness* and *openness* which must be resolved and brought into balance if ways of conceptualizing and practicing transcendence are not to be taken prisoner by ethnic and chthonic loyalties which thereby acquire a false absolutism. If the universalist traditions of the metacosmic religions can teach us that we have here on earth no lasting abode, no ultimate right of possession, the biocosmic religions of indigenous peoples can make us aware of the extent to which we are nevertheless profoundly at one with the earth and at home in its physical and spiritual fabric. Out of this dual heritage must be shaped a religious consciousness which, while aspiring to liberate us by pointing beyond, yet nourishes us on the wisdom of earthly belonging and human relationships, thus laying the foundation for the eventual — and practical — transcendence of violence. Narrative traditions rather than conceptual systems now seem to offer the better prospect of achieving this. Both Western Christianity and Asian Buddhism could be said to have lost at different times the balance between *mythos* and *logos*, the symbolic and the cognitive, the natural and the human, which ideally allows religion to integrate all aspects of human and cosmic life into a coherent universe of meaning which, while no stranger to conflict, no longer has any place for violence as a way of resolving it.

The much-vaunted "global ethic," as an attempt to formulate a basic ethical consensus to which all people of faith could subscribe, is also an attempt, though necessarily a minimalist one, to stake out the parameters of such a new config-uration of religion. At present the global ethic takes the very general form of a "thin," because necessarily abstract and inclusive, ethical *code*, whereas the very least that is needed is a profound ethical *reorientation*, which was perhaps better captured by Hans Küng's original term "global ethos."[2] Ethical traditions, like the religious traditions which have engendered and nurtured them, have developed largely independently of one another and now appear culturally incompatible. The steps to be taken towards a global ethic, however, are not simply:

1. Deduction of universal principles of a common ethic from the ethical traditions of the religions;

2. Application of these previously agreed principles to the moral dilemmas of post-modernity,

but rather:

1. The practice of non-violent communication among the religions them-selves;

2. Gradual growth in mutual respect and understanding, overcoming meliorism and abandoning unilateral declarations of definitiveness and superiority;

3. Distinctive but complementary contributions, not only to a putative "ethic of survival" for all, but to the sharing of distinctive visions of transcendence.[3]

Each religious tradition, in its own "cultural dialect," provides very particular stories and symbols of transcendence. In the new context of globalization these stories and symbols need to be mutually translatable without the threat of alienation or identity loss.

The religions, in sorting out the apparent incompatibilities between the culture-bound symbolic languages in which they speak about the meaning of poverty, suffering and death and celebrate creation, life and hope, must already be exemplars of non-violent communication. In learning to translate one another's symbolic languages, the religions are not only clarifying their visions of transcendence-in-immanence to the point where they could eventually share them, they are enacting ethically what they proclaim symbolically. Their stories, rituals and metaphors, always with particular reference to times and places, make us aware of what lies "beyond" the space-time of history *as a dimension of history itself.* In their particular cultural contexts they were each able to do this separately in the past; in the new context of globalization they can only do it, if at all, together. The thesis we have developed throughout this book is that if they succeed they can provide a foretaste of liberation from the unceasing cycles of violence and vengeance, whereas if they fail, it is hard to see where such a liberation could come from, given the human capacity to rationalize violence.

The Christian name for transcendence-in-immanence is "eschatology," which though it transcends time itself is symbolized as the "end time." Christianity's rootedness in the Jewish story of salvation invites us to think of "meaning" in terms of an "outcome," an "ending," which is at the same time the fulfillment of a purpose. Eschatology includes both senses of the word "end"; it is a finality which transcends time yet delimits it and gives it a sense of direction and completion. Not every religious tradition is similarly structured, though several, as we have seen, possess incipient eschatologies (the emergence of historical awareness in Aboriginal religion; the symbolic meaning of the "cargo cults" in Melanesian religion; the role of Maitreya, the future Buddha, in various strains of Buddhism). In Mahayana Buddhism, in particular, the vision of transcendence is not conceived teleologically but a-historically, for a teleological construction would re-involve the self. There is a growing realization, however, that the dimension of spatiality not only anchors Buddhist practice to particular places with all their cultural tonalities but roots the timelessness of transcendence in historicity.[4] The ancient

Indian idea of the "last age" of decline was inherited by Buddhism and has been particularly influential in Japan.

What concerns us here, however, is not the particularity of the symbolism but the element of vision which provides a context for ethics. Even if the imagined final realization transcends the ethical, it nevertheless provides the everyday practice of morality with a home, a nurturing context which ensures that people *see the point* of being moral. This "meaning" of morality, though immanent within the moral act itself, is in danger of not being realized if its intrinsic orientation to transcendence is not dramatized in metaphor, symbol and story. This is not simply to say that one narrative context can be substituted for another or that a number of them may be pooled or combined in order to enhance the ethical result. But it does suggest that the element of vision, whether temporally or spatially structured, is as intrinsic to ethics as ethics itself is fundamental to an orientation towards transcendence. Ethics has both *normative* and *visionary* dimensions.[5]

Reconciliation, like politics, is always local. The liberal political order of pluralist democracy, which has established fragile bridgeheads wherever Western influence has reached, is by definition secular; it offers, not a substantive view of the world, but a procedural arrangement for formulating consensus and mediating conflict. Given that virtually every society now contains representatives of most of the existing religious traditions, it is up to the religions themselves to find an interrelationship within the public space created by secular pluralism which will of itself bear witness to their potential for peace-building. But this view of interreligious relationships *ad extra,* in the public space of secular societies, does not necessarily imply that the pluralist paradigm is the solution to the problem of interreligious relationships *ad intra,* as the religions themselves conceive them. A pluralism which entails dualism, "objectifying" and "constructing" the Other as Stranger or restricting relationships to a carefully defined and "safe" minimum, is inadequate to both Buddhist and Christian understandings of ultimate truth. The "position" from which pluralism becomes possible for the religions, it has been suggested, must be "positionless" with respect to each and all of them; it is therefore intrinsically transcendent and challenges each of their conceptions of transcendence without itself being susceptible to absolutism.[6]

Debate about the "truth" of the religions' widely disparate views of the world is not incidental to their interrelationships but integral to them. The questions at issue between religious traditions, though they may seem archaic and irrelevant, encode the answers these traditions have given to the deepest yearnings of the human heart, including the practical problems of reconciliation and peace building. To the members of the respective traditions this is likely to seem like an invitation to disloyalty because it appears to place all on an equal footing for purely pragmatic purposes. Our task is to learn, together, that this need not be so, that the actual acceptance of people of other faiths and traditions is itself a religious act which must spring from a spirituality of non-violence. We are thus faced with the task of creating a global non-violent way of life which will come to seem as natural and inevitable as violence does now. This is an ethical task, but ethics alone cannot accomplish it. Those who can commit themselves together to a credible vision of hope, however, may be able to sustain it.

As an ecumenical program, at no matter what level and in what context — local religious communities, worldwide religious families, religious traditions of all kinds whether indigenous or trans-cultural — these *desiderata* might be summed up under three headings:[7]

1. Acknowledging the Other;

2. Welcoming the Stranger;

3. Reconciling the Enemy.

Each step in this program represents an increasing degree of difficulty, for making the Other into the Stranger is the first step towards creating the Enemy and is intrinsically violent.

1. The theologies (or Buddhologies or other equivalents) of the world's religions have always found ways of asserting that their respective traditions are superior to all others; relations with other religions are therefore conceived as talking down to spiritual inferiors. Christianity, right through to the Christological core of its doctrines, has been one of the worst offenders, but Buddhism too is not immune to this temptation. Acknowledgment of the autonomous existence of the religious Other, owing nothing to us yet not threatening us, is the first and fundamental step towards an ethic of non-violence.

2. Common to the ethics of all religions is the injunction to offer hospitality to the Stranger, especially the religious Stranger, because to be religious is in some sense to share a common exile, estranged from the world yet experiencing the absence of God or the unreality of the Self. "Dialogue" therefore becomes an intrinsically religious act of opening one's mind and heart to what is unfamiliar, and therefore seems threatening, in the religious identity of the Other.

3. Though the religions — not least Christianity, but also Buddhism in certain contexts and the primal traditions as well — are all too often associated with the justification and motivation of violence, they are also involved in peace processes which try to translate repentance and forgiveness into the practical politics of redemption and liberation, exemplary cases being

Northern Ireland, Sri Lanka and various parts of Southeast Asia.[8] Reconciliation, where one is oneself caught up in the cycle of retribution for ancient wrongs and resentment at present sufferings, is surely the sternest ecumenical test of all.[9]

To rise to this threefold challenge, in Christian terms, is to celebrate the sacrament of the Stranger; to fail this test, as European Christianity and Asian Buddhism so often did in the past, is to remain sub-Christian, un-Buddhist and ultimately irreligious. Yet if overcoming dualism, not in the sense of abolishing difference but of learning to live with it, is the irreplaceable contribution of the religions, whether "universal" or "primal," to the creation of a non-violent global way of life, then the traditions we have studied, despite their many failings and inadequacies, will inevitably form an integral part of the "global ethos" which is slowly but surely emerging.

COMPETING MISSIONARIES AND RELUCTANT ECUMENISTS IN MELANESIA

The Pacific Islanders' initial contacts with Europeans were traumatic. The Spaniards, sometimes with Christian missionaries on board, were the first to arrive in their quest to locate the spice islands of Indonesia and the Philippines. Ferdinand Magellan sailed across the whole Pacific from South America to the Mariana Islands east of the Philippines in 1521. For the first time, Christian symbols were displayed and the mass was celebrated. In 1595 Mendaña and Quiros came upon islands which they took to be King Solomon's treasure trove, so they named them the Solomon Islands. The Spaniards also visited Tahiti in the Society Islands. But when, in the course of colonial expansion, the English and French arrived, commercial interests overrode all else. Traders scoured the islands for sandalwood, establishing plantations and shifting the inhabitants from one island to another for economic reasons. Escaped convicts from the British penal settlements in Australia were scattered all over the South Pacific. In religious terms the Pacific became a distorted mirror image of the national and denominational rivalries of Europe.[1]

The incentive for the evangelization of the Pacific came from the evangelical revivals in England — and in New England — during the eighteenth century. The women and men who were influenced by John Wesley and Jonathan Edwards were not only spiritually awakened but were also children of the Enlightenment. The Anglicans John Eyre and Thomas Haweis and the independent Christian David Bogue formed the London Missionary Society (LMS) in 1795. By the time its members reached the Loyalty Islands in 1840 the Society was coming under the influence of British Congregationalism.[2] They went to the Pacific with the firm purpose of bringing to the as yet untouched peoples of Polynesia both the light of the gospel and British Protestant civilization. The French, whose aim was to extend their sphere of influence as well as to establish the Roman Catholic Church in the Pacific region, usually arrived later, which made their missionary

155

activity in areas already evangelized by Protestants all the more provocative. The mutual ignorance of these two spearheads of the Christian mission with respect to one another's missionary motives and methods was boundless. All the hereditary enmity of their two peoples and the post-Reformation intolerance of Europe culminated in the opposition between "Methodists" and "Papists." Nothing could have been more irrelevant to the Pacific Islanders on the threshold of a new era.

The murder of the LMS missionary John Williams at Erromanga in the New Hebrides on 20 November 1839 was a profound shock to the optimism of the south sea missionaries.[3] Until then only a few whites had made contact with the inhabitants of the "black islands" stretching from New Caledonia to New Guinea. Even for Polynesians this area was foreign, unhealthy and dangerous. The Marists, who arrived first — for once! — on the Solomon Islands, had to leave by 1855 because of the animosity of the indigenes and the tropical diseases; only in 1898 did Catholics attempt a new start there. The Anglican missionary Bishop Patteson founded a seminary for Pacific Islanders in New Zealand so that the young men could pursue their studies far from the distractions of village life; later (1866–1920) it was moved to Norfolk Island. His goal was that the Melanesians themselves should become missionaries to their own peoples. But even Bishop Patteson, who had expended so much effort and love on the reconciliation of European and Pacific cultures, was murdered on a remote atoll to the north of the New Hebrides in 1871, probably in revenge for the interference of white arms dealers in local tribal conflicts.[4]

While the English and French missionaries rivaled one another in their competition for the souls of the inhabitants of New Caledonia and the New Hebrides (now Vanuatu), New Guinea, by far the largest but also the least known island of Melanesia, was irresistibly attracting the more far-sighted Pacific missionaries. Others, too, were already casting greedy eyes on New Guinea: German colonizers, Australian gold seekers, even the government of the scarcely established colony of Queensland. It was some of the most experienced missionaries, with the active help of Cook Islanders, Samoans and Fijians, who set about the task of evangelizing Melanesia. The Methodist George Brown established himself among the Tolai on the easternmost extremity of New Britain; Lawes (1873) and Chalmers (1877) went to Papua for the LMS, though it was a group of Cook Islanders led by Ruatoka who were the first to set foot on the mainland. Polynesian missionaries such as Ruatoka, Maretu, Ta'unga and Joeli Bulu played an important part in spreading Christianity throughout the Pacific region.[5]

At about this time, despite previous failures, the Catholic Church once again began to take an interest in Melanesia. Ironically, it was the tragic duplicity of the Marquis de Rays, who enticed a band of starry-eyed French utopians to New Ireland and left them to their fate, that triggered off the new missionary efforts of the Vatican. The Missionaries of the Sacred Heart (M.S.C.), founded in 1854 to counteract the rise of secularism in France, were given the task in 1881 of countering the Protestants in Papua. When the LMS, the Methodists and the Anglicans agreed at conferences held in Port Moresby in 1890 and 1893 to demarcate their mission territories, share Pacific Island evangelists among themselves and discuss difficulties such as "native marriages, Sabbath observance and principles of Bible translation,"[6] the French Catholics would have none of it. In their view, no misguided respect for agreements between heretics and worldly governments was to be allowed to hinder the spread of the gospel.[7] In New Guinea, too, there was scope for boundary disputes, this time between Lutherans and Catholics. Johann Flierl, the pioneer missionary from Neuendettelsau in Bavaria, landed in 1886 at Simbang near Finschhafen on the north coast, much to the annoyance of the *Deutsche Neuguinea-Compagnie,* which had no interest in having Christian moralists in the vicinity of the plantations it administered with an iron hand after annexing land in 1884. After great privations Flierl and his companions founded one of the most soundly based missions in the whole Pacific. Like the Anglicans, who set up their mission further east at Dogura,[8] the Lutherans counted on the collaboration of the Melanesian evangelists from the very beginning. It was they who later opened up the highlands for missionary work. Even in the 1930s Catholic and Lutheran missionaries quite literally raced one another to secure territory as the highlands became accessible to whites. After two Catholic missionaries were murdered the Australian administration prohibited further expansion into "unpacified" areas. For the first time, the churches — who had always been the first to penetrate into the most difficult areas — had to wait impatiently until the secular arm put things in order before they could take up the work of Christian instruction.[9]

It needed the upheavals of two world wars to force the competing mission churches into openness and cooperation with one another. The rise of Japan to become an industrial and military power after the First World War created an insatiable demand for raw materials. The countries of the southwest Pacific were to satisfy this demand by forming a "Southeast Asia Co-Prosperity Sphere" under Japanese leadership, which would have absorbed them into a Pacific version of the Thousand Year Reich. The Koreans and the Chinese were the first to feel the merciless blows of the Japanese war machine, whereas Indians, Malays and Indonesians were more inclined to welcome the humiliation of their British and Dutch colonial masters by a rising Asian power. The Japanese advance towards the mineral wealth of Australia finally came to grief, as had so many explorers and missionaries, in the malaria-infested jungles and impenetrable mountains of New Guinea.[10] One of the side effects of the united efforts of Australians and Americans to repulse the Japanese from the southwest Pacific was that the white peoples of the Pacific seaboard became aware of the Islanders, their cultures, their lively Christian faith and not least their strategic importance. Many missionaries of all denominations were executed by the Japanese or killed in Allied attacks on prison camps or transport ships.[11] Catholics and Protestants everywhere, no matter how different their backgrounds, found that they belonged together, and the indigenous Christian communities proved themselves not only under the onslaught of the war itself, but equally in the face of the overwhelming cultural impact of economic power and technical superiority, not forgetting the impression made by the Afro-American soldiers. Their ability to fend for themselves sowed the seeds of the indigenous churches that were to emerge after the war.

With these developments, however, the missionary history of the churches in the Pacific was far from over. If it was the great evangelical revivals of the nineteenth century that provided the motivation for the Free Churches to set out for the unknown and unevangelized world of the South Pacific, in the twentieth century their Evangelical, Pentecostal and Adventist successors were just as strongly drawn there.[12]

Even experienced church leaders in the Pacific have understandable difficulty in distinguishing between all these competing offers of salvation. Hardly had they learned to cope with the ecumenical bodies set up by the Western churches, which had previously shown such enmity towards one another, when they had to face this new challenge from sectarian groups, in which many of their own members have found a new religious home, a solution to the loss of their identity and a refuge from the trauma of rootlessness. In the meantime, the missionary history of the Pacific, which oscillates between arrogance towards the Islanders and solidarity with them, has already become church history. In 1973 the United Church in Papua New Guinea and Solomon Islands elected Leslie Boseto from the Solomon Islands as its first indigenous moderator. The first Melanesian to be made a bishop was the Anglican George Ambo, ordained in 1960 as archbishop of the Anglican Church in Papua New Guinea; the second was Bishop Leonard Alufurai from the Solomon Islands in 1964. The first Papuan Catholic priest, Louis Vangeke, M.S.C., succeeded the great missionary pioneer Archbishop Alain de Boismenu. At the time of its transition from mission to church in 1976 — which provides a veritable case study of all the problems involved — the Evangelical Lutheran Church of Papua New Guinea chose Pastor Zurewe Zurenuo as its head bishop.[13] In ways and to degrees which depend on the theological principles of the mission churches from which they stem, most of the former "missions" have become autonomous churches.[14] Bishop Leslie Boseto — as so often — spoke for all Pacific Islanders when he exclaimed at an ecumenical meeting: "We are no longer mission territory!"

Appendix II

CHINA'S PROBLEMS
WITH THE "FOREIGN RELIGION"

Some time during the Later or Eastern Han dynasty (25 B.C.E. — 220 C.E.), knowledge of Buddhist teachings began to percolate from India into China through its vast western hinterland. Around 68 C.E., the Emperor Ming (58–75) is said to have had a dream which was interpreted by his minister Fu Yi as a vision of the Indian sage known as the Buddha. Though we are still in the realm of legend, there is evidence that Buddhism was known at least as early as 65 C.E. and that contacts between outlying parts of China and Central Asia, perhaps even North India, had been taking place.[1] Emperor Ming's mission to bring back Buddhist *sutras* to his capital Lo-yang is not beyond the bounds of possibility, for relations certainly existed between China and the western regions,[2] though the first Chinese known to have traveled abroad in search of Buddhist texts is the monk Chi Shih-hsing, who is said to have gone to Khotan in 260.[3] "In actual fact," concludes Zürcher,

> it is unknown when Buddhism entered China. It must have slowly infiltrated from the North-West, via the two branches of the continental silk-road which entered Chinese territory at Tunhuan, and from there through the corridor of Kansu to the "region within the Passes" and the North China Plain, where in Later Han times the capital Loyan was situated. This infiltration must have taken place between the first half of the first century B.C. — the period of consolidation of Chinese power in Central Asia — and the middle of the first century A.D., when the existence of Buddhism is attested for the first time in contemporary Chinese sources.[4]

Brought in haphazard fashion by "merchants, refugees, envoys, hostages," Buddhism must have existed "among scattered foreign families, groups and settlements at a rather early date," and some short Sanskrit texts must have been in circulation as early as the beginning of the third century.[5]

Though we cannot be sure how Buddhist monks from India, Parthia, Sogdia and Scythia managed to get to China, there is evidence that three distinct centers of Buddhist learning developed during the Later Han dynasty: at Lo-yang in the north, P'eng-ch'eng on the lower Yangtze in the east, and at Chiao-chou (Tonkin, now Vietnam) in the south.[6] The result was a Buddhist-Taoist syncretism based on the legend of Lao-tzu's having gone to India to convert the barbarians, after which he became the Buddha.

> Therefore, the founders of Buddhism and Taoism were one and the same person, for the Buddha was but an incarnation of Lao-tzu. Since the two religions originated from the same source, there was no difference between them, so that it was quite proper for the deities Buddha and Huang-Lao to be worshipped on the same altar.[7]

This is attested in a Memorial submitted to the emperor by Hsiang K'ai in 166, in which he daringly contrasts the emperor's "sacrifices... to Huang-lao and the Buddha" with his actual moral practice.[8] We may conclude with Zürcher that there was a "close connection between Taoism and Buddhism in Later Han times" and that the *sangha* "was not an isolated enclave of foreign culture."[9]

But one major problem remained: "Buddhism was offering answers to questions the Chinese were not asking! It was only with the collapse of the Han empire almost two centuries later that the Chinese situation began to change sufficiently for Buddhism to be relevant."[10]

> The Chinese were after a way out of the growing social and political chaos accompanying the disintegration of the Chou empire, which led to attempts at articulating the Way (Tao) of socio-political order and stability. The Indians, on the other hand, were seeking a way of coping with a human existence characterized by suffering and frustration, and apparently doomed to an interminable series of re-births....[11]

The Chinese, unfamiliar with foreign languages, "very naturally fell back upon Taoist terms to express Buddhist ideas," proposing for translation the Buddhist texts that corresponded to their interests.[12] After the collapse of the Han Dynasty and the sack of Lo-yang (311) and Ch'ang-an (316), literati, officials and learned monks fled to the south, regarding themselves as "the true heirs and preservers of Chinese culture."[13] The "barbarian" north was now open to cultural — including Buddhist — influences from far to the west and southwest, while in the cultural isolation of the south Buddhism became the preserve of certain educated gentry and intellectuals.[14] Falling back on pre-existing transcription systems which assigned foreign phonetics to the Chinese characters as developed by the Former Han to facilitate administration of the western regions,[15] a method of translation known as "matching the meanings" or "reaching meaning" (*ko-i*) was developed, which appears to have correlated "the numerical categories of the sutras and ... (terms from) secular literature."[16] The very earliest translations seem to have been those of Lokaksema (who in the years 168–88 made the "Perfection of Wisdom" literature and thus the Mahayana accessible for the first time) and Dharmaraksa (whose highly specialized team translated the all-important *Lotus Sutra* in 286).[17] As the Chinese gained some knowledge of Sanskrit and their Indian guests began to master Chinese, techniques were developed involving teams of translators who checked and cross-checked one another's work, a far cry from the crude "matching of meanings."[18] The Buddhist converts, many of whom belonged to the educated gentry, were thus enabled to make some sense of these important Buddhist texts which articulated in highly paradoxical language the insubstantiality or "emptiness" (*sunyata*) of all things.[19]

This was the period of the so-called "Dark Learning" (*hsüan-hsüeh*)[20] by which Confucianist literati assimilated the Taoist paradoxes of being and non-being or action and inaction (*wu-wei*), speculated on the absolute principle which must be at the origin of universal harmony, and developed "the concept of *wu* or non-being that is the basis of all things."[21] Complementing the more legalistic and conservative "Doctrine of Names" (*ming-chiao*), the Dark Learning or "Study of the Mystery" "represents the more abstract, unworldly and idealistic tendency in medieval Chinese thought" and manifests "a profound interest in ontological problems."[22] It grappled with the age-old question whether there lies beneath the world of change, where "being" (*yu*) is perceived as limited and nameable, an unlimited, unchangeable and unnamable principle of "non-being" (*wu*). "This implies that 'being' and 'non-being,' though different, do not form a pair of mutually exclusive opposites."[23] The concept of a basic principle (*li*) or Great Ultimate (*t'ai-chi*) underlying and producing the Two Modes (*yin* and *yang*), and the impossibility of expressing this ultimate reality in language, are well established in the classical commentaries on the Book of Changes (*I-ching*).[24] The attempt to reconcile the "realistic" and "idealistic" viewpoints by Hsiang Hsiu (ca. 221–ca. 300) and Kuo Hsiang (d. 312) "forms the classical expression of Dark Learning in its last creative phase just before the impact of Mahayana Buddhism upon Chinese thought" and issues in the denial even of *wu*, "non-being," as a permanent substrate:

> There is no substrate at all; there is nothing which underlies diversity but the principle of diversity itself, and in this all things are one.... "Being" (as a totality) can simply not have been "produced" at all, for "non-being" is by definition unable to produce anything, and any other way of production presupposes the previous existence of "being."[25]

In the political and social sphere the Dark Learning maintained that spontaneous "non-activity" can be realized in the midst of mundane affairs, albeit in the framework of the rigid class distinctions of medieval society, which were allotted to individuals for no apparent reason as their "natural share." "It is exactly here that Buddhism came to fill one of the most serious lacunae with its theory of universal retribution (*karman* and rebirth) which supplied an ideological justification for this seemingly haphazard distribution of 'natural shares.' "[26]

After the violent repression of the "rebellion of the Yellow Turbans" in 184 and the ensuing "period of the Three Kingdoms" (220–265/280), which was characterized by "collapse of the central government, decentralized military control of the provinces, famine, large-scale banditry and messianic-revolutionary peasant movements,"[27] the travels of Buddhist scholars seeking texts and teachers in central Asia were blocked, but in the course of the fourth century both travel and translation once more became possible. The monk Fa-hsien set out on his epic journey to India to procure original *sutras*, particularly the *Vinaya* or monastic discipline, in 399. In the meantime, Tao-An (312–85) had devised provisional rules of discipline and drawn up a catalogue of *sutras*, bringing the cult of the Bodhisattva Maitreya to Ch'ang-an in 379. He had been struggling on his own with the Perfection of Wisdom literature, using the Chinese Dark Learning and his own experience of *dhyana* meditation to interpret it. The first of the great translators, Kumarajiva (d. 413), a Kuchanese convert from the Theravada, had begun to provide reliable renderings of some of the most important Perfection of Wisdom texts as well as the influential *Vimalakirti-Nirdesa* and the *Lotus Sutra*, revealing the true import of their meaning, especially the concept of "emptiness" (*sunyata*), for the first time. Though Tao-An had come close to this, "he still fails to realize the absolute identity of emptiness and phenomena, of Nirvana and samsara, a truth which only dawned upon the Chinese exegetes after the introduction of the Madhyamika treatises by Kumarajiva and his school."[28] Hui-yüan (344–416), who corresponded with Kumarajiva, investigated the practice of *dhyana* meditation (*Ch'an-an* in China and later *Zen* in Japan) and followed Tao-An's interest in devotion to the future Buddha Maitreya by encouraging the cult of Amitabha (the focus of Pure Land Buddhism).[29] Tao-sheng (ca. 360), through close study of the *Nirvanasutra*, boldly affirmed that all beings, even those sunk in desires (known as *icchantikas* and regarded as incapable of enlightenment), have the universal Buddha nature and may discover their True Self (*chen-wo*) through sudden enlightenment.[30] These "heresies" were to lay the foundation for some of the most characteristic doctrines of indigenous Chinese Buddhism.

The political turmoil of the Three Kingdoms period saw non-Chinese (*T'o-pa*) dynasties inimical to Buddhism established in the north. The controversy over the autonomy of the *sangha* and the attitude of the anti-Buddhist members of the gentry "give us an impression of the immense ideological and practical obstacles which the Buddhist Church met when it began to penetrate into the higher strata of society and to attract the attention of the ruling classes."[31] The Confucian minister Ts'ui Hao (381–450) wanted to set up the ideal Confucian state and conspired with his Taoist friend K'ou Ch'ien-chih (d. 448) to incite a persecution of Buddhism in 446. In the south, Emperor Wu (Ching-ling, 502–49) favored Buddhism against the opposition of Confucian critics, modeling himself on Asoka, the famous Buddhist ruler of India. Though there was no outright perse-cution, Taoist contempt for the non-Chinese "barbarians" and Confucian hostility to monasticism incited anti-Buddhist propaganda.[32] First at Yün-kang and later, after the Northern Wei capital had been transferred to Lo-yang, at Lung-men, hundreds of images were carved in caves portraying not only the Buddha Sakya-muni and the future Buddha Maitreya, but also the Buddha Amitabha and the Bodhisattva Avalokitesvara. After renewed acrimonious debates between Taoists and Buddhists, Buddhism was again suppressed in 574 by the northern Emperor Wu, though the Taoists too were proscribed for having introduced forgeries. A more sympathetic ruler succeeded Wu in 578, and in 589 Yang Chien conquered the southern Ch'en Dynasty and reunified China for the first time in three cen-turies, proclaiming himself Emperor Wen of the Sui Dynasty (581–618).[33] There followed a revival of Buddhism as the unifying ideology of the restored empire. Emperor Wen, convinced that he owed his ascendancy to the Buddhist *dharma,* styled himself a universal monarch and a lay disciple on the Indian model, order-ing the erection of *stupas* (reliquaries) throughout the realm in expiation of the damage caused to Buddhist temples by his military campaigns. Buddhism was now the religion of the common people as well as the gentry. Emperor Wen eventually overreached himself with grandiose construction works including two capitals, Ch'ang-an and Lo-yang, and the T'ang Dynasty that succeeded him after his assassination in 618 reverted to Confucianism as the state ideology, but Bud-dhism was now established as "the most powerful religion of the realm. It must have been; otherwise Emperor Wen would not have been so bold as to use it as the official ideology to unify the empire."[34] It was this example of imperial patronage that so impressed the Koreans, who asked for relics to take back to their kingdoms of Kokuryo, Paekche and Silla, and the Japanese prince Shotoku Taishi, who thereupon encouraged the introduction of Buddhism to Japan as the religion that could unify and civilize his fragmented and isolated country.[35]

The stage was now set for Buddhism to flourish as never before under the T'ang Dynasty (618–907), whose confident cosmopolitanism is demonstrated by the tolerance it extended to the Nestorian Christians, Muslims and Manicheans who came within its purview. Buddhism appealed to all classes, but by the same token it became more and more integrated into the state, which eventually took control of ordination under the Vinaya rules. The famous pilgrim Hsüan-tsang (ca. 596–664), upon his return from his (illegal) journey to India, found favor with Emperor T'ai-tsung, and he was followed by many others attracted by the brilliance of Indian teachers.[36] The inevitable result of such wide acceptance was the accumulation of wealth and influence which instigated Han Yü's anti-Buddhist Memorial of 819 and led to renewed persecution in 845, observed by the Japanese traveler Ennin. But popular forms of Buddhism such as the cult of Amitabha and the more ascetic Ch'an schools survived the seizure of temple lands and the purging of state officials to become authentically Chinese inculturations of Buddhism. An old Chinese expression classifies four of them: "T'ien-t'ai and Hua-Yen schools for teachings; Ch'an and Ching-t'u schools for practice!"[37] Because it was the fully developed and historically tested Buddhism of the T'ang period which exercised such a lasting influence on Japan, it will repay some further attention.[38]

Buddhism, as Ninian Smart remarks, "has played a specially dynamic role in the evolution of Chinese thought. Its very foreignness was an advantage, for it brought something new and difficult into Chinese civilization, and the resultant dialectic with native forces could be very fruitful."[39] One example is the Hua-yen school's interpretation of the central Buddhist doctrine of the "mutually dependent co-origination" (*pratityasamutpada*) of all things, usually expressed in the twelve-fold chain of causation governing rebirth in successive lives. The Mahayana version of this was that it implies the absence of "own being" (*svabhava*) in all constituents of reality (*dharmas*). While acknowledging the teaching on emptiness, the Chinese preferred the more positive interpretation given by Fa-tsang (643–712) when he was summoned before the emperor to explain the Hua-yen teachings in 699. These are based on the *Avatamsaka* or *Garland Sutra*, allegedly preached by the Buddha immediately after his enlightenment but not understood until much later. The *sutra* explains the emptiness of all *dharmas* by the simultaneous arising of all things out of the universal principle or *dharma-dhatu*. In an essay written in 704 Fa-tsang illustrated his point by referring to a golden lion, all parts of which, though different, are contained in all others because all are gold, and in teaching the doctrine to his students he surrounded a Buddha image with mirrors, each of which reflected all the others. The Hua-yen school, which had no equivalent in India, classified the Buddhist doctrines into five stages, from the Hinayana to the fully developed Mahayana, which is interpreted as teaching that all phenomena (*qi* in Confucian terminology) equally manifest the ultimate principle (*li*, now interpreted as the Buddha-nature). "A totalistic system is thus established, with everything leading to one point, the Buddha, in the center. It is no wonder that Empress Wu Tse-t'ien and the Japanese emperors favored the system, since it provided a religious sanction for their totalitarian schemes."[40] Hua-yen indeed reappeared in medieval Japan as Kegon and is symbolized by the huge bronze statue of Vairocana, the Buddha of Illumination, in the Todai-ji temple in Nara.[41]

One of several Buddhist texts which captured the imagination of the Chinese and became the basis of widespread popular devotion was the *Pure Land Sutra* (*Sukhavativyuha*), in which the monk Dharmakara asks to be reborn as the Buddha Amitabha in a Western Paradise or "Pure Land."[42] In the shorter version of this text only faith and prayer are necessary to achieve this, in other words: the causal chain of *karma* can be broken by intense devotion. Because of the limitless compassion of the Bodhisattva Avalokitesvara (whose name was loosely rendered "The One Who Hears the Cries of the World," in Chinese *Kuan-shih-yin*),[43] enlightenment is thus possible for all creatures. This universal compassion was represented by Kuan-yin or the Bodhisattva's female consort Tara, until under Tantric influence in the tenth century Kuan-yin became female, "The Giver of Children."[44] In the multi-ethnic north of China this devotion, particularly the repetition of the name of Buddha *(nien-fo)*, was popularized by Shan-tao and T'an-luan (476–542), while Tz'u-min (680–748) combined meditation with devotion and criticized the more astringent Ch'an, which diminished the importance of learning and discipline and advocated meditation alone.[45]

Though native Chinese such as Tao-an (312–85) and Hui-yüan (334–416) had experimented with Indian *dhyana* meditation and had recognized its complementarity with *prajña* (wisdom),[46] it is traditionally the arrival of Bodhidharma in 520 which initiates the Ch'an lineage in China. There developed northern and southern schools, which became bitterly divided over the question of gradual and sudden enlightenment. The southern school eventually prevailed in the person of Hui-neng, who according to legend was secretly elevated by Hung-jen to become the Sixth Patriarch, although he was only a humble rice pounder, because of his insight into original nothingness. He could not assume his patriarchal role openly until 676.[47] Though at first sight it may seem too abstruse to have appealed to the Chinese, it was in fact Ch'an with its teaching that the mind is the Buddha-nature, the ultimate emptiness which gives unity to all things but is inconceivable and inexpressible, which became the authentically Chinese expression of Buddhism. The Liu-chi (Jap. Rinzai) branch used techniques such as the *kung-an* (Jap. *koan*), the rationally unsolvable "case" or "riddle," to shock its adepts into awakening (Chin. *wu*, Jap. *satori*), while the Ts'ao-tung (Jap. Soto) school preferred to guide the adept though sitting meditation (*zazen*). These developments came as the flowering of the arts under the T'ang Dynasty reached its peak, exemplified in the poetry of Li Po (701–62) and Tu Fu (712–70), whose spontaneity and creativity were matched by the poets' libertarian and unconventional lifestyles.[48]

The Ch'an movement is but one aspect of the whole liberating tendency that characterized the age. This is one of the reasons why it became so popular in China. The school was not so speculative as the T'ien-t'ai, Hua-yen and Wei-shih Schools, and hence appealed more to the practical tendency in Chinese thought. It did not antagonize Confucian thought, and it bore a close affinity with Taoism in its philosophical ramifications.[49]

The naturalness and spontaneity of Ch'an have much in common with the thought of Lao-tzu and Chuang-tzu, for whom the ineffable Tao is everywhere and in everything, no matter how lowly.[50] The Taoists' mistrust of talking about the Tao has affinities with the Ch'an rejection of scriptures, images and rituals. It was this, and the rule introduced by Huai-hai (720–814) that all monks should engage in productive labor, that helped them survive the severe persecution of 845.[51]

The great epic of translation and assimilation was substantially complete by the time the rebellion of An Lu-shan (d. 757?) rudely shattered the peace and prosperity of the T'ang and initiated the turbulent transition through the period of the "Five Dynasties" (907–70) to the Sung Dynasty (960–1127). After various attempts at classification and periodization of texts according to the respective weight given them by the emerging Chinese schools, certain *sutras* had established themselves as definitively important in the eyes of the Chinese. The *Vimalakirti Nirdesa Sutra* — first translated around 188, again in the third century and by Kumarajiva in 406 — in which the worldly-wise layman Vimalakirti outwits the sanctimonious Hinayana monks, was understandably very popular among the anti-clerical Chinese. But it was the *Saddharmapundarika Sutra,* "The Sutra of the Lotus of the Wonderful Law," which had perhaps the most profound effect of all because of its claim to be the final revelation of the eternal Buddha-nature and hence to contain the message of universal salvation. Translated by Dharmaraksa in 286 and definitively by Kumarajiva in 406, its teaching of the partial concealment and gradual disclosure of the true *dharma* by the Buddha's use of *upaya,* "skilful means," according to the capacity of his listeners, helped to resolve the Chinese perplexity about the relative status of the different texts and offered the philosophical distinction between "worldly" (*samvrti*) and "transcendent" (*paramartha*) levels of truth. The *sutra* seemed to resolve the rivalry of the schools by proclaiming the "One Vehicle" (*ekayana*) that contains and transcends them all. The movements emanating from Mt. T'ien-t'ai regarded it as the basic Buddhist text, and its status was if anything enhanced in the Tendai School which brought this tradition to Japan. Whereas Confucianism and Taoism always carried the implication that they were for the superior Chinese only, Buddhism, whether Ch'an, Pure Land or T'ien-t'ai, transcended ethnicity and presented itself as equally accessible to all. At the same time, however, it must be remembered that the early Chinese Buddhists were "forced to be eclectics by the circumstances under which the doctrine was presented to them," for only a few foreign *acaryas* could freely express themselves in Chinese, whereas before the late fourth century no Chinese seems to have had any knowledge of Sanskrit.... All these factors must have contributed to the thorough sinization of Buddhism ... to the formation of a Buddhism in Chinese guise, digested by Chinese minds, translated into Chinese patterns of thought.[52]

This was to be Buddhism's great strength as the next stage of its Asian journey opened.

NOTES

Introduction

1. The violent legacy of monotheism informs the sociologist Rodney Stark's analysis of the historical data, *One True God: Historical Consequences of Monotheism* (Princeton, N.J.: Princeton University Press, 2001). Such analyses tend to assume that there are discrete "entities" labeled "this religion" and "that religion" which can be compared with one another as coherent wholes. Language constrains us to use the shorthand of the various "isms," which can easily create this impression, but Stark himself admits in chap. 1 that monotheism is rarely if ever encountered in pure form, whereas Buddhism acquired quasi-theistic elements.

2. I am aware, of course, that a more symmetrical comparison could be achieved by studying the history of Christianity's enculturation into Europe. But in this book I want to concentrate on the Asia-Pacific region, presuming in my readers a general knowledge of Christianity's European history, whereas the behavior of *this* Christianity once it expanded into the Pacific is much less known.

3. See the introduction to J. D. May, *Christus Initiator: Theologie im Pazifik* (Düsseldorf: Patmos, 1990). Samuel Huntington, *The Clash of Civilizations and the Remaking of World Order* (New York: Simon & Schuster, 1996), tends to dismiss attempts at Asia-Pacific regionalization, whereas Manuel Castells, *End of Millennium: The Information Age: Economy, Society and Culture*, vol. 3 (Malden and Oxford: Blackwell, 1998), chap. 4, sees the Asia-Pacific developing as its economic centers and distinctive cultures interact independently with the trilateral power centers (US, EU, Japan) and become integrated into the global economy, see 206–15. This is of course a predominantly economic perspective.

4. For some varied and stimulating treatments of these and other questions involved in such research, see Robert Borofsky, ed., *Remembrance of Pacific Pasts: An Invitation to Remake History* (Honolulu: University of Hawai'i Press, 2000); K. R. Howe, R. Kiste and Brij Lal, eds., *Tides of History: The Pacific Islands in the Twentieth Century* (Honolulu: University of Hawai'i Press, 1994).

5. Without being able to go into this in detail here, it is the philosophical theologies of Karl Rahner and Bernard Lonergan, pioneered by the "transcendental Thomism" of their fellow-Jesuit Joseph Maréchal, which have developed this tradition most impressively in dialogue with the post-Enlightenment thought of Kant, Husserl and Heidegger.

6. Jan van Bragt, "Begegnung von Ost und West: Buddhismus und Christentum," in Hans Waldenfels and Thomas Immoos, eds., *Fernöstliche Weisheit und christlicher Glaube* (Mainz: Matthias-Grünewald-Verlag, 1985), 268–88, 277–78; see also Perry Schmidt-Leukel, *"Den Löwen brüllen hören": Zur Hermeneutik eines christlichen Verständnisses der buddhistischen Heilsbotschaft* (Munich: Schöningh, 1992), 538, n. 31.

7. Joseph O'Leary, *Religious Pluralism and Christian Truth* (Edinburgh University Press, 1996). See also the quixotically personal, engagingly off-beat, but unfailingly stimulating dialogue with Derrida conducted by Robert Magiola, *On Deconstructing Life-Worlds: Buddhism, Christianity, Culture* (Atlanta: Scholars Press, 1997).

8. David Loy, *Lack and Transcendence: The Problem of Death and Life in Psychotherapy, Existentialism, and Buddhism* (Amherst, Mass.: Humanity Books, 1999).

9. See the summary in ibid., 50, and the following chapter on "The Pain of Being Human."

10. See ibid., 92–93.

11. Loy's Conclusion on "Transcendence East and West," in ibid., 154–72, develops this typology brilliantly; see also his more recent *A Buddhist History of the West: Studies in Lack* (Albany: State University of New York Press, 2002). To these questions, too, we must return in Part III.

12. These views are associated with the powerful hypothesis of René Girard in such works as *Violence and the Sacred* (Baltimore: Johns Hopkins University Press, 1977) and *The Scapegoat* (London: Athlone Press, 1986); see the discussion in Robert G. Hamerton-Kelly, ed., *Violent Origins: Walter Burkert, René Girard, and Jonathan Z. Smith on Ritual Killing and Cultural Formation* (Stanford, Calif.: Stanford University Press, 1987).

13. See Thich Nhat Hanh, *Vietnam: The Lotus in the Sea of Fire* (London: SCM, 1967) with a sympathetic Foreword by Thomas Merton. The story of their brief but significant relationship has now been told by Robert H. King, *Thomas Merton and Thich Nhat Hanh: Engaged Spirituality in an Age of Globalization* (New York and London: Continuum, 2001).

14. An indication that this may in fact be so is the profound meditation on Buddhist and Quaker suicides in protest against the war in Vietnam by Sallie B. King, "They Who Burned Themselves for Peace: Quaker and Buddhist Self-Immolators during the Vietnam War," *Buddhist-Christian Studies* 20 (2000): 127–50. Following the self-immolation of Thich Quang Duc (11 June 1963), the first of its kind for hundreds of years, the incidents on which King concentrates are those involving the student and disciple of Thich Nhat Hanh, Nhat Chi Mai (16 May 1967) and the American Quaker pacifist Norman Morrison (2 November 1965), though there were others. The moral issues of interior motivation and public example are acute in each case.

15. I do not wish to overlook the equally terrible fate of political dissidents such as communists, nor of what the Nazis called the *unwertes Leben* of the mentally defective, homosexuals or Roma and Sinti. I concentrate on the attempted extermination of the Jews because it contains a certain theological quality which is pertinent to our study.

16. See Johann Baptist Metz, "Christen und Juden nach Auschwitz: Auch eine Betrachtung über das Ende bürgerlicher Religion," in idem, *Jenseits bürgerlicher Religion: Reden über die Zukunft des Christentums* (Munich: Kaiser; Mainz: Grünewald, 1980), 29–50; Metz's answer to Adorno's famous saying is more precisely: "We can pray *after* Auschwitz because there was prayer *in* Auschwitz," 31.

17. A recent study by Lucia Scherzberg, *Kirchenreform mit Hilfe des Nationalsozialismus. Karl Adam als kontextueller Theologe* (Darmstadt: Wissenschaftliche Buchgesellschaft, 2001), shows how the prominent Catholic theologian of the Tübingen School, Karl Adam, not only entertained explicit Nazi sympathies but "forgot" them after the war as if they were of no consequence or had never existed. Much more such research remains to be done.

18. See David Sorkin, *The Transformation of German Jewry, 1780–1840* (Detroit: Wayne State University Press, 1999). Stark, *One True God,* chap. 3, develops the thesis that both Christianity and Islam tolerated Jews in their respective European spheres of influence until they themselves came into conflict (Spanish *reconquista,* crusades), at which point the Jews became "collateral victims," as did heretics.

19. For more precise references see J. D. May, " 'The Only Great Ecumenical Question': Christian-Jewish Relations," *Studies* 77 (1988): 300–308, 301.

20. For what follows, I am especially indebted to Peter [Schüttke-]Scherle, *From Contextual to Ecumenical Theology? A Dialogue between Minjung Theology and "Theology after Auschwitz"* (Frankfurt: Peter Lang, 1989); John Pawlikowski, *Jesus and the Theology of Israel* (Washington: Catholic University of America Press, 1989); Birte Petersen, *Theologie nach Auschwitz? Jüdische und christliche Versuche einer Antwort* (Berlin: Institut Kirche und Judentum, 1998).

21. See John B. Cobb and Christopher Ives, eds., *The Emptying God: A Buddhist-Jewish-Christian Conversation* (Maryknoll, N.Y.: Orbis, 1990).

22. See Richard Gombrich, *Buddhist Precept and Practice: Traditional Buddhism in the Highlands of Ceylon* (London: Kegan Paul International, 1995), 34.

23. *Mahavamsa* XXV, 108–11, cited by Richard Gombrich, *Theravada Buddhism: A Social History from Ancient Benares to Modern Colombo* (London and New York: Routledge & Kegan Paul, 1988), 141.

24. See S. J. Tambiah, *Buddhism Betrayed? Religion, Politics and Violence in Sri Lanka* (Chicago: University of Chicago Press, 1992); idem, "Buddhism, Violence, and Politics in Sri Lanka," in Martin E. Marty and R. Scott Appleby, eds., *Fundamentalisms and the State: Remaking Politics, Economics, and Militance* (Chicago: University of Chicago Press, 1993), 589–619; J. D. May, "Christian-Buddhist-Marxist Dialogue in Sri Lanka: A Model for Social Change in Asia?," *Journal of Ecumenical Studies* 19 (1982): 719–43; François Houtart, *Religion and Ideology in Sri Lanka* (Bangalore, 1974).

25. The re-Hinduization of Singhalese Buddhism affected courtly and social rituals, e.g., the marriage ceremony, at times going so far that monks had to be brought from Thailand to restore the *upasampada* ordination and the *uposatha* assembly; see Gombrich, *Precept and Practice,* 23–43; *Theravada Buddhism,* chap. 6. Lynn de Silva, *Buddhism: Beliefs and Practices in Sri Lanka,* 2d rev. ed. (Colombo: Wesley Press, 1980), gives a detailed account of the role of Buddhism in Singhalese "popular" religion.

26. The point is made by Ninian Smart in contrasting the role of religion in India and Sri Lanka, "India, Sri Lanka and Religion," John P. Burris, ed., *Reflections in the Mirror of Religion* (London: Macmillan, 1997), 130–47, 135.

27. See Tambiah, *Buddhism Betrayed?,* in which the writings and reports of the period such as Walpola Rahula, *The Heritage of the Bhikkhu* (1946); Buddhist Commission of Enquiry, *The Betrayal of Buddhism* (1956); and D. C. Vijayawardhana, *The Revolt in the Temple* (1953) are critically assessed; Ulrich Dornberg, *Searching Through the Crisis: Christians, Contextual Theology and Social Change in Sri Lanka in the 1970s and 1980s* (Colombo: Logos, 1992), 30–41, 49–54; Peter Harvey, *An Introduction to Buddhism: Teachings, History and Practices* (Cambridge: Cambridge University Press, 1990), 290–93; Richard Gombrich and Gananath Obeyesekere, *Buddhism Transformed: Religious Change in Sri Lanka* (Princeton, N.J.: Princeton University Press, 1988); James Manor, "Organizational Weaknesses and

the Rise of Singhalese Buddhist Extremism," in Martin E. Marty and R. Scott Appleby, eds., *Accounting for Fundamentalism: The Dynamic Character of Movements* (Chicago: University of Chicago Press, 1994), 770–84. See also Iain Atack, "Social Conflict and Human Rights Abuses in Sri Lanka 1987–89," M.Phil. thesis, Irish School of Ecumenics, Trinity College Dublin, 1992.

28. The term "Protestant Buddhism," which is not uncontroversial, is used by Gombrich, *Theravada Buddhism,* chap. 7.

29. Donald K. Swearer, "Fundamentalistic Movements in Theravada Buddhism," in Martin E. Marty and R. Scott Appleby, *Fundamentalisms Observed* (Chicago: University of Chicago Press, 1991), 628–90, 639, see also 640, 647, 648.

30. Ibid., 650. The problem to be explored in this book could hardly be better expressed.

31. See James Manor, "Organizational Weakness and the Rise of Singhalese Buddhist Extremism," in Marty and Appleby, *Accounting for Fundamentalisms,* 770–84. The Theravada proved sufficiently politically multivalent to be exploited by all shades of opinion, but the fact that extremist views were articulated by monks placed them beyond criticism, 774–76.

32. See Aloysius Pieris, "Faith Communities and Communalism," in S. Arokiasamy, ed., *Responding to Communalism: The Task of Religions and Theology* (Anand, Gujarat: Gujarat Sahitya Prakash, 1991), 37–60. For Pieris religion needs ideology if it is not to remain utopian, but it must also be able to divest itself of harmful ideology, which can "contaminate" the "collective memory of an Absolute Future" preserved by religion, 46, 50. In an interesting gloss he notes that the original Buddhist and Tamil rivals had the popular nicknames "Duttha-Gamini (Wicked Gamini)" and "Dharmistha Elara" (the Just Elara). This indicates that the Singhalese masses have never been racist!, 57.

Part I: Christianity's Pacific Voyage

1. Norman Habel, who grew up a few miles away on the shores of Lake Linlithgow, makes exactly the same observation, *Reconciliation: Searching for Australia's Soul* (Sydney: HarperCollins, 1999), 66–67.

2. In what follows I shall be referring to Jan Critchett, *A "Distant Field of Murder": Western District Frontiers 1834–1848* (Melbourne: Melbourne University Press, 1990). She bases her analysis of what happened on a thorough study of the journals of George Augustus Robinson, who, though compromised by his role in the attempt to subdue the Aborigines of Van Diemen's Land (Tasmania), made the first systematic survey of race relations in the Western District of Victoria in 1841at the behest of Superintendent Charles Joseph La Trobe (3, 6), and on other primary sources such as the study published by James Dawson in 1881 after long first-hand observation with the help of his daughter Isabella, who could speak Aboriginal languages (3).

3. Ibid., 4.

4. Ibid., 6, 24, 129. She estimates the Aboriginal population of the District at about 3500 (74). By the 1840s there would have been roughly equal numbers of white men and Aboriginal men, not counting women and children: 1102 and 1167 respectively (76).

5. John Power to Lord John Russell, 30 Nov. 1840, quoted by Critchett, ibid., frontispiece.

6. Critchett, ibid., 92, 130; the casualties on both sides are named and listed in Appendices 2 and 3.

7. Ibid., 137.

8. Ibid., 91. By 1842 the situation in the District was "in turmoil" (107) with constant attacks on homesteads and stock.

9. Ibid., 86–67.

10. Ibid., 61, 63, 94, 103–13.

11. See Critchett's discussion of the not entirely reliable tribal and language boundaries established by Dawson and Tindale, ibid., 42–51, with maps, and the detailed listing of tribes and their localities drawn from extant sources in Appendix 1. See also Gib Wettenhall, *The People of Gariwerd: The Grampians' Aboriginal Heritage* (Victoria: Aboriginal Affairs Victoria, 1999), 3, and the detailed language map of Aboriginal Australia published by the Australian Institute of Aboriginal and Torres Strait Islander Affairs, 2000.

Chapter 1: Internalizing the Primal Other

1. E.g., the film *First Contact,* made by Bob Connolly and Robin Anderson in 1983 using film material shot by the Leahy brothers on their journey through the highlands of New Guinea in 1932–33, which formed the basis of a book of the same title (Ringwood, Vic., Australia: Viking Penguin, 1987); and *L'Ombre Blanche au Pays des Papous,* shown on the French-German channel Arte in 1996.

2. Robert Hughes, *The Fatal Shore: A History of the Transportation of Convicts to Australia 1787–1868* (London: Pan Books, 1988), chap. 3.

3. Much of what follows is a reworking of a lecture I gave at Trinity College, Dublin, on 7 November. 1996, entitled "Internalizing the Primal Other: Aboriginal Religion and European Christianity," which is to be published in a *Festschrift* for Gabriel Daly.

4. I should perhaps note that as an Australian of Irish descent, a "Pacific Islander" who has lived for many years in Europe, I have a certain ambivalence towards both the Old World and the New, especially since my awareness of how the Irish were treated in Britain and its colonies, beginning with Northern Ireland, has been sharpened by living in Ireland; the parallels between the Aboriginals and the Irish in this respect have been explored by the Melbourne historian Val Noone in a number of papers and in his magazine *Táin.*

5. See John N. Molony, *The Penguin Bicentennial History of Australia: The Story of Two Hundred Years* (Ringwood, Vic., Australia: Viking, 1987), 6, 16–17, and, for a very full account, Bob Reece, *The Origins of Irish Convict Transportation to New South Wales* (Basingstoke, U.K.: Palgrave, 2001).

6. Cited by John Harris, *One Blood: Two Hundred Years of Aboriginal Encounter with Christianity: A Story of Hope* (Sutherland, N.S.W., Australia: Albatross Books, 1990), 37.

7. Cited by W. E. H. Stanner, "The History of Indifference Thus Begins," in *White Man Got No Dreaming: Essays 1938–1973* (Canberra: Australian National University Press, 1979), 165–91, 165.

8. Harris, *One Blood,* 37; see also Hilary M. Carey, *Believing in Australia: A Cultural History of Religion* (St. Leonards, N.S.W., Australia: Allen & Unwin, 1996).

9. Lieutenant William Dawes at first refused to take part in the expedition at all; see Henry Reynolds, *This Whispering in Our Hearts* (St. Leonards, N.S.W., Australia: Allen &

Unwin, 1998), 1–2. John Molony, *The Native-Born: The First White Australians* (Melbourne: Melbourne University Press, 2000), gives a moving account of the situation from the settlers' point of view, while W. E. H. Stanner introduces his Boyer Lectures, *After the Dreaming: Black and White Australians — An Anthropologist's View* (Sydney: Australian Broadcasting Corporation, 1969), 1–11, with a step-by-step summary of Governor Phillip's ineptitude as misunderstandings mounted.

10. Francis X. Hezel, S.J., *The First Taint of Civilization: A History of the Caroline and Marshall Islands in Pre-Colonial Days, 1521–1885* (Honolulu: University of Hawai'i Press, 1983).

11. See the extensive documentation compiled by Henry Reynolds, *Dispossession: Black Australians and White Invaders* (Sydney: Allen & Unwin, 1989), esp. chap. 4.

12. On this see Gideon Goosen, "Christian and Aboriginal Interface in Australia," *Theological Studies* 60 (1999): 72–94, 76.

13. Cited in Harris, *One Blood,* 22; see Anne Pattel-Gray, *The Great White Flood: Racism in Australia* (Atlanta: Scholars Press, 1998), 133–36 on the "flogging chaplain."

14. See Harris, *One Blood,* 33–34; Reynolds, *Whispering,* chap. 2

15. See Reynolds, *Dispossession,* chap. 3; this is the theme of Reynolds, *Whispering,* and of the first history of Australia written entirely from the point of view of the Europeans' moral right to occupy the land: David Day, *Claiming a Continent: A History of Australia* (Sydney: Angus & Robertson, 1996), chaps. 4–7.

16. See Harris, *One Blood,* 27–28.

17. On this see the thought-provoking essay by Stanner, "Caliban Discovered," in his *White Man Got No Dreaming,* 144–64, 150.

18. See the landmark report by the Human Rights and Equal Opportunity Commission, *Bringing Them Home: Report of the National Inquiry into the Separation of Aboriginal and Torres Strait Islander Children from Their Families* (Sydney: Human Rights and Equal Opportunity Commission, 1997).

19. Harris, *One Blood,* 71.

20. See Stanner, "History of Indifference."

21. See Harris, *One Blood,* 72–75.

22. See ibid., 148, and the extensive documentation in Pattel-Gray, *Great White Flood.*

23. See Harris, *One Blood,* 23–24.

24. See ibid., 182.

25. Stanner, *After the Dreaming,* 18–29; see also Denis Edwards, "Sin and Salvation in the South Land of the Holy Spirit," Peter Malone, ed., *Discovering an Australian Theology* (Homebush, N.S.W., Australia: St. Paul Publications, 1988), 89–102, 96–97.

26. Harris, *One Blood,* 184.

27. See ibid., 39–40.

28. The Rainbow Spirit Elders in collaboration with Robert Bos, Norman Habel and Shirley Wurst, *Rainbow Spirit Theology: Towards an Australian Aboriginal Theology* (Blackburn, Vic., Australia: HarperCollins, 1997), 44, 51, and extensively in Pattel-Gray, *Great White Flood,* see 199–201.

29. Regina M. Schwartz, *The Curse of Cain: The Violent Legacy of Monotheism* (Chicago: University of Chicago Press, 1997), 47, reflecting on the claim that "horrific acts of human violence have been committed and continue to be committed in the service of what is

after all an idea: the notion that a 'group' (an imagined community) must 'possess' (how can land be owned?) a 'piece' (note how the earth is imagined in pieces) of land," 40.

30. Schwartz, *The Curse of Cain*, 62, see 51–54.

31. Cited by Harris, *One Blood*, 150, with even more eloquent Aboriginal testimonies, e.g., "Why me have lubra? Why me have piccaninny? You have all this place, no good have children, no good have lubra, me tumble down and die very soon now."

32. Jan Critchett, A *"Distant Field of Murder": Western District Frontiers 1834–1848* (Melbourne: Melbourne University Press, 1990), 38. She notes that in the Western District, more isolated from European contact, the decline in births and the onset of disease were delayed.

33. See Henry Reynolds, *The Other Side of the Frontier* (Ringwood, Vic., Australia: Penguin, 1982).

34. These have been reconstructed by Tony Swain, *A Place for Strangers: Towards a History of Australian Aboriginal Being* (Cambridge: Cambridge University Press, 1993).

35. Molony, *History of Australia*, 11, estimates 750,000, though both lower and higher figures are also given.

36. Personal communication from the priest-archaeologist Eugene Stockton, since confirmed by Day, *Claiming a Continent*, who considers 120,000 years to be a likely figure; Pattel-Gray, *Great White Flood*, 86, gives 140,000; and Goosen, "Interface," 72, cites thermoluminescence datings of 116,000 years.

37. Tony Swain, *Interpreting Aboriginal Religion: An Historical Account* (Adelaide: Australian Association for the Study of Religions, 1985), 14; see also 75ff., 102–3, 106–23.

38. It is Swain's achievement in *A Place for Strangers* to have opened up this area of research; see his concluding summary, 276–96, and his contribution to Tony Swain and Garry Trompf, *The Religions of Oceania* (London and New York: Routledge, 1995), part 1.

39. Max Charlesworth, introducing the anthology edited by him with Howard Morphy, Diane Bell and Kenneth Maddock, *Religion in Aboriginal Australia* (St. Lucia: University of Queensland Press, 1986), 2, 4.

40. See Stanner, "Some Aspects of Aboriginal Religion," in Robert Crotty, ed., *The Charles Strong Lectures 1972–1984* (Leiden: E. J. Brill, 1987), 3–20, and A. P. Elkin, *Aboriginal Men of High Degree: Initiation and Sorcery in the World's Oldest Tradition* (Rochester: Inter Traditions, 1994 [1997]). Pattel-Gray, *Great White Flood*, 142–44, is dubious about Elkin's objectivity, alleging "collusion with the government." The pioneering research of E. A. Worms, revised and augmented by Helmut Petri and in a new English translation edited by Martin Wilson, *Australian Aboriginal Religions* (Sydney: Nelen Yubu, 1998), though its phenomenology of religion methodology is now somewhat dated, is still informative.

41. Stanner, "The Dreaming," in *White Man Got No Dreaming*, 23–40, 23. Many now regard this as a mistranslation of words which mean "eternal" or "uncreated" and connote Law; see the detailed study by Lynne Hume, *Ancestral Power: The Dreaming, Consciousness and Aboriginal Australians* (Melbourne: Melbourne University Press, 2002). Charlesworth dislikes the term because of its poetic vagueness and its implied lack of subjectivity, but in his introduction to *Religion in Aboriginal Australia*, 9–12, explaining its origins and the different senses in which it may be used, he concedes that it does express the element of transcendence in Aboriginal religion; see also his "Anthropology and Australian Aboriginal Religion," *Religious Traditions* 13 (1990): 7–22. The Rainbow Spirit Elders speak of the

"Creator Spirit," and Norman Habel prefers "Spirit of the Land," *Reconciliation: Searching for Australia's Soul* (Sydney: HarperCollins, 1999), 95–105.

42. Stanner, "Aboriginal Religion," 4.

43. Roland M. Berndt and Catherine H. Berndt, *The Speaking Land: Myth and Story in Aboriginal Australia* (Ringwood, Vic., Australia: Penguin, 1988).

44. Charlesworth, *Aboriginal Religion*, 7.

45. Roland M. Berndt, "Good and Bad in Australian Aboriginal Religion," in Crotty, ed., *The Charles Strong Lectures 1972–1984*, 21–36, 22–23; for a discussion of the Berndts' "charter theory" of the Dreaming, see Swain, *Interpreting Aboriginal Religion*, 112–14.

46. Tony Swain, "Reinventing the Eternal: Aboriginal Spirituality and Modernity," in Norman C. Habel, ed., *Religion and Multiculturalism in Australia: Essays in Honour of Victor Hayes* (Adelaide, Australia: AASR, 1992), 122–36, 130.

47. Eugene Stockton, *The Aboriginal Gift: Spirituality for a Nation* (Sydney: Millennium Books, 1995), 18.

48. Charlesworth, *Religion in Aboriginal Australia*, 13–14, encourages the use of the term for Aboriginal religion, though James L. Cox, "The Classification 'Primal Religions' as a Non-Empirical Christian Theological Construct," *Studies in World Christianity* 2 (1996): 55–76, questions its legitimacy as a research tool. The fact that it was endorsed by missiologists such as John V. Taylor and Andrew Walls does not impugn its usefulness as an indicator of fundamental religious needs, values and forms of expression.

49. Guboo Ted Thomas, "The Land Is Sacred: Renewing the Dreaming in Modern Australia," Garry W. Trompf, ed., *The Gospel Is Not Western: Black Theologies from the Southwest Pacific* (Maryknoll, N.Y.: Orbis, 1987), 90–94, 93.

50. One of the group of Rainbow Spirit Elders who collaborated to produce *Rainbow Spirit Theology*, 4.

51. *Rainbow Spirit Theology*, 4–5.

52. Sidney Nolan and Russell Drysdale in their severe depictions of the land and its legends; Roland Robinson in his translations of Aboriginal poetry, some of which are reproduced in Les Murray's *Anthology of Australian Religious Poetry* (Blackburn, Vic., Australia: CollinsDove, 1986); poets such as Les Murray and Bruce Dawe (see Peter Kirkwood, "Two Australian Poets as Theologians: Les Murray and Bruce Dawe," Malone, *Discovering an Australian Theology*, 195–216); Patrick White (*Voss*; *A Fringe of Leaves*) and Thomas Keneally (*The Chant of Jimmie Blacksmith*) in their imaginative reconstructions of traumatic historical incidents; and films such as Peter Weir's *Picnic at Hanging Rock* and *The Last Wave* have insisted on the wider human dimensions of the European encounter with the land itself as the "sacred site" of Aboriginal religion. Perhaps this is nowhere more vividly captured than in Xavier Herbert's sprawling epic *Poor Fellow My Country*, in which the great mythical figures of Aboriginal cosmology such as the Rainbow Serpent are, in a sense, characters. But no one, in my view, has plumbed these depths more sensitively than David Malouf. In *An Imaginary Life* he uses the fictional autobiography of the poet Ovid, exiled from imperial Rome to the wild shores of Dalmatia, to examine the re-education of a sophisticated European as he learns to communicate with a captured boy who had lived wild, privy to the secrets of nature. In *Remembering Babylon* the theme is varied to probe the reactions of settlers in western Queensland to a white boy who has lived with the Aborigines, who is both "of us" and "of them." Reviewing these works, the critic Veronica Brady

says that they embark on a journey into the self which bears comparison with the quest for the *atman* in Indian religious philosophy ("A Properly Appointed Humanism: Australian Culture and the Aborigines in Patrick White's *A Fringe of Leaves*" and "Malouf's *An Imaginary Life*," Veronica Brady, *Caught in the Draught: On Contemporary Australian Culture and Society* [Sydney: Angus & Robertson, 1994, 139–52, 233–57]. David Tacey, *Edge of the Sacred: Transformation in Australia* [Blackburn, Vic., Australia: HarperCollins, 1995]), has traced the rediscovery of the sacred in a wide range of Australian artists, both European and Aboriginal, in the framework of Jungian psychology. Of particular interest is the profound disturbance evoked in the visiting English novelist D. H. Lawrence by his intuition of the sacredness of the Australian landscape, which inspired his novel *Kangaroo;* see Tacey, chap. 4.

53. Tacey has ably defended himself against the charge of appropriation, see Mitchell Rolls, "The Jungian Quest for the Aborigine Within: A Close Reading of David Tacey's *Edge of the Sacred: Transformation in Australia*," *Melbourne Journal of Politics* 25 (1998): 171–87; David Tacey, "What Are We Afraid Of?: Intellectualism, Aboriginality, and the Sacred," ibid., 189–94. James Tulip, "Spirituality and the Centre: A Review Essay," *Uniting Church Studies* 7, no. 1 (2001): 41–50, comments on more recent developments, including Tacey's book *ReEnchantment: The New Australian Spirituality* (Sydney: HarperCollins, 2000). Interestingly, Thomas Keneally now admits that he would not attempt to get inside the mind of the Westernized but alienated Aborigine Jimmie Blacksmith today, "A New Chant for Jimmie Blacksmith," *The Sydney Morning Herald, Spectrum,* 25–26 August 2001, 4–5.

54. This is developed by David Tracy, *Dialogue with the Other: The Inter-Religious Dialogue* (Louvain: Peeters Press, 1990), chap. 3. White Australian theologians such as Denis Edwards, Eugene Stockton, Frank Fletcher, Martin Wilson, Norman Habel, Don Carrington and Robert Bos are experimenting with different approaches, some philosophical, others biblical, to this lost dimension of European theology; for an assessment see Goosen, "Interface," 76–82.

55. Stockton, *Aboriginal Gift,* 4.

56. Ibid., 169; idem, "A Bush Theologian Goes His Way," Peter Malone, ed., *Developing an Australian Theology* (Strathfield, Australia: St. Paul's Publications, 1999), 249–64.

57. Frank Fletcher, "Finding the Framework to Prepare for Dialogue with the Aborigines," *Pacifica* 10 (1997): 25–38, 26; see also idem, "Towards a Dialogue with Traditional Aboriginal Religion," *Pacifica* 9 (1996): 164–74; "Does Spirituality Need Some Concrete Rootedness in Our Land?," *Compass Theology Review* 33 (Spring 1999): 31–34; "Imagination for the Australian Spiritual Journey," Malone, ed., *Developing an Australian Theology,* 265–78; "Is Aboriginal Spirituality Relevant to the Mystery of Christ?," *The Australasian Catholic Record* 78 (2001): 271–78.

58. Fletcher, "Framework," 34.

59. Ibid., 38.

60. Cited in Stockton, *Aboriginal Gift,* 113.

61. On the psychology of racism from the receiving end see Pattel-Gray, *Great White Flood,* 213.

62. Stockton, *Aboriginal Gift,* 95. For a religiously sensitive interpretation of Aboriginal art, see Rosemary Crumlin, ed., *Aboriginal Art and Spirituality* (Blackburn, Vic., Australia: Dove Communications, 1991).

63. Djiniyini Gondarra, *Let My People Go: Series of Reflections on Aboriginal Theology* (Darwin, N.T., Australia: Bethel Presbytery, 1986); *Father You Gave Us the Dreaming* (Darwin, N.T., Australia: Bethel Presbytery, 1988).

64. Patrick Dodson, "The Land Our Mother, the Church Our Mother," Malone, *Discovering an Australian Theology*, 83–88.

65. Reproduced in Stockton, *Aboriginal Gift*, 179–84 and chap. 10; see also the reflections by Dan O'Donovan, *Dadirri* (Sydney: Nelen Yubu Missiological Unit, 2001) and the conference papers by Aboriginal speakers edited by Anne Pattel-Gray, *Aboriginal Spirituality: Past, Present, Future* (East Melbourne: HarperCollins Religious, 1996).

66. Anne Pattel-Gray and Garry W. Trompf, "Styles of Australian Aboriginal and Melanesian Theology," *International Review of Mission* 82 (1993): 167–88, 168. Though still strongly influenced by the "missionized Christianity" implanted by the early missionaries, Aboriginal theologians are slowly finding their voice in the public sphere. They are conscious of their debt to the "forgotten theologians" of the past: the first converts, beginning with the son of Bennelong; the first ordained ministers (James Noble, Anglican, 1925; Patrick Dodson, Roman Catholic, 1975; Liyapidiny Marika, the first Uniting Church Aboriginal woman minister, 1991); and the early Bible translators, whose achievements went largely unrecognized. See also Goosen, "Interface," 82–93.

67. Pattel-Gray and Trompf, "Styles of Australian Aboriginal and Melanesian Theology," 172.

68. Ibid., 176.

69. Fletcher, "Framework," 36.

70. *Rainbow Spirit Theology*, 5, 11.

71. Human Rights and Equal Opportunity Commission, *Bringing Them Home: Report of the National Inquiry into the Separation of Aboriginal and Torres Strait Islander Children from Their Families* (Sydney: Human Rights and Equal Opportunity Commission, 1997), 266.

72. Ibid., 583.

73. Ibid., 140.

74. William Ferguson and John Patten, 1938, *Bringing Them Home*, 46.

75. Van Krieken, *Bringing Them Home*, 252.

76. *Bringing Them Home*, 12.

77. Ibid., 13.

78. Ibid., 130.

79. Ibid., 152.

80. Ibid., 200.

81. See ibid., 205–7; 222; 233–34.

82. "There is no uniform view about reparation, but there is a consistent view of indigenous people as to the necessity for apologies...an apology must be matched by a commitment to rectify past mistakes through reparation and compensation," Aboriginal and Torres Strait Islander Commission, *Bringing Them Home*, 285.

83. Western Australian Baptists, *Bringing Them Home*, 291.

84. Uniting Church National Assembly, 1996, *Bringing Them Home*, 290.

85. Catholic Church, Darwin, *Bringing Them Home*, 405.

86. NCCA, Media Release, 21 May 2001.

87. On the problems of "reconciliation," see Pattel-Gray, *Great White Flood,* chap. 5. Norman Habel, in *Reconciliation,* has given a very personal and public example of coming to terms with one's own inherited racism and devising healing rites at the sites of atrocities. See also John Wilcken, S.J., "Reconciliation in Australia: An Ethical Challenge," *Compass Theology Review* 33 (Spring 1999): 15–22; J. D. May, "A Rationale for Reconciliation," *Uniting Church Studies* 7 (March 2001): 1–13. The complex legal and religious issues involved in securing Aboriginal land rights on the basis of a treaty would take us too far afield here, but some key texts are: Frank Brennan, *Sharing the Country* (Ringwood, Vic., Australia: Penguin, 1991); H. C. Coombs, *Aboriginal Autonomy: Issues and Strategies* (Cambridge: Cambridge University Press, 1994); Henry Reynolds, *Aboriginal Sovereignty: Reflections on Race, State and Nation* (St. Leonards, N.S.W., Australia: Allen & Unwin, 1996).

88. See David H. Turner, "Aboriginal Religion as World Religion: An Assessment," *Studies in World Christianity* 2 (1996): 77–96, where he calls this methodology "Nothinging," 79–80, 91; see also "Australian Aboriginal Religion as 'World Religion,'" *Studies in Religion* 20 (1991): 165–80; "The Incarnation of Nambirrirrma," in Swain and Rose, *Aboriginal Australians and Christian Missions,* 470–83. In progressive steps Turner argues that Aboriginal religion belongs to all humanity as much as Hindu or Buddhist religion, and has at least as much capacity for peacemaking. His analysis of the story of Nambirrirrma as a "Christ-event" arising from the land itself, which is "imbued with Eternity" (475), portrays the culture hero as "simultaneously particular and general, self and other, a part and the whole" (477) and sets up a dialectical relationship between the love embodied in Aboriginal social structures and the personalizing of love-relationships in St. John's Gospel which is decidedly different from the one-way model of missionary preaching.

89. Goosen, "Interface," gives some indication of this; see also chapter 6 below. Discussions with Frank Fletcher and Eugene Stockton during a recent visit to Australia have made clear to me the extent to which European theology's cognitive bias has made it virtually incapable of integrating the symbolic (Fletcher, September 13, 2001) and the pre-conceptual images that are much more creative than logical argument because they spring from the archetypes that structure stories and pictures (Stockton, September 15, 2001).

90. *Rainbow Spirit Theology,* 18.

Chapter 2: Initiation Into the Future

1. See Margaret Jolly, "Epilogue: Further Reflections on Violence in Melanesia," in Sinclair Dinnen and Allison Ley, eds., *Reflections on Violence in Melanesia* (Annandale, N.S.W., Australia: Hawkins Press; Canberra: Asia Pacific Press, 2000), 305–24, 307. Most contributors to this volume point out how the reputation of being "violent savages" was foisted upon Melanesians — often in contrast to the fairer-skinned Polynesians and certainly as the antithesis of noble-minded Europeans — by the early missionaries and anthropologists, a reputation which distorts research into violent behavior there to this day.

2. See Günther Renck, *Contextualization of Christianity and Christianization of Language: A Case Study from the Highlands of Papua New Guinea* (Erlangen: Verlag der Ev.-Luth. Mission, 1990), 6: "In the New Guinea area (in the wider sense) well over 1,000 languages, that is roughly one-fifth of the known languages on earth, are spoken by about five million

people, which means that the average number of speakers per language is somewhere between four and five thousand."

3. Garry Trompf, *Payback: The Logic of Retribution in Melanesian Religions* (Cambridge: Cambridge University Press, 1994), 460.

4. See for example Mogola Kamiali, "Missionary Attitudes: A Subjective and Objective Analysis," *Melanesian Journal of Theology* 2 (1986): 145–73. The story of Christian missionary penetration of the Pacific is summarized in Appendix I.

5. Patrick Gesch, "Cargo Cults: The Village-Christian Dialogue," in Wendy Flannery, ed., *Religious Movements in Melanesia Today* vol. 3 (Goroka, Papua New Guinea: Melanesian Institute, 1984), 1–13. It made a considerable difference whether the missionaries concerned were Catholic or Protestant: whereas Catholics seemed to take for granted the effects of sacramental symbolism on Melanesian sensibilities, Protestants tended to work intensively on Bible translation and cultural assimilation, thus helping to prepare the ground for later modernization (Theo Ahrens, personal communication).

6. See Roland M. Berndt and Catherine H. Berndt, *The Speaking Land: Myth and Story in Aboriginal Australia* (Ringwood, Vic., Australia: Penguin Books, 1989); Roland M. Berndt, "A Profile of Good and Bad in Australian Aboriginal Religion," Robert B. Crotty, ed., *The Charles Strong Lectures, 1972–1984* (Leiden: E. J. Brill, 1987), 21–36.

7. See Paul Brennan, *Let Sleeping Snakes Lie: Central Enga Traditional Religious Belief and Ritual* (Adelaide: Australian Association for the Study of Religions, 1977), 17–18; Roderic Lacey, "Heroes, Journeys and Change: Precolonial Religious Life in Papua New Guinea," in Norman C. Habel, ed., *Powers, Plumes and Piglets: Phenomena of Melanesian Religion* (Adelaide: Australian Association for the Study of Religions, 1979), 194–209, 198; Maria Dlugosz, *Mae Enga Myths and Christ's Message: Fullness of Life in Mae Enga Mythology and Christ the Life (Jn 10:10)* (Nettetal: Steyler Verlag, 1998), 32–33.

8. The 230,000 Enga, with their nine mutually intelligible dialects living in ten thousand square kilometers of mountainous country, are by far the largest ethno-linguistic group and thus the great exception in Melanesia, see Dlugosz, *Mae Enga Myths,* 12.

9. In what follows I shall be drawing on J. D. May, *Christus Initiator: Theologie im Pazifik* (Düsseldorf: Patmos, 1990), chaps. 2 and 3.

10. Patrick Gesch, *Initiative and Initiation: A Cargo Cult-Type Movement in the Sepik Against its Background in Traditional Village Religion* (St. Augustin: Anthropos-Institut, 1985), 182, 268 ff.

11. This is the theme of Trompf, *Payback;* see also his essay, "Melanesian Religion in All Its Aspects," *Catalyst* 18 (1988): 155–62, and his contribution to Tony Swain and Garry Trompf, *The Religions of Oceania* (London and New York: Routledge, 1995).

12. Reported by the Bible translator Barry Irwin in Darrell Whiteman, "Melanesian Religions: An Overview," in Ennio Mantovani, ed., *An Introduction to Melanesian Religions: A Handbook for Church Workers* (Goroka, Papua New Guinea: Melanesian Institute, 1984), 87–121, 110–11.

13. See Richard Giddings, "Land Tenure," in Whiteman, ed., *An Introduction to Melanesian Cultures* (Goroka, Papua New Guinea: Melanesian Institute, 1984), 149–72, 151–53.

14. I owe this observation to Theo Ahrens (personal communication).

15. Few have grasped these relationships so profoundly as the missionary anthropologist of New Caledonia, Maurice Leenhardt, *Do Kamo. La personne et le mythe dans le monde mélanésien* (Paris: Gallimard, 1971 [1947]), 54, 61ff. The recent study by Jane Goodale, *To Sing with Pigs Is Human: The Concept of Person in Papua New Guinea* (Seattle: University of Washington Press, 1995), based on fieldwork among the Kaulong of West New Britain in the 1960s and 1970s, is a reminder of how difficult it is to generalize about Melanesia, yet despite some striking differences from ethnology based on the peoples of the New Guinea Highlands it complements Leenhardt's observations of New Caledonia in interesting ways.

16. Leenhardt, *Do Kamo*, 66, 68.

17. See Gernot Fugmann, "Fundamental Issues for a Theology in Melanesia," in Brian Schwarz, ed., *An Introduction to Ministry in Melanesia: A Handbook for Church Workers* (Goroka, Papua New Guinea: Melanesian Institute, 1985), 72–103, 74–78.

18. See Ennio Mantovani, "Traditional Values and Ethics," Darrel Whiteman, ed., *An Introduction to Melanesian Cultures,* 195–212.

19. See Donald E. McGregor, *The Fish and the Cross* (Goroka, Papua New Guinea: Melanesian Institute, 1982).

20. See Ennio Mantovani, "A Fundamental Melanesian Religion," in Theodor Ahrens and James Knight, eds., *Christ in Melanesia* (Goroka, Papua New Guinea: Melanesian Institute, 1977), 154–65; "Celebrations of Cosmic Ritual," idem, ed., *An Introduction to Melanesian Religions,* 147–68; "Mipela Simbu! The Pig Festival and Simbu Identity," Victor C. Hayes, ed., *Identity Issues in World Religions: Selected Proceedings of the Fifteenth Congress of the IAHR* (Adelaide: Australian Association for the Study of Religions, 1986), 104–205; James Knight, "Bona Gene: The Pig-Kill Festival of Numai (Simbu Province) — Tradition and Change," Habel, ed., *Powers, Plumes and Piglets,* 173–93.

21. As my colleague Gernot Fugmann once remarked, for Melanesians there can be no such thing as an "accident."

22. See J. D. May, "The Ethics of Multiculturalism: An Ecumenical Challenge for Australia," *St. Marks's Review* no. 160 (1995): 25–31; "Human Rights as Land Rights in the Pacific," *Pacifica* 6 (1993): 61–80.

23. For this and much of what follows see Garry Trompf, *Melanesian Religion* (Cambridge: Cambridge University Press, 1991), chap. 4.

24. Patrick Gesch, "Magic as a Process of Social Discernment," in Habel, ed., *Powers, Plumes and Piglets,* 137–48.

25. Mary MacDonald, "Magic, Medicine and Sorcery," in Ennio Mantovani, ed., *An Introduction to Melanesian Religions: A Handbook for Church Workers* (Goroka, Papua New Guinea: Melanesian Institute, 1984), 195–211, 196.

26. See Gernot Fugmann, "Magic: A Pastoral Response," in Ennio Mantovani, ed., *An Introduction to Melanesian Religions: A Handbook for Church Workers* (Goroka, Papua New Guinea: Melanesian Institute, 1984), 213–30.

27. MacDonald, "Magic, Medicine and Sorcery," 203–4.

28. See the pioneering study by Bernard Narokobi, *Lo bilong yumi yet: Law and Custom in Melanesia* (Goroka, Papua New Guinea: Melanesian Institute; Suva: University of the South Pacific, 1989).

29. See Gernot Fugmann, "Salvation Expressed in a Melanesian Context," in Ahrens and Knight, eds., *Christ in Melanesia,* 122–33; "Salvation in Melanesian Religions," in

Mantovani, ed., *An Introduction to Melanesian Religions*, 279–96; "Fundamental Issues for a Theology in Melanesia," in Schwarz, ed., *An Introduction to Ministry in Melanesia*, 72–103, 88ff.

30. In addition to the works of Fugmann cited above, see Trompf, *Melanesian Religion*, 68–73.

31. This was first discovered by Theo Ahrens, "Christian Syncretism in the Southern Madang District," *Catalyst* 4 (1974): 3–40, 13ff.; "Kirche, Volkschristentum und Volksreligion in Melanesien," in Theodor Ahrens and Walter Hollenweger, *Volkschristentum und Volksreligion im Pazifik: Wiederentdeckung des Mythos für den christlichen Glauben* (Frankfurt/Main: Verlag Otto Lembeck, 1977), 11–72, 25ff., 51–55.

32. See Fugmann, "Fundamental Issues," 90–96. Melanesians are not alone, of course, in finding it difficult to grasp the idea of a love that transcends retribution.

33. See Hermann Janssen, "Religion und Säkularisierung," in Rolf Italiaander, ed., *Heisses Land Niugini: Beiträge zu den Wandlungen in Papua Neuguinea* (Erlangen: Verlag der Ev.-Luth. Mission, 1974), 183–96; "What to Do? Missionary Attitudes to Cargo Cult Movements," in Theodor Ahrens and Kevin Murphy, eds., *The Church and Adjustment Movements* (Goroka, Papua New Guinea: Melanesian Institute, 1974), 157–75.

34. In his historical and geographical survey of these movements Friedrich Steinbauer, *Melanesische Cargo-Kulte. Neureligiöse Heilsbewegungen in der Südsee* (Munich: Delp, 1971), 199–206, notes the Mansren movement in West Irian from 1857; the Tokeriu movement in Papua around 1893; an early movement in the Sepik region of New Guinea about 1930; pre-Christian cargo expectations inspired by the Russian scientist Mikloucho-Maclay — see Nikolai Mikloucho-Maclay, *The New Guinea Diaries, 1871–1883* (Madang, Papua New Guinea: Kristen Press, 1977) — on the Rai Coast south of Madang from 1871; further movements on the Huon Peninsula and in the Morobe District from 1921, in the Highlands from 1943, and in the Bismarck Archipelago from 1929; in the Solomon Islands around 1913 and again in 1932; in the New Hebrides from 1923 and in New Caledonia since 1878. Altogether he mentions 186 historically documented cult movements. The real number is certainly higher, just as the real origins must be much earlier, but even this overview shows that we are dealing with a remarkable though not unique cultural phenomenon. In his pioneering study V. Lanternari, *The Religions of the Oppressed: A Study of Modern Messianic Cults* (New York: Mentor Books, 1963) places the Melanesian movements in a much wider context — see also Bryan Wilson, *Magic and the Millennium* (London: Heinemann, 1973) — but Trompf, *Melanesian Religion*, 199, warns against his assumption that the cults represent the "return of the dead" at the "New Year festival" — hardly a regular feature of Melanesian life! — to bring about "cosmic renewal," which also influenced Mircea Eliade's study of cargo cults, see 192–201. See the very full comparative study of the cults, with copious examples, in Trompf, *Payback*, Part II.

35. An observation made by Thomas Merton, *Love and Living* (New York: Farrar, Strauss, Giroux, 1979), 83–86, cited by Lamont Lindstrom, *Cargo Cult: Strange Stories of Desire from Melanesia and Beyond* (Honolulu: University of Hawai'i Press, 1993), 196.

36. Trompf, *Melanesian Religion*, 129–30, records an eyewitness account, interpreted by a psychologist as "mass hysteria," which he finds "all too glib."

37. See the critique of "one-track" explanations such as those of Worsley, Walters, Guiart, Wilson and Brunton in Trompf, *Melanesian Religion*, 191.

38. Patrick Gesch, "Cargo Cults: The Village-Christian Dialogue," in Flannery, ed., *Religious Movements in Melanesia*, 1–13.

39. See Ron Crocombe, *The Pacific Way: An Emerging Identity* (Suva, Fiji: Lotu Pasifika, 1976), 108–10.

40. Texts in Theodor Ahrens, *Unterwegs nach der verlorenen Heimat. Studien zur Identitätsproblematik in Melanesien* (Erlangen: Verlag der Ev.-Luth. Mission, 1986), 14–28; John Strelan, "New Challenges: Traditional and New Religious Movements," in Herwig Wagner and Hermann Reiner, eds., *The Lutheran Church in Papua New Guinea: The First Hundred Years, 1886–1986* (Adelaide: Lutheran Publishing House, 1986), 469–95, 471; Ahrens and Hollenweger, *Volkschristentum und Volksreligion im Pazifik*, 75–80; Rufus Pech, *Manub and Kilibob: Melanesian Models for Brotherhood Shaped by Myth, Dream and Drama* (Goroka, Papua New Guinea: Melanesian Institute, 1991), 79–87.

41. Like so many other cult leaders, Yaliwan had worked outside his home province in Lae and Madang and had served with the police; his companion Daniel Hawina also had outside experience in Wewak and Rabaul; see Patrick Gesch, *Initiative and Initiation*, 27ff.

42. Gesch, *Initiative and Initiation*, 128ff., discerns no less than 17 phases through which the movement has evolved. Within the ambit of traditional religion there were a millenarian phase, a cargo cult properly so called, fertility cults and cults of the dead; politically the movement experimented with civil disobedience, nationalism and participation in national and local politics; women's groups and a school were founded; and finally the movement went through an explicitly Christian phase as the New Apolstolic Church. See also Gesch, "Initiation and Cargo Cults: The Peli Case," in Wendy Flannery, ed., *Religious Movements in Melanesia Today*, vol. 1 (Goroka, Papua New Guinea: Melanesian Institute, 1983), 94–103.

43. See Trompf, *Payback*, 389–90. See also J. D. May, "Economics and Culture in the South Pacific," in Lucia A. Reisch, ed., *Ethical-Ecological Investment: Towards Global Sustainable Development* (Frankfurt: IKO-Verlag für Interkulturelle Kommunikation, 2001), 117–22.

44. See Trompf, *Payback*, 391–92, and 406 on the "secularization of reciprocity."

45. See ibid., 411, 416.

46. See ibid., 416. Ahrens goes to far as to say that "the tribal society is recolonizing the modern nation state" (personal communication), because the "gift" system of exchange continues despite the demands of the money economy. The opposition to "globalization," which led to the deaths of student demonstrators at the University of Papua New Guinea in 2001, is in reality a protest against individualization of the economy in a fundamentally group-orientated society.

47. Is not money "the world's most cherished fetish," "the god of this world," the apotheosis and sacrament of power? asks Garry Trompf in his stimulating essay *Religion and Money: Some Aspects* (Adelaide: Australian Association for the Study of Religions, 1980); on Yali, see 7, and for a fuller treatment, see *Payback*, chap. 8.

48. See Pech, *Manub and Kilibob*, 171–75.

49. See Peter Lawrence, *Road Belong Cargo* (Manchester: Manchester University Press, 1964), 116–21; Ahrens, "Christian Syncretism"; John Strelan, *Search for Salvation: Studies in the History and Theology of Cargo Cults* (Adelaide, Australia: Lutheran Publishing House, 1977), 202; idem, "New Challenges," 476–77; Pech, *Manub and Kilibob*, 189–93.

50. See Strelan, "New Challenges," 482; Pech, *Manub and Kilibob*, 205–10.

51. See Brian Schwarz, "Cargo Movements," in Ennio Mantovani, ed., *An Introduction to Melanesian Religions: A Handbook for Church Workers* (Goroka, Papua New Guinea: Melanesian Institute, 1984), 231–53, 238–39.

52. For the text see J. D. May, ed., *Living Theology in Melanesia: A Reader* (Goroka, Papua New Guinea: Melanesian Institute, 1985), 31–43.

53. See Schwarz, "Cargo Movements," 237.

54. Peter Worsley, *The Trumpet Shall Sound* (London: MacGibbon and Kee, 1957); see Schwarz, "Cargo Movements," 237.

55. E.g., Br. Andrew, "A Psychiatrist Looks at Religious Movements," in Wendy Flannery, ed., *Religious Movements in Melanesia Today*, vol. 3 (Goroka, Papua New Guinea: Melanesian Institute, 1983), 80–91, and several contributors to Carl Loeliger and Garry Trompf, eds., *New Religious Movements in Melanesia* (Suva, Fiji: University of the South Pacific; Port Moresby: University of Papua New Guinea, 1985).

56. Schwarz, "Cargo Movements," 243.

57. The first theological interpretations of cargo were attempted by Gottfried Oosterwal, *Modern Messianic Movements as a Theological and Missionary Challenge* (Elkhart, Ind.: Institute of Mennonite Studies, 1973), and John Strelan, *Search for Salvation: Studies in the History and Theology of Cargo Cults* (Adelaide, Australia: Lutheran Publishing House, 1977).

58. Keysser, a significant missionary innovator, was also something of an individualist; on his difficult legacy see Theo Ahrens, "Die Aktualität Christian Keyssers," idem, *Der neue Mensch im kolonialen Zwielicht: Studien zum religiösen Wandel in Ozeanien* (Münster and Hamburg: LIT Verlag, 1993), 29–44.

59. See Strelan, "New Challenges," 473–76.

60. See ibid., 480.

61. The Eemasang movement and the Kukuaik movement on the islands of Karkar and Bagabag to the north of Madang produced hymns in which the first generation of Christians strove to find a relationship to Christ as Melanesians, see Strelan, "New Challenges," 478, and Gernot Fugmann, ed., *The Birth of an Indigenous Church* (Goroka, Papua New Guinea: Melanesian Institute, 1986), 180–238. In the years of intensive cargoist activity, from about 1932 to 1942, the Bel-speaking Christians of Madang composed a large number of beautiful and theologically profound hymns, including some that warned against the seduction of the cults; see the pioneering study by Rufus Pech, "An Early Indigenous Theology — Expressed in Worship," in Ahrens and Knight, eds., *Christ in Melanesia,* 87–121, with original texts and translations, and the selection of revised translations in May, ed., *Living Theology in Melanesia,* 9–16; see also May, *Christus Initiator,* 127–31.

62. Ahrens, *Unterwegs,* 47, 128–34.

63. See Garry Trompf, ed., *Prophets of Melanesia: Six Essays* (Port Moresby: Institute of Papua New Guinea Studies; Suva, Institute of Pacific Studies, 1977).

64. The original documents edited by Fugmann, *The Birth of an Indigenous Church,* 159–76, show this very clearly.

65. See Ahrens, *Unterwegs,* 180–92.

66. Lynn Giddings, "Social Impact Study of the Yonki Hydro Scheme: Youth Rehabilitation Services Report," in Gernot Fugmann, ed., *Ethics and Development in Papua New Guinea* (Goroka, Papua New Guinea: Melanesian Institute, 1986), 149–201, 153.

67. It is for this reason that the Melanesian Institute in Goroka has carried out two major research projects in recent years, one on Marriage and Family Life in Melanesia and a second on Young Melanesians.

68. Leenhardt, *Do Kamo*, 100; the all-pervasiveness of "mythic thought" came home to him when his wife's pupils expressed amazement that Jerusalem was a "real" place: the geography lesson was the occasion of their stepping out of the mythic time in which they instinctively located the Christian story, 277. I remember Melanesian travelers to the Holy Land having just the same shock effect on their compatriots after their return home.

69. Leenhardt, *Do Kamo*, 155. According to Leenhardt, the "I" *(moi)* is not fixed; "l'action et moi, moi faire," 153, and the related morpheme *to* "agit à la manière d'un propulseur qui lance acteur et action dans l'avenir," 154. Goodale, *To Sing with Pigs*, chap. 2, found that among the Kaulong of West New Britain the *enu*, the "soul, self, spirit, or shadow," is used of the *potunus*, the "living whole person" in contrast to the *iwun* or "ghost" of the dead. The self, "which permeates the entire skin, flesh, bone, and blood of the body, is the part of one's being that experiences knowledge and in which knowledge is internalized." The expansion of the self through knowledge is reflected in the healthy state of the body, but the *enu* can become detached from the living person, who must not be awakened abruptly lest the shock of being bereft of self prove too great, 37–41.

70. Leenhardt, *Do Kamo*, 212, discovered that the root, *va*, of the Kanak for "word" derives from Indonesia. "Ainsi ces deux temps que nous séparons, acte et parole, se confondent en un seul dans la pensée canaque. Ils constituent ensemble la parole. Et l'élément essentiel est l'acte. La formulation n'est qu'un élément contingent," 216; "la parole est pensée, discours, action," 220. "Discours et objets ne sont pas pour eux formules et signes, voire langage, mais tradition, c'est-à-dire manière de traduction de la parole en sa pérennité, manifestation de l'être en sa continuité," 246. The singing contests documented by Goodale, *To Sing with Pigs*, would seem to perform a similar function.

71. See Leenhardt, *Do Kamo*, 248–49. "Ainsi la personne mélanésienne ne procède pas seulement de l'affectif individuel, ou de la société, ou de la pensée, mythique ou non, mais elle se manifeste au travers d'eux tous, elle a besoin d'eux tous pour être porté; elle est participative . . . le 'lui,'" 261.

72. See Leenhardt, *Do Kamo*, 280ff., 294–95, 300. For him history, whether for Europeans or for Melanesians, is "intégration de la personne dans le monde," 288; consequently "Il n'apparaît pas de différence intrinsèque entre le mythe de l'homme moderne et ceux du primitif mélanésien," 290.

73. This term, introduced by John V. Taylor, *The Primal Vision: Christian Presence Amid African Religion* (London: SCM, 1965) and advocated by the Scottish missiologist Andrew Walls, has been criticized for being theologically "loaded," see James L. Cox, "The Classification 'Primal Religions' as a Non-Empirical Christian Theological Construct," *Studies in World Christianity* 2 (1996): 55–76, but it is certainly an improvement on "primitive" and it can be taken to refer to what is both universal and fundamental in religious practices wherever they exist, see Taylor, 18.

74. See Ennio Mantovani, "What Is Religion?," idem, ed., *An Introduction to Melanesian Religion*, 23–47; "Is There a Biocosmic Religion? A Reply to Dr. Garland," *Catalyst* 16 (1986): 352–66. What constitutes "Life," of course, varies from culture to culture, and the

interpretation proposed here for the Melanesian concept is an attempt to mediate between this and literal and symbolic Western understandings.

75. The term "metacosmic" is used to good effect by Aloysius Pieris, "Towards an Asian Theology of Liberation: Some Religio-Cultural Guidelines," Virginia Fabella, ed., *Asia's Struggle for Full Humanity: Towards a Relevant Theology* (Maryknoll, N.Y.: Orbis, 1980), 75–95; I thereupon made it the basis of chap. 7 of *Christus Initiator.*

76. Lest there be any misunderstanding, Mantovani quotes a recent anthropological description of a highlands culture by Anna Meigs:

> It is a religion of physiological fitness and survival. Religious goals of heightened vitality and sexual potency are achieved without recourse to sacrifice, obeisance, mediation, worship, prayer. Spirits, deities and the supernatural in general play no role.... Physical life itself, uncontrollable and frightening, is the central mystery of the religious thought of Hua males.

Mantovani, "Is There a Biocosmic Religion?," 360–61.

77. See Dlugosz, *Mae Enga Myths,* 124–25.

78. See Ennio Mantovani and Mary MacDonald, *Christ the Life of Papua New Guinea* (Goroka, Papua New Guinea: Melanesian Institute, 1983); Ennio Mantovani, *Divine Revelation and the Religions of PNG: A Missiological Manual* (Goroka, Papua New Guinea: Melanesian Institute, 2000), chap. 9; and see below.

79. The paradox of the cross, the belief that the suffering of Christ is not capitulation to the forces of evil but the victory of gratuitous love, is in the end no easier for Melanesians to accept than for anyone else. Nevertheless the wood carvings and hymns of the early Catholic and Lutheran Christians show a profound grasp of this belief, and in the Huon Peninsula of New Guinea the new order of inter-tribal peace brought about by accepting it came to be known as the *miti.* We must not forget, however, that the relationships which led to violence against missionaries, whether European or indigenous, were often quite complex and by no means one-sided, see Christine Weir, "'The Gospel Came ... Fighting Is Ceasing among Us': Methodist Representations of Violence in Fiji and New Britain, 1830–1930," in Dinnen and Ley, *Reflections on Violence in Melanesia,* 35–52.

80. See my account of the debate between Ennio Mantovani and Christopher Garland in J. D. May, "The Trinity in Melanesia: Understanding the Christian God in a Pacific Culture," in James M. Byrne, ed., *The Christian Understanding of God Today* (Dublin: Columba Press, 1993), 154–65. Garland, "Is Traditional Religion in Papua New Guinea Theistic?," *Catalyst* 16 (1986): 127–45, contests Mantovani's view that Melanesian religion is non-theistic and makes an ingenious proposal of his own:

> In the first place it is possible to describe communal relationships in traditional religion according to a three-fold pattern which can be used as a symbol of the Holy Trinity. The "memory," primordial being which is the symbol of the Father, consists of the wisdom of the ancestors, to whom offerings and prayers are made in order to bring them into relationship. The "understanding," expressive being which is the symbol of the Son, is the means of salvation, the plentiful supply of food produced by an effective relationship with the ancestors. The "will," unitive being which is the symbol of the Holy Spirit is the dynamic energy, the "mana" which flows through the relationship, making it effective. (135–36)

Mantovani roundly rejects this, asserting that Melanesian religion cannot be critiqued using the "grammar" of Christian dogmatics and that Melanesians already possessed, in their own religious "language," the essentials of creation, sacrifice and redemption made explicit in Christian preaching, "Is There a Biocosmic Religion?," 353.

81. Conceding that Mantovani does not use the *word* "sacrifice," Ahrens insists that Mantovani's construal of the *dema* ritual as a "memorial" making present the source of life amounts to the same thing, which would imply that violent death is somehow transcendentally necessary in order to perpetuate "Life," see Theodor Ahrens, "On Grace and Reciprocity: A Fresh Approach to Contextualization with Reference to Christianity in Melanesia," *International Review of Mission* 89 (2000): 515–28; Mantovani's reply, *IRM* 90 (2001): 462–64, in which he vigorously objects to this interpretation of his work; and Ahrens's rejoinder, ibid. 464–66.

82. Garry Trompf makes the fascinating observation that it was Nietzsche who first made "a brilliant if poetic and highly speculative attempt to link revenge, the language of barter, and the dawn of religious notions," according to which " 'revenge was sanctified under the name of justice' " and "warlike 'instincts were devalued and suspended' by the peace of more developed social organization," which "opens up the fascinating question as to whether religion was born in the womb of violence rather than in the hushed, eerie encounter with the numinous," *Payback,* 16.

83. See Ahrens, "Grace and Reciprocity," 518–20, discussing Mantovani's influence on Dlugosz, *Mae Enga Myths* in connection with the theories of Girard. The point is controversial, not to say provocative; see the extended and energetic discussion in Robert G. Hamerton-Kelly, ed., *Violent Origins: Walter Burkert, René Girard, and Jonathan Z. Smith on Ritual Killing and Cultural Formation* (Stanford, Calif.: Stanford University Press, 1987), in which Adolf Jensen's account of sacrifice as a retrospective rationalization of ritual killing plays an important part, especially for Smith, who quite plausibly claims that the ritual killing of animals only occurs among pastoralists and has nothing to do with either hunting (Burkert) or a "primordial sacrifice" (Girard).

84. See David Lochhead, "Monotheistic Violence," *Buddhist-Christian Studies* 21 (2001): 3–12, referring to episodes such as those portrayed in Num 25:1–5, 11–13 and making the point that this still a *heno*theistic text, 4–5.

85. See Lochhead's discussion of the theories of René Girard, in ibid., 8–9.

86. Ahrens, "Grace and Reciprocity," 524–25.

87. Theodor Ahrens, "Studying Religion in Melanesia: Some Questions for Discussion" (unpubl. ms.), 21.

88. See J. D. May, *Christian Fundamentalism and Melanesian Identity* (Goroka, Papua New Guinea: Melanesian Institute Occasional Paper No. 3, 1986); Manfred Ernst, *Winds of Change: Rapidly Growing Religious Groups in the Pacific Islands* (Suva, Fiji: Pacific Conference of Churches, 1994); and the discussion in *The Pacific Journal of Theology* 12 (1994).

Part II: Buddhism's Asian Journey

1. Conscription was introduced by the Liberal-Country Party coalition government led by R. G. Menzies on 10 November 1964. His successor, Harold Holt, continued the policy under the demeaning slogan "All the way with LBJ!," as if Australians did not even

need to think about the rights and wrongs of the prosecution of the war by Presidents Johnson and Nixon. See Val Noone, *Disturbing the War: Melbourne Catholics and Vietnam* (Richmond, Vic., Australia: Spectrum Publications, 1993) 83, 100–104. Noone is able to draw intriguing parallels between incipient Catholic opposition to the Vietnam war and half-forgotten memories of Irish resistance to British colonialism.

2. See ibid., 144–47.

3. Santamaria thought in terms of an Asia-Pacific region in which communist China had taken the place of imperialist Japan and where Australia and New Zealand had the mission of being the Christian presence in a new community of peoples, see B. A. Santamaria, *The Price of Freedom* (Melbourne: Campion Press, 1964).

4. The Catholic right in Australia, oblivious of the voices of Vietnamese Catholic dissidents, was uncompromising in its rejection of Buddhist "neutralism," see Noone, *Disturbing the War,* 123–24, 274–75. The self-immolations have been studied in depth by Sallie B. King, "They Who Burned Themselves for Peace: Quaker and Buddhist Self-Immolators during the Vietnam War," *Buddhist-Christian Studies* 20 (2000): 127–50.

5. See the account by Neil Sheehan, *A Bright Shining Lie: John Paul Vann and America in Vietnam* (London: Pan Books, 1990), 144–68.

6. See the contemporary attempt to explain all this to an uncomprehending West by Thich Nhat Hanh, *Vietnam: The Lotus in the Sea of Fire* (London: SCM, 1967), chap. 2 — a book I would dearly like to have read at the time, though I probably would not have understood most of it. See also the first-hand observations and reflections of John Pilger, *Heroes* (London: Pan Books, 1987), chaps. 15, 16.

7. Thich Nhat Hanh, *Love in Action: Writings on Nonviolent Social Change* (Berkeley, Calif.: Parallax Press, 1993), 83, 150, the latter in the context of a parable inspired by his former student Mai about a bird in search of time, who says: "Time, if I could find you, certainly I could find myself," because it has been told by a monk: "Time is stilled in Eternity. There Love and Beloved are One. Each blade of grass, each piece of earth, each leaf, is one with that love." Does it matter whether those lines were written by a Buddhist or a Christian?

8. Ibid., 99.

9. Ibid., 101–6; see pp. 83ff.

10. Ibid., 125: "When we are wholly ourselves, we can see how one person by living fully demonstrates to all of us that life is possible, that a future is possible"; see also pp. 132ff.

11. Ibid., 139–40.

Chapter 3: The Buddha in Sacred Space

1. See Dogen, *Shobo-Genzo,* 3; *Gakudo Yojin-shu* ("Points to Watch in Buddhist Training"), 7: "The situation in remote countries like this one [Japan] is truly regrettable . . . China, however, has already taken refuge in the True Law of the Buddha," Yuho Yokoi and Daizen Victoria, *Zen Master Dogen: An Introduction with Selected Writings* (New York and Tokyo: Weatherhill, 1976), 105, 55.

2. *Shobo-Genzo,* 10; Yoko and Victoria, *Zen Master dogen,* 159, 161, 164.

3. See Ninian Smart, *Buddhism and Christianity: Rivals and Allies* (London: Macmillan, 1993), 35.

4. See Kenneth Ch'en, *Buddhism in China: A Historical Survey* (Princeton, N.J.: Princeton University Press, 1964), 476–78, 477.

5. This centuries-long process needs to be understood, not only because of its intrinsic interest in the light of contemporary attempts to "indigenize" and "contextualize" Christianity, but because we need to know what happened to Buddhism in China if we are to appreciate the problems inherited by the Japanese. This long and complicated history would interrupt the argument if recounted here, so I have summarized it in Appendix II.

6. As in the case of Korea, Buddhism must have been known in Japan by contact with immigrants and travelers long before official records took note of it, see Allan Grapard, *The Protocol of the Gods: A Study of the Kasuga Shrine in Japanese History* (Berkeley: University of California Press, 1992), 20–21.

7. Francis H. Cook, "Introduction of Buddhism to Japan and Its Development during the Nara Period," in Charles S. Prebish, ed., *Buddhism: A Modern Perspective* (University Park: Pennsylvania State University Press, 1975), 218–22; on Korea, see Lewis R. Lancaster, 212–14, and in more detail Robert Evans Buswell Jr., "Buddhism in Korea," Joseph M. Kitagawa and Mark D. Cummings, eds., *Buddhism in Asian History: Religion, History and Culture Readings from the Encyclopedia of Religion* (New York: Macmillan, 1989), 151–58.

8. See Araki Michio, "The Schools of Japanese Buddhism," Kitagawa and Cummings, *Buddhism and Asian History,* 267–75, 267–68, and W. G. Beasley, *The Japanese Experience: A Short History of Japan* (London: Weidenfeld & Nicholson, 1999), 24, 42–48.

9. Shotoku was himself a devout Buddhist with a reputation for learning, which formed the basis of his alliance with the Soga clan; see Beasley, *Japanese Experience,* 20–30 on the adoption of "Chinese-style government."

10. See S. N. Eisenstadt, *Japanese Civilization: A Comparative View* (Chicago: University of Chicago Press, 1996), esp. chap. 10, "Some Aspects of the Transformation of Confucianism and Buddhism in Japan."

11. Tamaru Noriyoshi, "Buddhism in Japan," in Kitagawa and Cummings, *Buddhism and Asian History,* 159–73, 162, and for a more detailed account, Beasley, *Japanese Experience,* chaps. 5 and 7.

12. Koyu Sonoda, "Saicho," in Yusen Kashiwahara and Koyu Sonoda, eds., *Shapers of Japanese Buddhism* (Tokyo: Kosei Publishing, 1994), 26–38, 30.

13. Sonoda, "Saicho," 36; on Saicho's conflict with the authorities on Mt. Hiei, who in concert with the ruling Fujiwara wished to keep the shrine-temples under their control for the protection of the state, see Grapard, *Protocol of the Gods,* 69–70.

14. Koyu Sonoda, "Kukai," in Kashiwahara and Sonoda, *Shapers,* 39–51, 51. Discreetly located just behind the main temple complex on Mt. Koya is a Shinto shrine dedicated to Koya as the original *kami* of the mountain, now given honorary status, as it were, as a *bodhisattva.* Erik Zürcher, *The Buddhist Conquest of China: The Spread and Adaptation of Buddhism in Early Medieval China* (Leiden: E. J. Brill, 1959), 207, notes "that the strong association between Buddhist monasteries and mountains — especially 'sacred' mountains — is a typically Chinese phenomenon" with a Taoist background, but it obviously appealed to the Japanese Buddhists as well.

15. Francis H. Cook, "Heian, Kamakura, and Tokugawa Periods in Japan," in Prebish, *Buddhism,* 223–28, 224.

16. See Yuishin Ito, "Kuya," in Kashiwahara and Sonoda, *Shapers*, 52–62, and the summary in Cook, 224.

17. Neil McMullin, "The *Lotus Sutra* and Politics in the Mid-Heian Period," in George J. Tanabe Jr. and Willa Jane Tanabe, eds., *The Lotus Sutra in Japanese Culture* (Honolulu: University of Hawai'i Press, 1989), 119–41, 119, 136–37.

18. Shan-tao, *Commentary on the Meditation Sutra*, cited in Yuishin Ito, "Honen," in Kashiwahara and Sonoda, *Shapers*, 63–75, 66.

19. Takehiko Furuta, "Shinran," in Kashiwahara and Sonoda, *Shapers*, 87–96, 93–94. The reader should be aware that these are hagiographic accounts of the great religious founders and that Japanese historical scholarship is beginning to question them. Galen Amstutz, *Interpreting Amida: History and Orientalism in the Study of Pure Land Buddhism* (Albany: State University of New York Press, 1997), examines at length the reasons for the neglect of Pure Land as a powerful current in medieval and contemporary Japanese Buddhism. Jacqueline I. Stone, *Original Enlightenment and the Transformation of Medieval Japanese Buddhism* (Honolulu: University of Hawai'i Press, 1999), reassesses the impact of Tendai thought in medieval Japan and questions the assumed discontinuity between the merely theoretical "old Buddhism" of Mt. Hiei and the more practical "new Buddhism" of Kamakura (58–59, 71–72 and the whole of chap. 2)

20. Cited by Manabu Fuji, "Nichiren," in Kashiwahara and Sonoda, *Shapers*, 123–34, 127.

21. Fuji, ibid., 130.

22. *Letter to Nichinyo Gozen*, Fuji, ibid., 133.

23. *Gokoku Shobo-gi*, see Yokoi and Victoria, *Zen Master Dogen*, 37.

24. See Aishin Imaeda, "Dogen," in Kashiwahara and Sonoda, *Shapers*, 97–122, 119, 121.

25. Yokoi and Victoria, *Zen Master Dogen*, 40.

26. Masao Abe, Art. "Dogen," in Eliade, ed., *Encyclopedia of Religion*, vol. 4 (New York: Macmillan, 1987), 388–89, 389; but see the more critical contextualization of Dogen's thought by Stone, *Original Enlightenment*, 72–77, 88–90.

27. Indeed, Yokoi and Victoria summarize Dogen's thought as a set of radical identities: Self=others, Practice=enlightenment; Precepts=Zen; Life=death; *Koan*=enlightenment; Time=being; Being=nonbeing; Zen Buddhism=the state; Men=women; Monks=lay people; *Sutras*=Zen, *Zen Master Dogen*, 39–41.

28. See Hakamaya Noriaki, "Scholarship as Criticism," in Jamie Hubbard and Paul L. Swanson, eds., *Pruning the Bodhi Tree: The Storm over Critical Buddhism* (Honolulu: University of Hawai'i Press, 1997), 113–44, 122, and Matsumoto Shiro, who in "The Meaning of 'Zen'" (242–50) claims that, whereas *dhyana* was a pre-Buddhist practice, the Buddha's radical innovation was the realization of *pratityasamutpada*; Zen is non-Buddhist, and "any 'Zen thought' that teaches the 'cessation of thinking'... is anti-Buddhist" (250). Stone, *Original Enlightenment*, places what the Critical Buddhists call the "substantialist heresy" interpretation of *hongaku* or "original enlightenment" thought in the "radical break" tradition, 66–85, alongside other interpretations which see medieval Tendai as the "matrix" of later developments or assert their "dialectical emergence" from Tendai.

29. See the long and technical article by Steven Heine, "Critical Buddhism and Dogen's *Shobogenzo*: The Debate over the 75-Fascicle and 12-Fascicle Texts," in Hubbard and

Swanson, *Pruning*, 251–85. The debate turns on whether or not Dogen had a radical change of mind after leaving Kamakura in 1248 which led to his rewriting the *Shobogenzo* in such a way as to eliminate all traces of "universal enlightenment" (*hongaku*) and reinstate karmic causality.

30. See Paul Groner, "The *Lotus Sutra* and Saicho's Interpretation of the Realization of Buddhahood with This Very Body," in Tanabe and Tanabe, *Lotus Sutra in Japanese Culture*, 53–74, 55, 61–62.

31. Kuroda Toshio, "Historical Consciousness and *Hon-jaku* Philosophy in the Medieval Period on Mount Hiei," in Tanabe and Tanabe, *Lotus Sutra in Japanese Culture*, 143–58, 143–44. Associated with this was the "tree theory" according to which Shinto was the root, Confucianism the branches and leaves, and Buddhism the fruits and flowers, 145.

32. Kuroda, "Historical Consciousness," 147, 150. This amounted to the assimilation of Kukai's Shingon esotericism by Tendai orthodoxy, 146. Kuroda, 154, identifies two distinct but interwoven trends in these texts:

> ... many texts belonging to the first trend deal with matters related to the "essence" (*honji*, i.e., Buddhism,) while those representing the second trend relate matters pertaining to the "hypostasis" (*suijaku*, i.e., Shinto).... Generally speaking, the first trend indicates a logic that develops spatially, symbolically, and as a mandala. It is doctrinal, mystical, and secretive while tending to indicate the "essence." The second trend evokes a logic that develops temporally, is descriptive, and partakes of the *engi* [interdependent origination] while tending to indicate the "hypostasis."

33. Allan G. Grapard, "The Textualized Mountain — Enmountained Text: The *Lotus Sutra* in Kunisaki," in Tanabe and Tanabe, *Lotus Sutra in Japanese Culture*, 159–89, 161, 164.

34. Ibid., 165.

35. Ibid., 172.

36. See Grapard, ibid., 180–86, see 187:

> Bearing such images and similitudes in mind, the Kunisaki ascetics would identify the space of their experience with a transcendental space. This being achieved, they engaged in the practices of penance to ensure that their ordinary experience would be engulfed in the remission of sins and thereby in the realm of undifferentiated suchness. This was what we would call the "religious" dimension of their experience. However, that experience was also closely related to the political dimensions of the formation of the state and of the national territory, which was regarded as being under the control of ruling agents who were seen as the native manifestations on earth (*suijaku*) of Buddhist figures (*honji*). In this sense, then, the ascetics' experience was neither purely religious nor purely political: it was what might be called "poligious."

37. This approach, starting with "actions" rather than "texts," is exemplified dramatically in Allan Grapard's study *The Protocol of the Gods*; see his Introduction on the "combinative" genius of Japanese religiosity. It is worth noting that the Chinese term *Shin-to* only came into use as a designation of the indigenous *kami no michi* ("way of the

kami") to demarcate it from the newly introduced *Butsu-do* ("way of the Buddha"), and that it was the social engineers of the Meiji Restoration who made it into a state religion.

38. See Brian (Daizen) A. Victoria, *Zen At War* (New York and Tokyo: Weatherhill, 1997), 5–10, where the points briefly summarized here and hereunder are extensively documented. The hostility to Buddhism in the reactionary Shintoist and imperialist circles of the time is powerfully evoked in Yukio Mishima's 1969 novel *Runaway Horses.* Gapard, *Protocol of the Gods,* reminds us that *Shinto* itself was a medieval Sinicization of the ancient "Way of the gods" (*Kami no Michi*) and had close affinities to Taoism, 12.

39. See Victoria, *Zen At War,* 14, 29.

40. Suzuki's position is documented at length in ibid., chap. 2 and *passim;* see 30–36.

41. See ibid., 104–10, once again citing Suzuki.

42. See ibid., 152–57, 162.

43. Only recently, thanks to correspondence with Professor Makoto Ozaki, have I realized the significance of Tanabe as a rigorous philosopher of Japan's religious experience, see Makoto Ozaki, *Introduction to the Philosophy of Tanabe According to the English Translation of the Seventh Chapter of* The Demonstratio of Christianity (Amsterdam: Editions Rodopi; Grand Rapids: Eerdmans, 1990); idem, *Individuum, Society, Humankind: The Triadic Logic of Species according to Tanabe Hajime* (Leiden: Brill, 2001); Taitetsu Unno and James W. Heisig, eds., *The Religious Philosophy of Tanabe Hajime: The Metanoetic Imperative* (Berkeley, Calif.: Asian Humanities Press, 1990). It seems, however, that Tanabe's personal crisis sprang from his perception of the failure of philosophy itself rather than his own moral failure; see the study by Johannes Laube, "Zur religionsphilosophischen Bedeutung der 'Metanoetik' des japanischen Philosophen Hajime Tanabe," *Zeitschrift für Missionswissenschaft und Religionswissenschaft* 65 (1981): 121–38, who insists: "Die Reue, die Tanabe meint, ist die Reue der Philosophie selbst, genauer: die Reue der autonomen philosophischen Vernunft, die Reue der theoretischen und praktischen Vernunft im Sinne Kants ... dass die persönlichen Erlebnisse Tanabes während der Kriegsjahre nicht der eigentliche Anlass der Reue sein können, die Tanabe meint ... Den eigentlichen Anlass bilden die kantischen Antinomien," 124.

44. See John W. Dower, *Embracing Defeat: Japan in the Wake of World War II* (New York: Norton, 1999), 496–504, on the attempts of Tanabe and others to use Buddhism in order to find "meaning" in Japan's tragedy, not unlike their European counterparts confronting Christianity with the Holocaust. Himi Kiyoshi, "Tanabe's Theory of the State," Unno and Heisig, *The Religious Philosophy of Tanabe Hajime,* 303–39, sheds valuable light on the social and political aspects of Tanabe's thinking.

45. See Yusa Michiko, "Nishida and Totalitarianism: A Philosopher's Resistance," in James W. Heisig and John C. Maraldo, eds., *Rude Awakenings: Zen, the Kyoto School, and the Question of Nationalism* (Honolulu: University of Hawai'i Press, 1994), 107–31, 118–19.

46. See the detailed assessments by Minamoto Ryoen, "The Symposium on 'Overcoming Modernity,'" in Heisig and Maraldo, *Rude Awakenings,* 197–229, and Horio Tsutomu, "The *Chuokoron* Discussions, Their Background and Meaning," ibid., 289–315.

47. See Hirata Seiko, "Zen Buddhist Attitudes to War," in Heisig and Maraldo, *Rude Awakenings,* 3–15, 5–8.

48. See Christopher Ives, "Ethical Pitfalls in Imperial Zen and Nishida Philosophy: Ichikawa Hakugen's Critique," in Heisig and Maraldo, *Rude Awakenings,* 16–39; Robert H. Scharf, "Whose Zen? Zen Nationalism Revisited," ibid., 40–57.

49. Cited in Kirita Kirohide, "D. T. Suzuki on Society and the State," in Heisig and Maraldo, *Rude Awakenings*, 52–74, 65.

50. See Andrew Feeberg, "The Problem of Modernity in the Philosophy of Nishida," in Heisig and Maraldo, *Rude Awakenings*, 151–73, 154, 156, 161.

51. Miwa Kimitada, referring to the state's attempt to "co-opt ethnic nationalism," cited by Keven M. Doak, "Nationalism as Dialectics: Ethnicity, Moralism and the State in Early Twentieth-Century Japan," in Heisig and Maraldo, *Rude Awakenings*, 174–96, 188–89.

52. Jan van Bragt, "Kyoto Philosophy — Intrinsically Nationalistic?," in Heisig and Maraldo, *Rude Awakenings*, 233–54, 246.

53. Ibid., 254.

54. See Victoria, *Zen At War*, 174–77.

55. See Paul L. Swanson, "Why They Say Zen Is Not Buddhism: Recent Japanese Critiques of Buddha-Nature," in Hubbard and Swanson, *Pruning*, 3–29, 5–6. Making the same point, Dan Lusthaus, "Critical Buddhism and Returning to the Sources," in Hubbard and Swanson, *Pruning*, 30–55, identifies the rejection by the Chinese of Hsüan-tsang's presentation of Indian ideas in the seventh century as a "pivotal" moment in Chinese Buddhist history, 35–36, for from that time on the Chinese insisted on retaining a metaphysical substrate akin to the *tao*, making even Nagarjuna into a *dhatu-vada* thinker.

56. See Hakamaya Noriaki, "Critical Philosophy versus Topical Philosophy," in Hubbard and Swanson, *Pruning*, 56–80, and the following essay by Jamie Hubbard, "Topophobia," 81–112, where the critical point I would wish to make is suggested: the whole position assumes a normative "true Buddhism" available to Critical Buddhists but denied their Buddhist opponents; this needs much further scrutiny.

57. Stone, *Original Enlightenment*, 81. She goes on: "*Hongaku* thought also undermines normative Buddhist teachings of impermanence by asserting that 'birth' and 'death' are functions of inherent principle."

58. Ibid., 81. Referring to Hakamaya's call for "critical use of intellect and language," she adds: "Moreover, without language, we would not only be unable to recall and reflect critically upon the past but would lose all sense of time itself, becoming locked in a timeless, eternal present — a loss of the very faculty that distinguishes us as humans." Such a position is significant in the context of interaction with "primal" traditions.

59. The point is made by Peter N. Gregory, "Is Critical Buddhism Really Critical?," in Hubbard and Swanson, *Pruning*, 286–97, 292, who asks by what right only Chih-i and Dogen are exempted from the general verdict of "naturalizing" and "essentializing" Buddhism.

60. See the measured and fair-minded assessment of the influence of the *Lotus Sutra's* teaching of harmony as interpreted by Nichiren on the wartime attitudes of Nikkyo Niwano, the founder of *Rissho-kosei-kai*, by Michio Shinozaki, "Peace and Nonviolence from a Mahayana Buddhist Perspective: Nikkyo Niwano's Thought," *Buddhist-Christian Studies* 21 (2001): 13–30, 20, 25. Niwano could not yet see "any critical principle for how Buddhist teachings can be used to protest an ideology that is derived from such collective egoism," 20.

61. Ibid., 24, 27.

62. This thesis is developed extensively by Eisenstadt, *Japanese Civilization*, see 212–14, 235, 306, 318, 320, 386–87; see also the extensive review by David Loy, "On Eisenstadt's

Japanese Civilization," *Cultural Dynamics* 10, no. 1 (1998): 84–90, in which he speaks of "a sophisticated textual tradition denying in principle its own logocentric focus: refuting the premises of Axial ideologies while constructed in terms derived from those ideologies, a self-conscious (and to that extent Axial) ideological effort to *de-Axialize* discourse," 89.

63. See Eisenstadt, *Japanese Civilization,* 243, quoting Thomas P. Kasulis.

64. See Eisenstadt, *Japanese Civilization,* 95.

65. The different responses of Buddhism and Christianity to this tension are masterfully exposed in Shusaku Endo's novel *Silence* (London: Peter Owen, 1969); see the illuminating introduction by William Johnston.

66. Eisenstadt, *Japanese Civilization,* 190, see 187–90.

67. Loy, "On Eisenstadt's *Japanese Civilization,*" 89.

68. See Eisenstadt, *Japanese Civilization,* 195. Though real power under the Tokugawa *bakufu* was in the hands of Shoguns, its legitimacy remained imperial, not Confucian, see 202.

69. These are treated in some detail by Werner Kohler, *Die Lotus-Lehre und die modernen Religionen in Japan* (Zürich: Atlantis-Verlag, 1962), chap. 6. See also Helen Hardacre, "The New Religions, Family, and Society in Japan," in Martin E. Marty and R. Scott Appleby, eds., *Fundamentalisms and Society: Reclaiming the Sciences, the Family, and Education* (Chicago: University of Chicago Press, 1993), 294–310, who stresses the patriarchalism of most of these groups, even those founded by women; and Winston Davis, "Fundamentalism in Japan: Religious and Political," in Martin E. Marty and R. Scott Appleby, eds., *Fundamentalisms Observed* (Chicago: University of Chicago Press, 1991), 782–813.

70. He was also extremely well informed about the Confucian, Taoist, Brahmin, Hinayana and inferior Mahayana teachings he was combating, see his *Kaimoku Sho* ("Opening of the Eyes") in Philip B. Yampolsky, ed., *Selected Writings of Nichiren* (New York: Columbia University Press, 1990), 50–147.

71. See Kohler, *Lotus-Lehre,* chap. 5.

72. See ibid., 193, citing Nichiren's use of the *Nirvana Sutra* to justify the bearing of weapons against the "false monks" who have brought Buddhism into discredit. The real source of this degree of intolerance, however, is the *Nichiren-Shoshu* stemming from the dissident monk Nikko, see 228–34. On the whole contentious issue see Murata Kiyoaki, *Japan's New Buddhism: An Objective Account of Soka Gakkai* (New York and Tokyo: Weatherhill, 1969); on *Soka-gakkai's* relationship to the political party *Komeito,* see Manfred Pohl, "Die politischen Parteien," in Hans Jürgen Mayer and Manfred Pohl, eds., *Länderbericht Japan* (Darmstadt: Wissenschaftliche Buchgesellschaft, 1995), 80–102, 91–95.

73. On this see Kohler, *Lotus-Lehre,* chap. 7.

74. See Jonathan Watts, "Is the Crisis Just Economic?," *Seeds of Peace* 15, no. 1 (1999): 22–24. The previous and the following paragraphs are adapted from a paper entitled "The *Lotus Sutra* as Sacred Space: The Social Functions of a Religious Text," read at the annual *Lotus Sutra* conference sponsored by *Rissho-kosei-kai* at Mt. Bandai in July 1999. I benefited greatly from this invitation, kindly extended by Dr. Gene Reeves, and from the criticism that the secular/sacred dichotomy around which my paper was constructed does not really apply to Japanese society.

75. Dower, *Embracing Defeat*, chap. 17, offers valuable insights into the "reverse course" by which the American occupation authorities (Supreme Command for the Allied Powers) curtailed democracy, targeted the Left, rehabilitated war criminals and favored both heavy industry and remilitarization as soon as the Cold War broke out. The American-Japanese (Dower says "SCAPanese") hybrid that resulted had at least as much as "cultural peculiarities" or "Asian values" to do with the fateful symbiosis of big business and big government that was eventually to cripple the Japanese economic giant.

76. These questions are an attempt to summarize the main lines of Gavan McCormack's analysis of Japan's economic and political weaknesses in his critical study *The Emptiness of Japanese Affluence* (St. Leonards, N.S.W., Australia: Allen & Unwin, 1996). The even more detailed, but also more restrained analyses in Mayer and Pohl, *Japan,* though aware of problems, are considerably more upbeat.

77. See McCormack, *Emptiness,* 66–67. "At this level, the problem of whether Japan has found an answer to the question of the meaning of life looks problematic," *Emptiness,* 141. Whereas Niwa Fumio in *The Buddha Tree* (1956) can portray small-town life deeply imbued with traditional piety and Buddhist devotionalism through the Shin priest Soshu, morally tortured by his secret liason with his mother in law in the precincts of an hereditary temple, Oe Kenzaburo's *The Silent Cry* (1967) probes with searing immediacy the distress of "modern" young people bereft of any discernible value orientation as they seek continuity with the past by vainly trying to reenact a rebellion that took place in their remote home village in 1860, while his protagonist Mitsu looks on appalled but without the resources to resist. These novels can also be read as parables of Japan's uncertainty as both its religious heritage and its newly imported secularity prove inadequate to resolve the contradictions of modernity.

78. McCormack, *Emptiness,* 290. The erosion of traditional agriculture by the adoption of American and Australian agribusiness methods only reinforces this, 141, a trend that is hardly compensated for by funding environmental protection in Southeast Asia, see Wolfram Wallraf, "Japan und Südostasien," in Mayer and Pohl, *Japan,* 370–83, 379. See also Helmut Weidner, "Entwicklungslinien und Merkmale der Umweltpolitik," 125–33, noting the environmental cost to neighboring Pacific countries, 132.

79. McCormack, *Emptiness,* 199.

80. Ibid., 226; on Japanese Buddhism's failure to transform the feudal system — even in the form of peasant rebellions (*ikki*), the "millenarizing" of the future Buddha Maitreya, and the Kamakura "Reformation" — and create a new political space from which social criticism could have emerged, see Eisenstadt, *Japanese Civilization,* 230–49.

81. McCormack, *Emptiness,* 232–36. The role of Emperor Hirohito, once supposed to be that of a helpless puppet of the military, is now being reassessed. According to Herbert P. Bix, *Hirohito and the Making of Modern Japan* (San Francisco: HarperCollins, 2000), this myth was manufactured in order to rehabilitate Hirohito sufficiently to preserve stability in post-war Japan. In reality, he bore direct responsibility for the fateful decisions that led to and helped prolong the war. See the review by Gar Alperovitz, *Guardian Weekly,* 14–20 September 2000, 37. Dower, *Embracing Defeat,* chaps. 9–11, unravels the diplomatic maneuvers that were necessary in order to remove the aura of divinity from the emperor while preserving the imperial institution, at the price, however, of allowing Hirohito to evade any admission of responsibility for either defeat or war crimes.

82. McCormack, *Emptiness*, 292.

83. Ibid., 169.

84. Ibid., 174–75.

85. See David Loy, "The Religion of the Market," *Journal of the American Academy of Religion* 65, no. 2 (1997): 275–90; see also his "Trying to Become Real: A Buddhist Critique of Some Secular Heresies," *International Philosophical Quarterly* 32 (1992): 403–25 on the construction of the desire-afflicted but necessarily unreal consumerist self as the centerpiece of this ideology: "The supreme irony is that our collective project to secure ourselves, technology, is what threatens to destroy us," 421; and his more comprehensive studies *Lack and Transcendence: The Problem of Death and Life in Psychotherapy, Existentialism, and Buddhism* (Amherst, Mass.: Humanity Books, 1999), and *A Buddhist History of the West: Studies in Lack* (Albany: State University of New York Press, 2002).

86. McCormack, *Emptiness*, 172.

87. Josef Kreiner, "Religionen heute," in Mayer and Pohl, *Japan*, 507.

88. This is the thesis advanced by Ogoshi Aiko, "Die dualistische Sicht der Natur in Japan: Eine buddhistisch-feministische Perspektive," in Hans Kessler, ed., *Ökologisches Weltethos im Dialog der Kulturen und Religionen* (Darmstadt: Wissenschaftliche Buchgesellschaft, 1996), 121–36, 122–29. When she accuses the *Lotus Sutra* of discriminating against women, however, she goes too far, for the story of the dragon princess can more plausibly be interpreted as asserting that women can possess the Buddha-nature and enter the Buddha Land, albeit on condition of being transformed into males, 125–26. The proposition that Shinto is dualistic also seems to me to be questionable; see Kreiner, Mayer and Pohl, *Japan*, 506. Ogoshi does, however, adduce other evidence of misogynist Buddhist texts such as the fourteenth-century *Ketsubon-kyo*, and Niwa's *The Buddha Tree* is dominated by an unresolved tension between sexual desire and religious devotion. See the fuller study by Masatoshi Ueki, *Gender Equality in Buddhism* (New York: Peter Lang, 2001).

89. This is the approach taken by Okano Haruko, "Das Problem 'Mensch und Natur' im japanischen Kontext: Eine Reflexion aus der ökologischen Perspektive," in Kessler, ed., *Ökologisches Weltethos*, 137–45. On the treatment of minorities see Hans Jürgen Mayer, "Minderheiten: Probleme und Perspektiven," in Mayer and Pohl, *Japan*, 119–24.

90. Tomatsu Yoshiharu, "The Secularization of Japanese Buddhism: The Priest as Profane Practitioner of the Sacred," *Think Sangha Journal* 1, no. 1 (1998): 46–56, 48–49. During the Russo-Japanese War and again during World War II, monks were drafted as foot soldiers; only doctors were exempted from military service, 49.

91. Tomatsu, "Secularization," 52–55.

Chapter 4: Development Without Violence?

1. The fascinating story of the emergence of modern Thailand, which need not detain us here, is told by Judith A. Stowe, *Siam Becomes Thailand: A Story of Intrigue* (Honolulu: University of Hawai'i Press, 1991); see also S. J. Tambiah, *World Conqueror and World Renouncer: A Study of Buddhism and Polity in Thailand against a Historical Background* (Cambridge: Cambridge University Press, 1976), esp. chap. 19. The name "Thai-land" was proposed by the nationalist propagandist Luang Vichitr Vadhakarn in order to give credence to a "pan-Thai movement" throughout the region; it was officially sanctioned by the dictator Phibul in 1939, Tambiah, *World Conqueror*, 477–79.

2. S. J. Tambiah, *Buddhism and the Spirit Cults in North-east Thailand* (Cambridge: Cambridge University Press, 1970), 377.

3. In what follows I rely principally on Phya Anuman Rajadhon, *Popular Buddhism in Siam and Other Essays on Thai Studies* (Bangkok: Thai Inter-Religious Commission for Development and Sathirakoses Nagapradipa Foundation, 1986), 13–22, and Tambiah, *Buddhism and the Spirit Cults,* 25–31; see also Tambiah's study of the relationship between forest-dwelling meditation masters and popular devotion, *The Buddhist Saints of the Forest and the Cult of Amulets: A Study in Charisma, Hagiography, Sectarianism, and Millennial Buddhism* (Cambridge: Cambridge University Press, 1984).

4. See Tambiah, *World Conqueror,* chap. 7.

5. See Tambiah, *Spirit Cults,* 40, 55, 59.

6. See ibid., 57–59. Interestingly, as we saw in the previous chapter, much the same applies in Japan, where death and burial are the province of Buddhist priests, while shamanistic practices from Japan's ancient past may still be used to get in touch with spirits.

7. See ibid., 53–55.

8. See ibid., 224–30, 243. Whereas in ancient India the *brahman* held the highest rank in the caste hierarchy because of his ritual purity, in Southeast Asia the concept of the divinized king or *devaraja* reversed the relationship between king and priest. In Thai village religion the *brahman* in the form of the *paahm* or village leader coexists with the *bhikkhu* as a kind of inverted *brahman:* accepting alms from anybody regardless of caste, wearing cast-off rags and positively seeking association with death, the major source of pollution, see Tambiah, 63–65, 252–60. "It is unthinkable in Thailand that a local *brahman* can be outside the Buddhist faith, or that his rites and those of the monk can be mutually exclusive," 256.

9. Ibid., 192, 268–69.

10. Ibid., 211, 280.

11. Ibid., 198, as a preface to his discussion of the *paritta* or recitations of canonical texts by the monks, where again "these textual sources reveal the remarkable paradox that the actual words said by the Buddha are not exorcistic but by and large ethical and moralistic, while in the "historical" circumstances of their enunciation they did yield practical effects against mortal dangers," 201. The word *paritta* comes from Pali via Sri Lanka, where similar ritual recitations are performed by Buddhist monks.

12. Ibid., 210.

13. Ibid., 219.

14. This terminology is proposed by Theo Sundermeier, "Implizite Axiome in der Religionsgeschichte: 'Primäre und sekundäre Religionserfahrung,'" W. Huber, E. Petzold and T. Sundermeier, eds., *Implizite Axiome: Tiefenstrukturen des Denkens und Handelns* (Munich: Chr. Kaiser, 1990).

15. Tambiah, *Spirit Cults,* 160.

16. Ibid., 172–73.

17. Ibid., 175; emphasis in original.

18. Ibid., 288.

19. Ibid., 292; interestingly, "the ritual license allowed dissolves the two most important hierarchical statuses in the village — the Buddhist monk, who normally is highly respected

and socially distinct, and the lay elder, who by virtue of his generational superiority and headship of the compound clusters is respected, wields a certain amount of authority, and occupies a position of leadership in the village," 293.

20. Ibid., 356.

21. See ibid., 338–39 (diagrammatic) and 346–49 (analytic).

22. Ibid., 368.

23. Michael von Brück and Whalen Lai, *Buddhismus und Christentum: Geschichte, Konfrontation, Dialog* (Munich: C. H. Beck, 1997), 590 (my translation).

24. On all this see extensively Tambiah, *World Conqueror,* esp. chap. 5.

25. See Tambiah, *Spirit Cults,* 74. For the following see also J. D. May, "Contested Space: Alternative Models of the Public Sphere in the Asia-Pacific," in Neil Brown and Robert Gascoigne, eds., *Faith in the Public Forum* (Adelaide: Australian Theological Forum, 1999), 78–108, 89–92, 93–95.

26. See Charles F. Keyes, "Buddhist Economics and Buddhist Fundamentalism in Burma and Thailand," in Martin E. Marty and R. Scott Appleby, eds., *Fundamentalisms and the State: Remaking Polities, Economics, and Militance* (Chicago: University of Chicago Press, 1993), 367–409.

27. See Tambiah, *World Conqueror,* 482–83. From the point of view of political science this is an astonishing achievement.

28. Ibid., 487, 503.

29. In societies that are communal rather than individualistic in character, democracy is bound to take different forms which may be no less democratic for not conforming to the liberal stereotype. "Freedom" here connotes not so much individual liberty as the collective independence of the nation, for which hierarchical authority and the maintenance of law and order are prerequisites, though such a mentality is not easy to justify to the West; see ibid., 431, 500, 513.

30. Tambiah, *Spirit Cults,* 26.

31. Ibid., 27.

32. Ibid., 27–28; see Rajadhon, *Popular Buddhism,* 14–15, with detailed examples of the cultural legacies inherited by the Thai, 16–22.

33. Detailed accounts can be found in Stowe, *Siam Becomes Thailand,* Tambiah, *World Conqueror,* chap. 11, and the writings of Sulak Sivaraksa, referred to below. Mongkut's reforms were continued by King Chulalongkorn around the turn of the twentieth century. Though the revolution of 1932 resulted in a succession of civilian and military rulers under a constitutional monarchy, it did not diminish the religious awe in which the royal family is held.

34. Especially by King Mongkut, Rama IV, 1851–68, a venerated scholar, and by his son King Chulalongkorn, Rama V, 1868–1910, who encouraged the use of reason in religious matters and abolished slavery and corvée labor. See Stowe, *Siam Becomes Thailand,* chap. 2.

35. "Public discussion about the key political, social, and economic issues in contemporary Thailand is often conducted through the medium of debates about Buddhist doctrine," for Buddhism "has a unique symbolic value in Thailand as a medium for expressing hopes and aspirations not only for religious salvation from suffering but also . . . for material prosperity and social and political success"; Peter A. Jackson, *Buddhism, Legitimation, and*

Conflict: The Political Functions of Urban Thai Buddhism (Singapore: Institute of Southeast Asian Studies, 1989), 3. On modern Thai Buddhism as a "religion of the bourgeoisie" see Tambiah, *World Conqueror,* 510.

36. Jackson, *Buddhism,* 55, continues: "Consequently, Buddhist justifications of democracy, economic development, human rights, women's rights, and so on represent much more than mere attempts to justify the relevance of Buddhism in the modern age. Rather, such middle-class analyses represent attempts to fashion an acceptable indigenous expression of their class's political, social, and economic aspirations."

37. Similar questions could be asked of the unfolding situations in Burma and Vietnam, the one a scene of cynical repression, the other a society with a high level of popular participation; of the unpredictable balance of Confucian values, Marxist doctrine and democratic aspirations in China; or of the extraordinary role of King Sihanouk throughout the vicissitudes of Cambodia's modern history. More such questions are raised in David Potter's detailed overview "Democratization in Asia," in David Held, ed., *Prospects for Democracy: North, South, East, West* (Cambridge: Polity Press, 1993), 355–79, especially with regard to Asia's numerous socialist countries, which seem remarkably unimpressed by recent developments in Eastern Europe, and the great exception to the overall gloomy trend, exuberantly democratic Papua New Guinea, though even here vote buying and political coercion are becoming endemic. For the following see J. D. May, "What Do Socially Engaged Buddhists and Christian Liberation Theologians Have to Say to One Another?," *Dialogue* 21 (1994): 1–18, 4–5, 9–12.

38. For the wider context of traditional saintly forest monks with a large popular following see Tambiah, *Buddhist Saints,* and on Buddhadasa, *World Conqueror,* 411–14, 423–25.

39. See Buddhadasa Bhikkhu, *Dhammic Socialism,* ed. Donald K. Swearer (Bangkok: Thai Inter-Religious Commission on Development, 1960).

40. See Jackson, *Buddhism,* 134; see also 133: "Phutthatat . . . oscillates between . . . two options . . . , at times supporting more explicitly democratic systems."

41. Buddhadasa Bhikkhu, *Handbook for Mankind* (Bangkok: The Dhamma Study and Practice Group, 1988), 16.

42. Buddhadasa, *Handbook,* 17, see 7. The other side of this coin is that the traditional "woeful states" also exist here and now, calling for action in the world motivated by *metta,* loving-kindness; see Tambiah, *World Conqueror,* 411–18. Tambiah still sees an unresolved tension in Buddhadasa's attempted reconciliation of meditation and service, and he is skeptical of such doctrinal innovations as the equivalence of *dhamma* and God, 425.

43. Buddhadasa, *Handbook,* 8, 13.

44. Jackson, *Buddhism,* 132–33.

45. See Sulak Sivaraksa, "My Personal Views on Education: A Buddhist-Christian Encounter," in idem, *A Socially Engaged Buddhism* (Bangkok: Thai Inter-Religious Commission for Development, 1988), 143–49; Herbert B. Phillips, "About the Author," S. Sivaraksa, *Siam in Crisis,* 2d rev. ed. (Bangkok: Santi Pracha Dhamma Institute and Thai Inter-Religious Commission for Development, 1990), 6–8.

46. These events are documented in the Appendices to Sulak Sivaraksa, *Siamese Resurgence: A Thai Buddhist Voice on Asia and a World of Change* (Bangkok: Asian Cultural Forum on Development, 1985), 337–463. See also the "Appreciation" by William L. Bradley and

the Introduction by David W. Chappell in Sulak Sivaraksa, *A Buddhist Vision for Renewing Society: Collected Articles by a Concerned Thai Intellectual* (Bangkok: Tienwan Publishing House, 1986), xi–xxvii.

47. See Sulak Sivaraksa, *Seeds of Peace: A Buddhist Vision for Renewing Society* (Berkeley, Calif.: Parallax Press, 1992), 119–126 and, for extensive documentation of his subsequent trial and acquittal on renewed charges of *lèse majesté*, *When Loyalty Demands Dissent: Sulak Sivaraksa and the Charge of Lese Majeste in Siam 1991–1993* (Bangkok: Santi Pracha Dhamma Institute, 1993).

48. See Sivaraksa, *Seeds of Peace*, 24–34.

49. See Jackson, *Buddhism*, chaps. 7 and 8; Donald K. Swearer, "Fundamentalistic Movements in Theravada Buddhism," in Marty and Appleby, eds., *Fundamentalisms Observed* (Chicago: University of Chicago Press, 1991), 628–90, 652–77; Keyes, "Buddhist Economics," 385–97.

50. See Sivaraksa, *Siam in Crisis*, 327–31.

51. See Swearer, "Fundamentalistic Movements," 676–77; on the movement as a whole, 667–77.

52. See ibid., 671.

53. Ibid., 657; see 656–67.

54. See Jackson, *Buddhism*, chap. 8, where he cites a student who "described the results of her training in almost pentecostal-like terms," using the expression "born again." He concludes: "There are many similarities to charismatic Christian movements," 212. Jackson interprets the opposition to Santi Asok and the acceptance of Wat Thammakay as a manifestation of the tension between middle class and establishment in urban Thailand, 219.

55. See Swearer, "Fundamentalistic Movements," 656, 668; Keyes, "Buddhist Economics," 399.

56. Keyes, "Buddhist Economics," 389, quoting Winston Davis.

57. See David Loy, "Buddhism and Money," in Sulak Sivaraksa, ed., *Radical Conservatism: Buddhism in the Contemporary World: Articles in Honor of Bhikkhu Buddhadasa's 84th Birthday Anniversary* (Bangkok: Thai Inter-Religious Commission for Development and International Network of Engaged Buddhists, 1990), 22–38; Ken Jones, *The Social Face of Buddhism: An Approach to Political and Social Activism* (London: Wisdom Publications, 1989).

58. The human and environmental effects of such "development" are movingly portrayed by the investigative journalist Sanitsuda Ekachai, *Behind the Smile: Voices of Thailand* (Bangkok: Thai Development Support Committee, 1990), and in the stories of prizewinning novelist Pira Sudham, *Siamese Drama And Other Stories from Thailand* (Bangkok: Shire Books, 1989).

59. Once again, Tambiah places these developments in the wider context of providing Buddhist legitimation for both nationalism and development by the "Thai-ization" of the hill tribes in more remote regions, involving both the promotion of the Thai language and proselytization by monks, see *World Conqueror*, 445–50.

60. For characterizations of spirit beliefs throughout Thailand see Rajadhon, *Popular Buddhism in Siam.*

61. See Yeshua Moser, "Trees in Monks' Clothing," *Peace Magazine* (November–December 1992): 17.

62. Cited by Seri Phongphit, *Religion in a Changing Society: Buddhism, Reform and the Role of Monks in Community Development in Thailand* (Hong Kong: Arena Press, 1988), 164. One is reminded of the Benedictine *laborare est orare;* but see below.

63. See Phongphit, *Religion in a Changing Society,* 177.

64. Charles F. Keyes, "Buddhist Practical Morality in a Changing Agrarian World: A Case Study from Northeastern Thailand," in Russell F. Sizemore and Donald K. Swearer, eds., *Ethics, Wealth, and Salvation: A Study in Buddhist Social Ethics* (Columbia: University of South Carolina Press, 1990), 170–89, 171.

65. Keyes, "Buddhist Practical Morality," 180.

66. Ibid., 171.

67. On the other hand, as I remarked in the Introduction, Theravada Buddhism finds it hard to develop a theory of the religious "other," possibly because its particular doctrine of transcendence suggests that it transcends all other conceivable "ways" (including Christianity and science) and therefore has no intrinsic ties to any particular religion, culture or political system, whereas Hinduism, at least until its recent fundamentalist phase, has tended to absorb minorities into itself, "tolerating" them by substituting a Hindu identity for their own (though Islam has resisted this). See Ninian Smart, "India, Sri Lanka and Religion," John P. Burris, ed., *Reflections in the Mirror of Religion* (London: Macmillan, 1997), 130–47, 134–36, 139–41, 145–47; and Tambiah, *World Conqueror,* 520–21, who goes so far as to speak of the "obtuseness" of missionary monks who did not realize that they were carrying out government policy of pacifying and assimilating the "inferior" hill tribes, 445. Notwithstanding these difficulties, David Chappell is able to propose "Six Buddhist Attitudes Toward Other Religions," Sivaraksa, *Radical Conservatism,* 443–58. I am grateful to Sallie King for challenging me to clarify this somewhat paradoxical point.

68. For the following see J. D. May, "Development without Violence? Some Buddhist and Christian Sources for Development Ethics," *Seeds of Peace* 13, no. 1 (1997): 18–25, 22–23.

69. There is thus, from the very beginning, scope for a "messianic" element in Buddhism, as we saw in some of its Japanese developments.

70. Some interesting ramifications of this "indirect" economic participation are followed up in Sizemore and Swearer, *Ethics, Wealth, and Salvation.*

71. Buddhadasa Bhikkhu, *Dhammic Socialism,* 88–92.

72. Joanna Macy, *World as Lover, World as Self* (Berkeley, Calif.: Parallax Press, 1991), 95–105.

73. For the following see J. D. May, "Gibt es eine buddhistische Wirtschaftsethik?," in Maria Hungerkamp and Matthias Lutz, eds., *Grenzen überschreitende Ethik: Festschrift für Prof. Dr. Johannes Hoffmann anlässlich seines 60. Geburtstags* (Frankfurt: IKO-Verlag für Interkulturelle Kommunikation, 1997), 65–82, 70–79.

74. See Sangharakshita, *Vision and Transformation: An Introduction to the Buddha's Eightfold Path* (Glasgow: Windhorse Publications, 1990); he prefers the translation "perfect" to the more usual "right," see 93–110. This specifically Buddhist economic ethic informs all the writings of Sulak Sivaraksa; for an overview of his thought see Donald K. Swearer, "Sulak Sivaraksa's Buddhist Vision for Renewing Society," in Christopher S. Queen and

Sallie B. King, eds., *Engaged Buddhism: Buddhist Liberation Movements in Asia* (Albany: State University of New York Press, 1996), 195–235.

75. See Santikaro Bhikkhu, "Buddhadasa Bhikkhu: Life and Society Through the Natural Eyes of Voidness," in Queen and King, *Engaged Buddhism,* 147–93; idem, "Möglichkeiten eines Dhamma-Sozialismus," Gerhard Köberlin, ed., *Wege zu einer gerechten Gesellschaft. Beiträge engagierter Buddhisten zu einer internationalen Debatte,* Weltmission heute No. 23 (Hamburg: Evangelisches Missionswerk, 1996), 86–133; see also Donald K. Swearer, "Das Vermächtnis von Buddhadasa Bhikkhu," 134–54.

76. See Santikaro Bhikkhu, "Buddhadasa," 159, 171; Donald K. Swearer, ed., Introduction, *Dhammic Socialism,* 19–41, 28.

77. See Swearer, *Dhammic Socialism,* 33; Santikaro, "Buddhadasa," 162, 169, with reference to the Buddhist emperor Asoka.

78. See Santikaro, "Buddhadasa," 166; Swearer, *Dhammic Socialism,* 28–29.

79. See Santikaro, "Buddhadasa," 155, 176; Swearer, *Dhammic Socialism,* 30–31.

80. See Santikaro, "Buddhadasa," 164, 170–71.

81. Swearer, *Dhammic Socialism,* 33.

82. See Santikaro, "Buddhadasa," 158.

83. See ibid., 173.

84. Swearer, *Dhammic Socialism,* 33–38.

85. In what follows I shall be referring to Sizemore and Swearer, *Ethics, Wealth and Salvation.* See also Charles F. Keyes, "Buddhist Economics and Buddhist Fundamentalism in Burma and Thailand," in Marty and Appleby, eds., *Fundamentalisms and the State,* 367–409.

86. This refers to the "Four Illimitables," lovingkindness (*metta*), compassion (*karuna*), altruistic love (*mudita*) and equanimity (*upekkha*); see the introductory essay by Phra Rajavaramuni, with copious textual references, in Sizemore and Swearer, *Ethics,* 29–53.

87. See the essays by John S. Strong, "Rich Man, Poor Man, *Bhikkhu,* King: Asoka's Great Quinquennial Festival and the Nature of Dana," in Sizemore and Swearer, *Ethics,* 107–23; Nancy Auer Falk, "Exemplary Donors of the Pali Tradition," ibid., 124–43. Persecution of avaricious monasteries by an envious state was particularly the case in China, as Sallie King has pointed out to me in a personal communication; see Appendix II.

88. Steven Kemper, "Wealth and Reformation in Sinhalese Buddhist Monasticism," in Sizemore and Swearer, *Ethics,* 152–69, 159. The refusal of alms has been used to good effect in Burma, where the word for "strike" is derived from it, see Keyes, "Buddhist Economics," 372–85, 377.

89. Phra Rajavaramuni, "Foundations of Buddhist Social Ethics," Sizemore and Swearer, *Ethics,* 29–53, 44.

90. See Frank E. Reynolds, "Ethics and Wealth in Theravada Buddhism: A Study in Comparative Religious Ethics," in Sizemore and Swearer, *Ethics,* 59–76; Charles F. Keyes, "Buddhist Practical Morality in a Changing Agrarian World: A Case from Northeast Thailand," ibid., 170–89.

91. Reynolds, "Ethics and Wealth," 59–86, 68–69.

92. David Little, "Ethical Analysis and Wealth in Theravada Buddhism: A Response to Frank Reynolds," in Sizemore and Swearer, *Ethics,* 77–86, 82.

93. See Keyes, "Buddhist Economics," 386–87.

94. See Robin W. Lovin, "Ethics, Wealth, and Eschatology: Buddhist and Christian Strategies for Social Change," in Sizemore and Swearer, *Ethics,* 190–208; Ronald M. Green, "Buddhist Economic Ethics: A Theoretical Approach," ibid., 215–34.

95. Lovin, "Ethics," 190–208, 191.

96. Ibid., 203–4.

97. Ibid., 208.

98. Tambiah, *World Conqueror,* 515.

99. Ibid., 518: "This dichotomy is also reflected elsewhere: the monk's vocation of learning and the vocation of meditation, monks dwelling in towns and those living in the forest, and monks implicated in monastic organization and those who remain apart as hermits or ascetics."

100. Ibid., 521–22.

101. These are studied in detail by Tambiah, *Buddhist Saints,* chaps. 19, 20.

Part 3: Strange Encounters

1. My first scholarly article took up this theme: "What Is Political Theology?," *Compass Theology Review* 4 (Melbourne, 1970): 88–94.

2. J. D. May, "Christian-Buddhist-Marxist Dialogue in Sri Lanka: A Model for Social Change in Asia?," *Journal of Ecumenical Studies* 19 (1982): 719–43; "Buddhist and Christian Responses to Social and Technical Revolution," *Dialogue* 7 (Colombo, 1980): 23–40.

3. As is evident in the work I produced, see J. D. May, "The Religious Construction of Meaning: Christianity and Buddhism as 'Problem-Solvers,'" in Victor C. Hayes, ed., *Australian Essays in World Religions* (Adelaide: Australian Association for the Study of Religions, 1977), 106–15; *Meaning, Consensus and Dialogue in Buddhist-Christian Communication: An Essay in the Construction of Meaning* (Berne: Peter Lang, 1984); "Einige Voraussetzungen interreligiöser Kommunikation am Beispiel Buddhismus und Christentum," *Neue Zeitschrift für Missionswissenschaft* 40 (1984): 26–35.

Chapter 5: Transcending Difference

1. Watsuji Tetsuro, *Fudo — Wind und Erde. Der Zusammenhang von Klima und Kultur* (Darmstadt: Primus Verlag, 1997), 4–5.

2. On the significance of the *ie* as the locus of all Japanese religiosity see Ian Reader, *Religion in Contemporary Japan* (Honolulu: University of Hawai'i Press, 1991), 12–13; the whole book is valuable for "situating" religion in Japanese life.

3. Watsuji, *Fudo,* 124–27.

4. Ibid., 129, see 144–45.

5. Ibid., 146–47. Watsuji can be forgiven, of course, for not anticipating the emerging borderless world of globalization, in which nation-states are beginning to go the way of medieval city-states.

6. Ibid., 133, see 128–32.

7. Ibid., 135. Watsuji was to develop this theme with ominous nationalistic overtones.

8. These have been researched by Armin Münch, *Dimensionen der Leere. Gott als Nichts und Nichts als Gott im christlich-buddhistischen Dialog* (Münster: LIT Verlag, 1998),

who takes as his guiding question: "What is lacking in our idea of God if we are ignorant of Buddhist experience," 5. I refer to his findings in what follows.

9. Münch, *Dimensionen,* calls these "immanentals" in analogy to the "transcendentals" of scholastic philosophy, 12–13. Münch's hypothesis is that while Buddhist thinking is "dorsal" or rearwards-directed, Christian theology is forwards-directed, though the dynamic of Buddhist transcendence is to leave behind all perspectivity, 130–33.

10. From now on I shall capitalize key terms such as Self, Other, Same, Stranger, Own, Enemy, Land, Life etc. when used in a systemic sense.

11. For the following see J. D. May, "Contested Space: Alternative Models of the Public Sphere in the Asia-Pacific," in Neil Brown and Robert Gascoigne, eds., *Faith in the Public Forum* (Adelaide: Australian Theological Forum, 1999), 78–108.

12. This theme from the thought of the German sociologist Niklas Luhmann is developed by Peter Beyer, *Religion and Globalization* (London: Sage, 1994).

13. This also applies to the forest-dwelling Buddhist meditation masters of Thailand, as we saw in chapter 4.

14. Those with experience of all three seem to think the differences are inconsequential, e.g., Dan O'Donovan, *Dadirri* (Kensington, Australia: Nelen Yubu Missiological Unit, 2001). O'Donovan, a Catholic priest who lives as a hermit in northwestern Australia but has practiced Zen meditation in India, is not afraid of complementarity: "I will be drawing on... Hindu Yoga; Buddhist Zen; Christian *Hesychasm;* Islamic *Dhikr*" in developing Miriam-Rose Ungunmerr's explanation of Aboriginal *dadirri,* 3, see 4–7.

15. See J. D. May, "The Trinity in Melanesia: Understanding the Christian God in a Pacific Culture," in James M. Byrne, ed., *The Christian Understanding of God Today* (Dublin: Columba Press, 1993), 154–65.

16. Without any reference to the exigencies of dialogue, Jean-Luc Marion, *God Without Being: Hors-Texte* (Chicago: University of Chicago Press, 1991) has recently proposed that the Christian tradition itself suggests that the divine love is theologically prior to being itself and should become the starting point for Christian "onto-theology." See also Oliver Davies, *A Theology of Compassion: Metaphysics of Difference and the Renewal of Tradition* (London: SCM, 2001), who similarly makes virtually no reference to the interreligious relevance of his extremely fruitful ideas.

17. See the lucid recapitulation of this history in Linda Hogan, *Confronting the Truth: Conscience in the Catholic Tradition* (Mahwah, N.J.: Paulist Press, 2000).

18. *Sunyata,* literally the hollow space inside an empty vessel, is of course a spatial metaphor, as is *nirvana,* derived from the absence of a flame after it has been extinguished, whereas temporality is crucial to the Jewish narrative structure of the Christian faith-story. This becomes particularly interesting if it is true, as some suggest, that spatial metaphors are as fundamental to post-modernity as temporal ones were to modernity (history, evolution, development, dialectical materialism etc.).

19. It would take us far beyond the scope of this book to pursue the question of the two truths in depth; suffice it to say that the idea, as deployed by Nagarjuna and Candrakirti, *is* the most radical imaginable overcoming of dualism. See Jay L. Garfield, *Empty Words: Buddhist Philosophy and Cross-Cultural Interpretation* (Oxford and New York: Oxford University Press, 2002), esp. chaps 2, 3 and 4 on causality, emptiness and positionlessness; and C. W. Huntington Jr. with Geshé Namgyal Wangchen, *The Emptiness of Emptiness: An*

Introduction to Early Indian Madhyamika (Honolulu: University of Hawai'i Press, 1989) on Candrakirti's *The Entry into the Middle Way*.

20. See Masao Abe, *Buddhism and Interfaith Dialogue* (London: Macmillan, 1995), where these themes are developed throughout Part One.

21. See ibid., 57–59, 100–102.

22. Ibid., 60.

23. On Abe's own admission, ibid., 61, because this would be a completely realized eschatology without any tension between already and non-yet.

24. For the following see J. D. May, "Strange Encounters: On Transcending Violence by Transcending Difference," *Studies in World Christianity* 6, no. 2 (2000): 224–44, 237–41.

25. I am reproducing here the fascinating cultural typology given by David Loy, *Lack and Transcendence: The Problem of Death and Life in Psychotherapy, Existentialism, and Buddhism* (Amherst, Mass.: Humanity Books, 1999), 154–72, here 156.

26. Ibid., 156.

27. Ibid., 155–56; 163.

28. Ibid., 156–57.

29. Ibid., 158–61.

30. Ibid., 165; see 163–65.

31. See May, "Contested Space," 78–108.

32. See J. D. May, "European Union, Christian Division? Christianity's Responsibility for Europe's Past and Future," *Studies* 89 (2000): 118–29.

33. I have at times referred to these as processes of "inculturation," a term borrowed from Christian missiology which is becoming controversial even there because it seems to presuppose a definitive — actually, European — Christianity which is then maneuvered into someone else's cultural context with as little displacement as possible. Yet the term is useful as a shorthand way of referring to transitions of religious identities, whether Christian, Buddhist, primal or other, into new cultural settings with new sets of semiotic correlates, resulting in mutual transformation. I shall continue to use the term in this "neutral" sense.

34. The following relies on the analysis of Peter Beyer, *Religion and Globalization*, who in turn draws on the work of the German sociologist Nicklas Luhmann; see 38–41.

35. Ibid., 45–50.

36. Ibid., 58, using an expression of Luhmann's.

37. See ibid., 63–66.

38. See ibid.: they are, in Luhmann's terms, "(at least potentially) systemic," 67 and chap. 3.

39. See the constructive proposals by Richard Falk, *Predatory Globalization: A Critique* (Cambridge: Polity Press, 1999).

40. See Beyer, *Religion and Globalization*, 82, 103–4.

41. The term was coined by Manuel Castells, *The Rise of the Network Society: The Information Age: Economy, Society and Culture*, vol. 1 (Oxford: Blackwell, 1996), 410–18, to characterize the "space of flows" in which the economy becomes an "economy of signs and space," see Scott Lash and John Urry, *Economies of Signs and Space* (London: Sage, 1994).

Chapter 6: Transcending Violence

1. Samuel P. Huntington, *The Clash of Civilizations and the Remaking of World Order* (New York: Simon & Schuster, 1996), based on the article "The Clash of Civilizations?," *Foreign Affairs* 72, no. 3 (1993): 22–49.

2. See Johan Galtung, *Peace by Peaceful Means: Peace and Conflict, Development and Civilization* (London: Sage, 1996).

3. The best-known exponent of this view is Hans Küng, *Global Responsibility: In Search of a New World Ethic* (London: SCM, 1990); *A Global Ethic for Global Politics and Economics* (London: SCM, 1997). I have explored this possibility in J. D. May, *After Pluralism: Towards an Interreligious Ethic* (Münster: LIT Verlag, 2000), though I am now less inclined to propose ethical agreement as the "solution" to doctrinal differences and cultural incompatibilities, see J. D. May, "Ethic of Survival or Vision of Hope? The Aim of Interreligious Dialogue," *Dharma World* 29 (September–October 2002): 25–28.

4. The term *Konvivenz* is used by Theo Sundermeier, *Den Fremden verstehen. Eine praktische Hermeneutik* (Göttingen: Vandenhoeck & Ruprecht, 1996), 226, who insists that it is not equivalent to the Latin American expression *convivencia,* nor to the "conviviality" celebrated by Ivan Illich, nor to the ecumenical term *koinonia,* but embraces mutual help, reciprocal learning and shared celebration in immediate relationship with the Stranger. This is consonant with ideas to be developed later in this chapter.

5. For the following see J. D. May, "Strange Encounters: On Transcending Violence by Transcending Difference," *Studies in World Christianity* 6, no. 2 (2000): 225–31.

6. Regina Schwartz, *The Curse of Cain: The Violent Legacy of Monotheism* (Chicago: University of Chicago Press, 1997), 5.

7. The discussion may be traced through B. Wilson, ed., *Rationality* (Oxford: Blackwell, 1970); M. Hollis and S. Lukes, eds., *Rationality and Relativism* (Oxford: Blackwell, 1984); M. Krausz, ed., *Relativism: Interpretation and Confrontation* (Notre Dame: University of Notre Dame Press, 1989); R. A. Mall, *Philosophie im Vergleich der Kulturen. Interkulturelle Philosophie — eine neue Orientierung* (Darmstadt: Wissenschaftliche Buchgesellschaft, 1995); M. Brocker and H. Nau, eds., *Ethnozentrismus: Möglichkeiten und Grenzen des interkulturellen Dialogs* (Darmstadt: Primus-Verlag, 1997).

8. See Dieter Mersch in Brocker and Nau, eds., *Ethnozentrismus,* 27–45, 27, 29, 36.

9. See Andreas Wimmer in Brocker and Nau, eds., *Ethnozentrismus,* 120–40, 121, 124; and May, *After Pluralism,* 65–68.

10. See Wolfgang Kluxen in Brocker and Nau, eds., *Ethnozentrismus,* 11–26, 18.

11. Wimmer, *Ethnozentrismus,* 128–29.

12. Ibid., 130.

13. Ibid., 132–33: Was alle Menschen miteinander verbindet und was es ihnen ermöglicht, die kulturelle Landschaft in Bewegung zu setzen und sich selbst in ihr zu bewegen, ist die Fähigkeit, auf der Suche nach einem Kompromiss Sinn und Nutzen in Übereinstimmung zu bringen. Dies möchte ich die Pragmatik der kulturellen Produktion nennen.

14. Ibid., 135. In contrast to Habermas, Wimmer's innovation is "that the validity of a norm may be doubted not only by reference to universal standards of rationality, but also, thanks to the fact of cultural heterogeneity, from within the culture (*kulturimmanent*)," 138, n. 36.

15. Martin Fuchs in Brocker and Nau, *Ethnozentrismus*, 141–52, 149–50.

16. R. A. Mall in Brocker and Nau, eds., *Ethnozentrismus*, 68–89, 71: Es mag Europa überraschen, dass Europa heute interpretierbar geworden ist. See also Mall, *Philosophie im Vergleich*.

17. See R. Friedli, *Fremdheit als Heimat: Auf der Suche nach einem Kriterium für den Dialog zwischen den Religionen* (Fribourg: Universitätsverlag, 1974), using examples from Biblical, Buddhist and African traditions.

18. A thesis developed by David Krieger, *The New Universalism: Foundations for a Global Theology* (Maryknoll, N.Y.: Orbis, 1991).

19. See Paul F. Knitter, "Catholics and Other Religions: Bridging the Gap between Dialogue and Theology," *Louvain Studies* 24 (1999): 319–54, where he gives evidence for this "gap" and recent attempts to bridge it.

20. On the contribution of Levinas, see May, *After Pluralism*, 35–43. Paul Ricoeur, *Oneself as Another* (Chicago: University of Chicago Press, 1992), Tenth Study, illuminates both the contrast and the complementarity between Husserl and Levinas in this respect: Husserl, intent on grounding the Self as *ipse*, suspends the evidence of otherness; Levinas, intent on demonstrating the priority of otherness over the Self as *idem*, suspends the evidence of self-knowledge (332). In Husserlian terms: "the gap can never be bridged between the presentation of my experience and the appresentation of your experience" (333). The gnoseological transfer from *ego* to *alter ego* is symmetrical with the ethical transfer from *alter ego* to *ego* (335). The word disclosed in the face of the other "comes to be placed at the origin of my acts. . . . Each face is a Sinai that prohibits murder . . . the face singularizes the commandment" (336). In Buddhist eyes, of course, this would be perceived as dualism: there is no "position" from which the priority of *gnosis* or *ethos* could be established, unless it be the "positionless position" beyond both but unattainable for conceptualization, see Masao Abe's discussion with Paul Knitter on the priority of prayer over action in Masao Abe, *Buddhism and Interfaith Dialogue* (London: Macmillan, 1995), 236–43. Perhaps this is precisely what Levinas's category "the infinite," which is not the conceptualization of a "third" position, is meant to envisage; perhaps, too, it is the point of Jean-Luc Marion's thesis that, without prejudice to the "existence" of God, love is more fundamental than Being as a category by which to "grasp" God if God is not to become an idol.

21. Sundermeier, *Den Fremden verstehen*, rightly insists that the specifically religious theme is not simply otherness as such but coming to understand strangeness: "Wenn Gott erwählt, heisst das, dass er trennt . . . Gott erscheint Israel wie ein Fremder (Jer 14,8)" (206); this problematic is "offensichtlich im Zentrum der Religion selbst angesiedelt" (215). I cannot agree with his criticism, however, that Levinas does not envisage the Stranger as Stranger, see 62–71 and the objections raised by Wulf-Volker Lindner and Susanna Kempin in Theo Ahrens, ed., *Zwischen Rationalität und Globalisierung: Studien zu Mission, Ökumene und Religion* (Ammersbek bei Hamburg: Verlag an der Lottbek, 1997), 249–63, 252, 256.

22. A striking recent example of it is the extraordinary Vatican document *Dominus Iesus*; see J. D. May, "Catholic Fundamentalism? Some Implications of *Dominus Iesus* for Dialogue and Peacemaking" in Michael Rainer, ed., *"Dominus Iesus": Anstössige Wahrheit oder anstössige Kirche?* (Münster: LIT Verlag, 2001), 112–33; also in *Horizons* 28 (2001): 271–93.

23. At this point, of course, the question of criteria arises: does what we have said apply to Scientology and Satanism? One way of answering this question is "by their fruits you shall know them," but even this begs the question of what counts as "good." Nevertheless, in practice we manage to distinguish between genuine and spurious religion about as well as we do between good and bad characters.

24. The perspective outlined here has been developed in a critical dialogue with Levinas by Michael Barnes, *Theology and the Dialogue of Religions* (Cambridge: Cambridge University Press, 2002), which I received too late to incorporate it adequately into the present discussion.

25. This is a central assertion of Huntington, *The Clash of Civilizations*, 217–18: "The underlying problem for the West is not Islamic fundamentalism. It is Islam, a different civilization whose people are convinced of the superiority of their culture and are obsessed with the inferiority of their power. The problem for Islam . . . is the West."

26. See Paul Knitter, "Responsibilities for the Future: Toward an Interfaith Ethic," in J. D. May, ed., *Pluralism and the Religions: The Theological and Political Dimensions* (London: Cassell, 1998), 75–89; more fully in Knitter, *One Earth, Many Religions: Multifaith Dialogue and Global Responsibility* (Maryknoll, N.Y.: Orbis, 1995). In making this case one must of course be wary of an ethical rigorism that would lend credence to Gavin D'Costa's accusation that theological pluralists are in fact Enlightenment exclusivists: the meliority they attack in other positions is intrinsic to their own! See G. D'Costa, *The Meeting of Religions and the Trinity* (Edinburgh: T. & T. Clark, 2000), 39. I believe Knitter successfully avoids this danger.

27. I am grateful to David Loy for clarifying this point in personal correspondence.

28. Krieger, *New Universalism*, alludes to Gandhi's principle of *satyagraha* ("soul force," lit. "living [=non-violently holding to] the truth [=God]"); this is perhaps the core of truth in Hans Küng's ambitious proposals for a "global ethic." The theme is developed further in May, *After Pluralism*. Jay L. Garfield, *Empty Words: Buddhist Philosophy and Cross-Cultural Interpretation* (Oxford and New York: Oxford University Press, 2002), 220–28 contrasts "theistic" Hindu and "atheistic" Buddhist interpretations of *satyagraha*.

29. See Wilfred Cantwell Smith, *The Meaning and End of Religion* (New York: Macmillan, 1962).

30. Maurice Leenhardt, *Do Kamo. La personne et le mythe dans le monde mélanésien* (Paris: Gallimard, 1971 [1947]), 261: Ainsi la personne mélanésienne ne procède pas seulement de l'affectif individuel, ou de la société, ou de la pensée, mythique ou non, mais elle se manifeste au travers d'eux tous, elle a besoin d'eux tous pour être porté; elle est participative . . . "le lui." On the plurality of names corresponding to social roles and status see also Jane Goodale, *To Sing with Pigs Is Human: The Concept of Person in Papua New Guinea* (Seattle: University of Washington Press, 1995), chap. 5, esp. 109–12 for examples of naming "big men" (*pomidan*) and "big women" (*polamit*) in songs.

31. S. Collins, *Selfless Persons: Imagery and Thought in Theravada Buddhism* (Cambridge: Cambridge University Press, 1982), 111–14. Interestingly, this is one of the very few accounts of non-Western theories of the self mentioned by Ricoeur, *Oneself as Another*, 39, n. 28.

32. See Collins, *Selfless Persons*, 153–56.

33. See the essays in Part II of Donald Swearer, ed., *Me and Mine: Selected Essays of Bhikkhu Buddhadasa* (Albany: State University of New York Press, 1989).

34. David Loy, *Lack and Transcendence: The Problem of Death and Life in Psychotherapy, Existentialism, and Buddhism* (Amherst, Mass.: Humanity Books, 1999), and *A Buddhist History of the West: Studies in Lack* (Albany: State University of New York Press, 2002).

35. Masao Abe, *Buddhism and Interfaith Dialogue* (London: Macmillan, 1995), 201.

36. Ibid., 201, quoting MK XXIV:18.

37. Ibid., 203.

38. For an impressive example of this see the conversation between Nagarjuna and Derrida set up by Joseph O'Leary, *Religious Pluralism and Christian Truth* (Edinburgh: Edinburgh University Press, 1996).

39. This was my thesis in May, *After Pluralism*. One of the most interesting recent developments of this line of thought is by Paul Knitter, *One Earth, Many Religions*.

40. See O'Leary, *Religious Pluralism and Christian Truth*.

41. See J. D. May, "What Do Socially Engaged Buddhists and Christian Liberation Theologians Have to Say to One Another?," *Dialogue* 21 (1994): 1–18; "Development without Violence? Some Buddhist and Christian Sources for Development Ethics," *Seeds of Peace* 13, no. 1 (1997): 18–25.

42. See Frank Fletcher, "Is There a Bridge?," *Nelen Yubu* no. 78 (2000/2): 7–16.

43. As O'Leary, *Religious Pluralism and Christian Truth*, 158, put it, the Fathers of the Church are "estranged from us by the questions they did not ask"; see also Roger Haight, *Jesus, Symbol of God* (Maryknoll, N.Y.: Orbis, 1999), who simply says that the traditional language has become "incredible," 292; and the contributions of Frances Young to John Hick, ed., *The Myth of God Incarnate*, 2d ed. (London: SCM, 1993), 13–47, 87–121. Aloysius Pieris, "Christ beyond Dogma: Doing Christology in the Context of the Religions and the Poor," *Louvain Studies* 25 (2000): 187–231, goes so far as to say "that the dogmas which were intended to ensure unity in the Christian *koinonia* ended up destroying it," 190, and "that the Conciliar doctrine is not only *irrelevant* but even *misleading* from the point of view of the Asian context," 194.

44. See John Hick, ed., *Myth*; John Hick and Paul Knitter, eds., *The Myth of Christian Uniqueness: Toward a Pluralistic Theology of Religions* (Maryknoll, N.Y.: Orbis, 1987); Gavin D'Costa, *Theology and Religious Pluralism* (Oxford: Blackwell, 1986); idem, ed., *Christian Uniqueness Reconsidered: The Myth of a Pluralistic Theology of Religions* (Maryknoll, N.Y.: Orbis, 1990); Paul Knitter, *No Other Name? A Critical Survey of Christian Attitudes Towards the World Religions* (London: SCM; Maryknoll, N.Y.: Orbis, 1985); idem, *Jesus and the Other Names: Christian Mission and Global Responsibility* (Maryknoll, N.Y.: Orbis; Oxford: Oneworld, 1996); idem, *Introducing Theologies of Religions* (Marykoll, N.Y.: Orbis, 2002).

45. See Wesley J. Wildman, *Fidelity with Plausibility: Modest Christologies in the Twentieth Century* (Albany: State University of New York Press, 1998) [I thank Paul Knitter for alerting me to this book, which I have not yet been able to obtain].

46. On the complex debates leading up to Chalcedon see Aloys Grillmeier, *Christ in Christian Tradition* (London: Mowbray, 1965), esp. 433–52, 456–60.

47. Text in J. Neuner and J. Dupuis, *The Christian Faith in the Doctrinal Documents of the Catholic Church* (London: Collins, 1982, rev.), 154. Taking up the key terms that had been used in the long-running debate, the council continued: "The distinction between

the natures was never abolished by their union but rather the character proper to each of the two natures was preserved as they came together in one person (*prosopon*) and one hypostasis," 154–55.

48. See Dermot Lane, *The Reality of Jesus: An Essay in Christology* (Dublin: Veritas, 1975), 111–15.

49. We can say "God is like Jesus" or "God is in Jesus," but not "Jesus is God," unless we take a leaf from the book of Buddhist Madhyamika dialectic and say "Jesus both is and is not God," see Haight, *Jesus, Symbol of God,* 112.

50. The analysis of this plurality of New Testament Christologies by Edward Schillebeeckx, *Jesus: An Experiment in Christology* (London: Collins, 1983, orig. 1974), 403–515, remains unsurpassed; see also Haight, *Jesus,* 17–26, 152–84.

51. These perspectives are developed in great detail by O'Leary, *Religious Pluralism,* and Haight, *Jesus,* and are roundly condemned in Ratzinger's *Dominus Iesus.* See especially Haight's groundbreaking chapter 14, "Jesus and the World Religions," *Jesus,* 395–423.

52. See the useful overview by Elizabeth Johnson, *Consider Jesus: Waves of Renewal in Christology* (London: Chapman, 1990), who identifies "transcendental" and "narrative" approaches in modern Christologies.

53. Jon Sobrino sets out his Chalcedonian credentials in *Christology at the Crossroads: A Latin American Approach* (London: SCM, 1978), chap. 10, whereas Aloysius Pieris, *An Asian Theology of Liberation* (Maryknoll, N.Y.: Orbis, 1988); *God's Reign for God's Poor: A Return to the Jesus Formula* (Kelaniya, Sri Lanka: Tulana Research Center, 1998), 66–77; and "Christ beyond Dogma," 201–16, does not shy away from identifying the methodological inadequacies of "*revolving the Christological discourse around the mystery of the 'incarnation' interpreted as the hypostatic union,*" 201. Mischievously, Pieris makes his case without "quoting a single Asian theologian," preferring to show that the Western tradition itself contains alternative ways of demonstrating Jesus' uniqueness as the fulfillment of God's promise to the poor, 195.

54. A relatively early example is Peter Schüttke-Scherle's Irish School of Ecumenics thesis, *From Contextual to Ecumenical Theology? A Dialogue between Minjung Theology and "Theology after Auschwitz"* (Bern: Peter Lang, 1989); a more recent one is Aloysius Pieris, *God's Reign for God's Poor,* especially the final chapter on "The Covenant Christology and Inter-Religious Dialogue," 67–77; see also his *Fire and Water: Basic Issues in Asian Buddhism and Christianity* (Maryknoll, N.Y.: Orbis, 1996), chaps. 7, 12, and "Christ beyond Dogma." For Pieris, the suffering masses of Asia *are* "Christ in Asia," whom the "Asian Christ" of intellectuals and the "Euro-ecclesiastical Christ" of church teaching vainly try to supplant; and the Christ is the full disclosure, in the death-resurrection-pentecost event, of who Jesus is as savior.

55. See Pieris, "Christ beyond Dogma," 192–93, 214–15; Christology is thus not so much *fides quaerens intellectum* as *fides sperans salutem,* 197.

56. As Pieris puts it in a characteristically striking formulation: "Christian soteriology condemns its own manner of furthering religion with the aid of colonial powers; its treatment of Jews; its continued injustice to women; its past incomprehension and persecution of other religions in Asia.... Each religion condemns its own institutional deviations, from the standpoint of its own basic spirituality," "Christ beyond Dogma," 219.

57. This approach is developed by Jon Sobrino, *Christology at the Crossroads*, though he is at pains to demonstrate his doctrinal orthodoxy, see the clarificatory essay "The Truth about Jesus Christ" in his collection *Jesus in Latin America* (Maryknoll, N.Y.: Orbis, 1987), 3–53.

58. The theme of a "suffering and dying" God, always suspected of the heresy of "patri-passianiam" in the framework of Chalcedonian Christology, has been brought back into currency by the work of Jürgen Moltmann in a critical dialogue with Hegel; the "self-emptying" God has been rediscovered in the dialogue with the Kyoto school of Zen philosophers, especially Masao Abe.

59. Rodney Stark, *One True God: Historical Consequences of Monotheism* (Princeton, N.J.: Princeton University Press, 2001), chap. 5, emphasizes the "religious civility" (rather than a vacuous "civil religion") that must prevail in the context of mutual recognition provided by pluralism if the monotheisms' absolute claims are not to result in violence, and asks whether this can be reduplicated under the conditions of globalization.

60. See Regina Schwartz, *The Curse of Cain: The Violent Legacy of Monotheism* (Chicago: University of Chicago Press, 1997) 21–38: covenants were symbolized by the cutting of sacrificial victims and were sealed in blood.

61. Pieris refutes any suggestion of "exclusivism": "a divine election is not a reason for exclusivism because election is for mission, that is to say, one is chosen not *above* others but *for* others," "Christ beyond Dogma," 200, though this would need to be argued further; I am less certain about a residual "inclusivism" in his "contention that the Asian Poor, the majority of whom are non-Christians, constitute the *true Body of Christ which has not [yet] recognized and named its Head*," 199: are they not then "anonymous Christians"? See also Aloysius Pieris, "Multi-Ethnic Peoplehood and the God of the Bible: A Comment on the True Nature of Yahweh's Election of Israel," *Dialogue* 28 (2001): 66–78, in which he argues that the transition from "Israel" to "the Jews" involved the realization that Yahweh was not another god of the powerful but *the* God of the slaves, whose "predilection (or 'option,' as the word election implies) seemed to be for *the oppressed as such, anywhere at any time*," 69. This is based on scholarly reconstructions of the emergence of Israel in Canaan which are not uncontroversial. The great virtue of Pieris's proposal, however, is that it does not involve itself in universalist accounts of "pluralism" as conceived by the Western academy. The "revision" and "reaffirmation" of Jesus' uniqueness proposed by Paul Knitter, *Jesus and the Other Names*, chaps. 4 and 5, addresses much the same agenda with a comparable methodology while stressing that this uniqueness is "relational": that Jesus is "truly" savior does not entail that he is the "only" savior.

62. Pieris, "Christ beyond Dogma," 217, summarizing the "twofold *Kraista Sutra*" he laid out at the beginning of this groundbreaking essay.

63. See Michael von Brück and Whalen Lai, *Buddhismus und Christentum: Geschichte, Konfrontation, Dialog* (Munich: Beck, 1997), 582. The concluding synthesis of this remarkable book, though drawing extensively on available scholarship, is in many respects highly speculative and open to further discussion. I shall also refer to a second book to which von Brück and Lai often turn for guidance, Perry Schmidt-Leukel, *"Den Löwen brüllen hören": Zur Hermeneutik eines christlichen Verständnisses der buddhistischen Heilsbotschaft* (Munich: Schöningh, 1992). Taken together, these two books represent a giant leap forward in Christian attempts to develop a hermeneutic for dialogue by *doing* "Buddhology."

64. Von Brück and Lai, *Buddhismus und Christentum*, 580–81.

65. Aloysius Pieris, "Millenniarist Messianism in Buddhist History," in Seán Freyne and Nicholas Lash, eds., *Is the World Ending?* (London: SCM; Maryknoll, N.Y.: Orbis, *Concilium* 1998/4), 106–15; "The *Mahapurisa* Ideal and the Principle of Dual Authority," *Dialogue* 23 (1996): 168–76, cites the *Cakkavatti-Sihanada-Suttanta* (*DN* III) as the source of the orthodox Theravada teaching on the necessity for *two* sources, not one, of wise rule: a "wheel-turner" or "universal person" (*cakkavatti*) in the religious sphere (*dhamma-cakka*) and a "secular" counterpart (*ana-cakka*), the former being the Buddha Metteyya (Maitreya) and the latter a non-violent world-conqueror named Sankha. He contrasts this ideal order with both Buddhist and Christian politico-religious monism, in which a prophetic or "messianic" corrective to worldly power is eliminated.

66. Von Brück and Lai, *Buddhismus und Christentum*, 591.

67. See ibid., 591–94.

68. Ibid., 596.

69. Ibid., 602–3; see 600–601.

70. See ibid., 604–5; the imagery is reminiscent of the adoptionist model in Christology, 606, even to the point of naming the king *devaputra*, "Son of God," 607.

71. Ibid., 606–7.

72. See ibid., 607–8; Schmidt-Leukel, *Löwen*, 605–54, on Shinran.

73. Ibid., 608–10, cite historical cases.

74. Among its main literary sources are the "Buddhocentric" *Lotus Sutra*, which grew up around the *stupa* cult of reliquaries, rejected the Hinayana *arhats* and *pratyekabuddhas* as inferior and proclaimed the One Vehicle (*ekayana*) centered on the revelation of the Buddha's "true nature"; the *Vimalakirti Sutra*, in which the wise layman Vimalakirti makes fun of the learned monk Sariputra but really seems to be questioning the elitism of forest monks in the tradition of Subhuti; the *Sukhavati-vyuha Sutra* on the Buddha Amitabha, which inspired the Pure Land tradition; the *Avatamsaka* literature, based on meditation practice and pilgrimage, in which the Buddha becomes assimilated to the sun-god Vairocana; and the *tathagatagarbha* ("womb of the Thus-gone" or "Buddha-nature") tradition of a "seed of enlightenment" in every being. See von Brück and Lai, *Buddhismus und Christentum*, 615–18; Schmidt-Leukel, *Löwen*, 522–604 on Nagarjuna and Dharmakirti.

75. Von Brück and Lai, *Buddhismus und Christentum*, 619–21. Schmidt-Leukel, *Löwen*, 655–74, is more interested in working out a basis for the unity of Buddhism in its thematization of the "basic human experiences" from which his hermeneutic stems.

76. See von Brück and Lai, *Buddhismus und Christentum*, 624–31.

77. For an incisive account of how this happened and how it was corrected by Nagarjuna's return to the authentic Buddhist tradition (neither "annihilationism" nor "eternalism," neither being nor non-being), see David Kalupahana, *A History of Buddhist Philosophy: Continuities and Discontinuities* (Honolulu: University of Hawai'i Press, 1992).

78. See Perry Schmidt-Leukel, "Buddha and Christ as Mediators of Salvific Transcendent Reality," *Swedish Missiological Themes* 90 (2002): 17–38, and my account of the discussion which followed this presentation at the Fourth Conference of the European Network of Buddhist-Christian Studies, Höör, Sweden, 4–7 May 2001, *Buddhist-Christian Studies* 22 (2002): 195–97.

79. Masao Abe, *Buddhism and Interfaith Dialogue,* 26–37, argues that the *sambhogakaya* corresponds to the mode of existence of the "deities" Yahweh, Allah, Isvara, Amida etc. who are manifested in Jesus, Muhammad, Krishna, and Gautama in the *nirmanakaya* or historical mode, see Diagram 2, 35. Leaving aside what Muslims might have to say about this, for Christians it poses the problem of the relation of the "formless and boundless reality of Emptiness" in the *dharmakaya* mode to God, which leads John Cobb to conclude that we are in fact dealing with *two* ultimates. It will be remembered that the "evangelical" Buddhist movement we studied in Thailand took the name *Thammakay=Dharmakaya.*

80. One of the most creative attempts to correlate these strands of tradition with one another and with Christian thinking is that of Tanabe Hajime, see Makoto Ozaki, *Introduction to the Philosophy of Tanabe: According to the English Translation of the Seventh Chapter of the* Demonstratio *of Christianity* (Amsterdam: Rodopi; Grand Rapids: Eerdmans, 1990); *Individuum, Society, Humankind: The Triadic Logic of Species according to Hajime Tanabe* (Leiden: Brill, 2001); "Christ in the Eternal Light of the Buddha," *Studia Missionalia* 50 (2000): 357–89; see also the discussion of Tanabe by Donald Mitchell, *Spirituality and Emptiness: The Dynamics of Spiritual Life in Buddhism and Christianity* (New York and Mahwah N.J.: Paulist Press, 1991), chap. 4, and the essays in Taitetsu Unno and James W. Heisig, eds., *The Religious Philosophy of Tanabe Hajime: The Metanoetic Imperative* (Berkeley, Calif.: Asian Humanities Press, 1990).

81. This is simply explained by Tanabe's disciple Takeuchi Yoshinori in his "Recollections of Professor Tanabe," in Unno and Heisig, *Religious Philosophy,* 1–11, 8–10; see also Ozaki, "The Logic of Species," *Individuum, Society, Humankind,* 5–15.

82. See Ozaki, "The World as the Active Presence of Eternity," *Individuum, Society, Humankind,* 27–39, 29–31.

83. Ibid., 36; see 34–37.

84. Ibid., 41–48. Interestingly, in view of our consideration of temporality and spatiality in chapter 5, Tanabe sees species as the "spatialization of time" orientated to the past, the acting individual as the "temporalization of space" orientated to the future, and genus as the present which unifies them, 49–50.

85. Whalen Lai, "Tanabe and the Dialectics of Mediation: A Critique," in Unno and Heisig, *Religious Philosophy,* 256–76, sketches with great sensitivity the Buddhological subtleties involved: Tanabe represents an asymmetrical relationship stressing other-power without denying self-power, which aligns him more with traditional Tendai than with either Dogen or Shinran (264); unlike Nishida, Nishitani and Abe, he advocates the *shikaku* teaching of incipient enlightenment rather than the *hongaku* or a priori "original" enlightenment (269, 274) because he wishes to remain a "realist" about the fragility and fallibility of human nature.

86. Jamie Hubbard, "Tanabe's Metanoetics: The Failure of Absolutism," in Unno and Heisig, *Religious Philosophy,* 360–79, 363–66, turns the spotlight on both the Western and Buddhist roots of this absolutism, leaving open the extent to which Tanabe took over the "original enlightenment" (*hongaku*) teaching from Shinran.

87. Though here, too, questions remain open. Shinran often spoke of "shame and guilt" (*zangi*) but never of "repentance and restitution" (*zange*) in the sense intended by Tanabe, according to Ueda Yoshifumi in Unno and Heisig, 134–49; the simplistic opposition of

"own-power" and "other-power," Zen and Shin is also questioned by several contributors to this volume.

88. This point is stressed repeatedly by Schmidt-Leukel, especially of the Theravada, see *Löwen,* 493–97.

Conclusion: Beyond Violence?

1. See the wide diversity of approaches to this issue in the papers edited by Joseph A. Camilleri, *Religion and Culture in Asia Pacific: Violence or Healing?* (Melbourne: Vista, 2001).

2. See Hans Küng, *Global Responsibility: In Search of a New World Ethic* (London: SCM, 1990).

3. See J. D. May, "Ethic of Survival or Vision of Hope? The Aim of Interreligious Dialogue," *Dharma World* 29 (September–October 2002): 25–28.

4. Masao Abe, *Buddhism and Interfaith Dialogue* (London: Macmillan, 1995), achieves this mediation not only by focusing on the *sambhogakaya* but by stressing the religious significance of both time and space as dimensions of the Bodhisattva's vow, which locates ethics in history, 59–61, 195–203. Whereas Christian ethics are future-oriented and exist in the tension between already and not-yet, Buddhist ethics presuppose a completely realized eschatology (the equivalence of *samsara* and *nirvana*), in which already and not-yet are co-extensive. See also Michio T. Shinozaki, "Peace and Nonviolence from a Mahayana Buddhist Perspective: Nikkyo Niwano's Thought," *Buddhist-Christian Studies* 21 (2001): 13–30; Mark T. Unno, "Questions in the Making: A Review Essay on Zen Buddhist Ethics in the Context of Buddhist and Comparative Ethics," *Journal of Religious Ethics* 27 (1999): 509–36; Jan van Bragt, "Reflections on Zen and Ethics," *Studies in Interreligious Dialogue* 12, no. 2 (2002): 133–47.

5. See Robert Gascoigne, *The Public Forum and Christian Ethics* (Cambridge: Cambridge University Press, 2001).

6. This theme is developed by Abe throughout *Buddhism and Interfaith Dialogue,* but it can be reciprocated by Christians in the dialogue relationship, see Rita M. Gross and Terry C. Muck, eds., *Buddhists Talk about Jesus, Christians Talk about the Buddha* (New York and London: Continuum, 2000); Perry Schmidt-Leukel with Gerhard Köberlin and Thomas Josef Götz, eds., *Buddhist Perceptions of Jesus: Papers of the Third Conference of the European Network of Buddhist-Christian Studies (St. Ottilien 1999)* (St. Ottilien: EOS-Verlag, 2001); *Swedish Missiological Themes* 90 (2002): special issue on "Christian Perceptions of Buddha."

7. See J. D. May, "European Union, Christian Divison? Christianity's Responsibility for Europe's Past and Future," *Studies* 89 (2000): 118–29. The ideas merely sketched here are developed much more fully with reference to the situation in Northern Ireland by my colleagues Joseph Liechty and Cecelia Clegg, *Moving Beyond Sectarianism: Religion, Conflict, and Reconciliation in Northern Ireland* (Dublin: Columba Press, 2001). Though the book's setting is poles apart from the vast Asia-Pacific context, frequent discussion with Joe and Cecelia has been of immense help in developing my own approach, especially their nuanced account of what sectarianism is, how it functions in a society, and what lessons may be learned from it for dealing with difference and ideological conflict.

8. For a comprehensive survey and analysis of the religions' contributions to both violent conflict and its resolution worldwide, see R. Scott Appleby, *The Ambivalence of the Sacred: Religion, Violence, and Reconciliation* (Lanham, Md.: Rowman & Littlefield, 2000).

9. See J. D. May, "A Rationale for Reconciliation," *Uniting Church Studies* 7 (2001): 1–13.

Appendix I: Competing Missionaries and Reluctant Ecumenists in Melanesia

1. The story has been told in gripping detail by, among others, John Garrett, *To Live among the Stars: Christian Origins in Oceania* (Geneva: World Council of Churches; Suva, Fiji: University of the South Pacific, 1982), with emphasis on Polynesia; Francis X. Hezel, *The First Taint of Civilization: A History of the Caroline and Marshall Islands in Pre-Colonial Days, 1521–1885* (Honolulu: University of Hawai'i Press, 1983), for events in Micronesia; and Rufus Pech, "The Acts of the Apostles in Papua New Guinea and Solomon Islands," in Brian Schwarz, ed., *An Introduction to Ministry in Melanesia* (Goroka, Papua New Guinea: Melanesian Institute, 1985), 17–71, on the decisive encounters in Melanesia. Some of what follows is drawn from J. D. May, *Christus Initiator: Theologie im Pazifik* (Düsseldorf: Patmos, 1990), here especially the Introduction and chapter 1.

2. See Paul Richardson and Theo Aerts, eds., *Romans and Anglicans in Papua New Guinea* (Goroka, Papua New Guinea: Liturgical Catechetical Institute, 1991), 2–3.

3. See Garrett, *To Live among the Stars,* 161ff.

4. See Pech, "Acts of the Apostles," 22ff.

5. Theo Ahrens speaks of the "geographically based ecumenicity" that resulted (personal communication); see his study "Bethlehem, Jerusalem und die 'Entdeckung des eigenen Körpers': Zum Beitrag polynesischer Missionare in der Christianisierung Ozeaniens," in Theodor Ahrens, Hans Joachim Kosmahl, Joachim Wietzke, eds., *Vom Gehorsam des Glaubens: Paul-Gerhardt Buttler zum 60. Geburtstag* (Ammersbek bei Hamburg: Verlag an der Lottbek, 1991), 17–27. The important story of Pacific Islanders as missionaries has now been documented by Doug Munro and Andrew Thornley, eds., *The Covenant Makers: Islander Missionaries in the Pacific* (Suva, Fiji: Pacific Theological College and Institute of Pacific Studies, 1996).

6. Richardson and Aerts, *Romans and Anglicans,* 6.

7. Bishops Verjus and de Boismenu in Papua and Louis Couppé in New Britain thus successfully opposed the mission boundaries proposed by the British and German colonial administrations, see Garrett, *To Live among the Stars,* 237ff.; Rainer Jaspers, "Colonialism and Catholic Mission Activity on New Britain between 1890 and 1899: The Problem of the Mission Districts," *Papers Prepared for the Visit of Pope John Paul II to Papua New Guinea* (Port Moresby, Papua New Guinea: Government Printer, 1982) 47–60; Garry Trompf, *Melanesian Religion* (Cambridge: Cambridge University Press, 1991) 148–49, with case studies of Roman Catholic missions in chaps. 6 and 7.

8. See Richardson and Aerts, *Romans and Anglicans,* 12–20; Timothy Kinahan, *A Church Is Born: A History of the Anglican Church in Papua New Guinea* (Port Moresby, Papua New Guinea: Anglican Church in Papua New Guinea, 1990 [1983]), 4.

9. See Brian Schwarz, "The Ecumenical Setting," in Herwig Wagner and Hermann Reiner, eds., *The Lutheran Church in Papua New Guinea: The First Hundred Years, 1886– 1986* (Adelaide, Australia: Lutheran Publishing House, 1986), 329–55, 335–38.

10. See Gavin Souter, *New Guinea: The Last Unknown* (Sydney: Angus & Robertson, 1974); Peter Ryan, *Fear Drive My Feet* (Melbourne: Melbourne University Press, 1960).

11. The missionary work of the German Lutherans and Catholics survived the war largely because their Australian and American fellow-Christians kept it going, though the fidelity and ingenuity of the indigenous Christians themselves played an important part, see Herwig Wagner, "Papua-Neuguinea — Ein Beispiel übernationaler Zusammenarbeit in der Mission," in Kurt-Dietrich Mrossko, ed., *Wok Misin: 100 Jahre deutsche Mission in Papua-Neuguinea* (Neuendettelsau: Missionskolleg im Missionswerk der ELKB, 1986), 123– 34; Gerhard O. Reitz, "Partnership across Oceans: The American Lutheran Church," in Wagner and Reiner, eds., *The Lutheran Church in Papua New Guinea*, 141–86.

12. Even before the outbreak of the First World War the South Seas Evangelical Mission, founded by the Australian Florence Young to evangelize the Melanesian cane cutters of north Queensland, arrived in the Solomon Islands (1904); the Seventh Day Adventists began work in Papua in 1908; and the Liebenzell Mission commenced operations on the Admiralty Islands north of New Guinea in 1914; see Pech, "The Acts of the Apostles," 20. The Assemblies of God were in Fiji as early as 1926, the Jehovah's Witnesses by 1939; after the Second World War they both spread like wildfire; see Charles W. Forman, *The Island Churches of the South Pacific* (Maryknoll, N.Y.: Orbis, 1982), 200. These churches were even less prepared to cooperate with one another than their forebears: the American Baptists, for example, wanted no fellowship with their Australian counterparts. Apart from Christian groups, the Mormons, established in Hawai'i since 1926, have been making their presence felt in Melanesia, and the Baha'is have achieved a remarkable degree of acceptance. In Fiji, Hindus and Muslims of Indian descent make up almost half the population, and even in Papua New Guinea Muslims are present in sufficient numbers to begin organizing themselves as a religion.

13. See J. D. May, "The Autonomous Church in Independent Papua New Guinea," in Wagner and Reiner, eds., *The Lutheran Church in Papua New Guinea*, 307–26.

14. See Forman, *Island Churches*; John Garrett, *Footsteps in the Sea: Christianity in Oceania to World War II* (Geneva: WCC; Suva, Fiji: University of the South Pacific, 1991), and *Where Nets Were Cast: Christianity in Oceania Since World War II* (Geneva, WCC; Suva, Fiji: University of the South Pacific, 1992).

Appendix 2: China's Problems with the "Foreign Religion"

1. Erik Zürcher, *The Buddhist Conquest of China: The Spread and Adaptation of Buddhism in Early Mediaeval China* (Leiden: E. J. Brill, 1959), 19, 22, stresses that this mention in an edict by no means implies that Buddhism was in any way established or even regarded as important and that the source for the story of Emperor Ming's dream, the Preface to the *Sutra in Forty-two Sections,* dates from the mid-third century. See also Zürcher's summary overview, "Buddhism in China," in Joseph M. Kitagawa and Mark D. Cummings, eds., *Buddhism and Asian History: Religion, History and Culture Readings from The Encyclopedia of Religion* (New York: Macmillan, 1989), 139–49; Arthur F. Wright, *Studies in Chinese Buddhism* (New Haven: Yale University Press, 1991), chap. 1.

2. See Kenneth Ch'en, *Buddhism in China: A Historical Survey* (Princeton, N.J.: Princeton University Press, 1964), 29–31.

3. Zürcher, *Buddhist Conquest,* 61.

4. Ibid., 22–23.

5. Ibid., 23–24.

6. See Ch'en, *Buddhism in China,* 40–44.

7. Ibid., 50. Huang-Lao was a compound of Huang-ti, the Yellow Emperor, and Lao-tzu; an altar was dedicated to the dual deity in the imperial palace. "To the emperor, Huang-Lao were the deities of a religion in which men were striving for immortality through dietetics, respiratory exercises, alchemy, and concentration," 27.

8. Zürcher, *Buddhist Conquest,* 37. Zürcher considers this "a basically Taoist ritual tinged with some Buddhist elements," not "court Buddhism" but "court Taoism slightly tinged with Buddhism" and in that sense nothing exceptional, 36–37. The Memorial does, however, quote from the *Sutra in Forty-two Sections,* showing that this text was already known, 38.

9. Zürcher, *Buddhist Conquest,* 38.

10. Fred Sturm, "Chinese Buddhist Philosophy," in Donald H. Bishop, ed., *Chinese Thought: An Introduction* (Delhi: Motilal Barnasidass, 1985), 184–234, 185; "Furthermore, both questions and answers were given in the grammatical framework of a highly inflected Indo-European language structure, fundamentally different from the linguistic structure of Chinese. . . . There were few, if any, equivalent concepts or distinctions in Chinese intellectual history up to that point, and the Chinese language, therefore, did not contain the vocabulary necessary for intelligible translation of Buddhist texts and discourse," 192.

11. Sturm, "Chinese Buddhist Philosophy," 185.

12. Ch'en, *Buddhism in China,* 49–50.

13. Ibid., 57.

14. See Zürcher, *Buddhist Conquest,* 4.

15. See ibid., 39–40.

16. The text, from the Biography of Chu Fa-ya, adds: "in order to make them understand," which suggests that there were difficulties to be surmounted! It is quoted by Ch'en, *Buddhism in China,* 68–69, and Zürcher, *Buddhist Conquest,* 184, here with the proviso that it is extremely difficult to know exactly what was meant over and above equivalences such as *bodhi=tao, nirvana=wu-wei* and other already well-known translations. Tao-an and Kumarajiva's disciple Hui-jui later disapproved of the method. See also Sturm, "Chinese Buddhist Philosophy," 194–95, 198.

17. See Zürcher, *Buddhist Conquest,* 35, 69.

18. For more detail see Ch'en, *Buddhism in China,* 365–72.

19. See ibid., 67–69.

20. Zürcher, *Buddhist Conquest,* 4, refuses to call this "Neo-Taoism" because it is "a Confucian recasting of early Taoist philosophy," 289.

21. Ch'en, *Buddhism in China,* 61.

22. Zürcher, *Buddhist Conquest,* 87.

23. Ibid., 87, remarking that "*Ming-chiao* and *hsüan-hsüeh* cannot simply be regarded as two rival schools of thought," as their respective preoccupations with "function" and

"substance" are both Confucian and foreshadow the two levels of truth, *samvrtisatya* (conventional level) and *paramarthasatya* (transcendent level), in Mahayana philosophy.

24. See ibid., 88–90.

25. Ibid., 90–92; see Sturm, "Chinese Buddhist Philosophy," 195.

26. Ibid., 92.

27. Ibid., 58, see 55–59.

28. Ibid., 192.

29. See ibid., 194. Tao-an and seven of his pupils had made a collective vow before an image of Maitreya; thirty years later, in 402, Hui-yüan and more than a hundred lay followers made a similar vow before a statue of Amitabha. In each case, the commitment was to support one another in striving for rebirth in Tushita heaven, a future realm of bliss.

30. For a more detailed account see Ch'en, *Buddhism in China*, chaps. 3, 4; see also Sturm, "Chinese Buddhist Philosophy," 200–201.

31. Zürcher, *Buddhist Conquest*, 108.

32. Sturm, "Chinese Buddhist Philosophy," lists the Chinese objections to Buddhism: "(i) Buddhism is not mentioned in the classics. . . . (ii) Buddhist monks renounce worldly joys. . . . (iii) Monks injure their bodies. . . . (iv) Monks do not marry. . . . (v) Buddhism teaches human souls do not die, but return to bodily existence [i.e., dualism]. . . . (vi) The ideas and practices of Buddhism come from barbaric lands of the west," 196–97.

33. For a fuller account see Ch'en, *Buddhism in China*, 184–99, and Jacques Gernet, *Buddhism in Chinese Society: An Economic History from the Fifth to the Tenth Centuries* (New York: Columbia University Press, 1995 [orig. 1956]).

34. Ch'en, *Buddhism in China*, 203.

35. See ibid., 201. For a much fuller study see Robert E. Buswell Jr., *The Formation of Ch'an Ideology in China and Korea: The Vajrasamadhi-Sutra, a Buddhist Apochryphon* (Princeton, N.J.: Princeton University Press, 1989).

36. See Ch'en, *Buddhism in China*, 235–38. It was Hsüan-tsang who successfully articulated Nagarjuna's logic of non-dualism, "the antithesis that everything is neither both existent and empty, nor neither existent nor empty," 201.

37. Sturm, "Chinese Buddhist Philosophy," 204

38. For a general overview, see Jan Yun-hua, *A Chronicle of Buddhism in China 581– 960 A.D.: Translations from Monk Chih-p'an's Fo-tsu T'ung-chi* (Santiniketan: Visva Bharati, 1966), Introduction.

39. Ninian Smart, *Buddhism and Christianity: Rivals and Allies* (London: Macmillan, 1993), 34.

40. Ch'en, *Buddhism in China*, 319; as Smart sums up the Hua-yen teaching, "the Buddha *is* the absolute . . . [all things are] wombs of the Thus-gone . . . we all possess the Buddha-nature," *Buddhism and Christianity*, 60. See also Sturm, "Chinese Buddhist Philosophy," 208–10.

41. Evoked by Smart, *Buddhism and Christianity*, 60. According to the — controversial — view of D. T. Suzuki, "Buddhism's Mahayana movement represents a new phase of Buddhist thought in which the idea of anatta (non-ego) was replaced by the concept of Buddhata (Buddha-nature), implying a transition from emphasis on individuality and personal liberation to an outlook which is cosmological in scope," Sturm, "Chinese Buddhist Philosophy," 214.

42. Zürcher, *Buddhist Conquest*, 219, sees Hui-yüan's vow before Amitabha, mentioned above, as being an "important landmark" on the way to this development, though not in the sense of founding a lineage. See also Heng-ching Shih, *The Syncretism of Ch'an and Pure Land Buddhism* (New York: Peter Lang, 1992).

43. Ch'en, *Buddhism in China*, 340, points out that this would be a correct translation of *Avalokitasvara*, which does in fact appear in a fifth-century manuscript of the *Lotus Sutra.*

44. See ibid., 342.

45. See ibid., 342–50.

46. See Zürcher, *Buddhist Conquest*, 222, adding that "pseudo-Buddhist or half understood Buddhist notions combined to bar the way to an understanding of the doctrine," especially "the high level of abstraction which characterizes these products of a subtle dialectical philosophy," 226.

47. See Ch'en, *Buddhism in China,* 350–57. This, at least, is the legend, designed to support the assertion that "the first public exposition of full Buddhist truth occurs on Chinese soil!" but probably also legitimating the outcome of a power struggle over the authenticity of the Ch'an lineage, see Sturm, "Chinese Buddhist Philosophy," 218–19.

48. See the illuminating introduction by Arthur Cooper to his translation, *Li Po and Tu Fu* (Harmondsworth: Penguin, 1973).

49. Ch'en, *Buddhism in China*, 361.

50. For sample texts see Zürcher, *Buddhist Conquest*, 88–92.

51. See Ch'en, *Buddhism in China*, 362–64.

52. Zürcher, *Buddhist Conquest*, 2.

INDEX

Also published by Continuum

Buddhists Talk about Jesus
Christians Talk about the Buddha
Edited by Rita M. Gross and Terry C. Muck

"Thought-provoking enough for specialists, these articulate views from informed followers of the 'other' faith are also accessible to general readers."

– *Library Journal*

"This is one of the most intriguing books that I have read in a long time.... Though not a large book, it has a great depth, and deserves to be read by anyone who has ever wondered about the relative message of two of the greatest teachers who have ever lived.... As a source of material for thought and for meditation, this book is thoroughly recommended."

– *Pure Land Notes*

Christians Talk about Buddhist Meditation
Buddhists Talk about Christian Prayer
Edited by Rita M. Gross and Terry C. Muck

This book adopts the format of *Buddhists Talk about Jesus, Christians Talk about the Buddha,* where scholar-practitioners — four of them Buddhist and four of them Christian — explore their relationship to the great religious leader of the other tradition. Then the remaining contributors, two from each tradition, address themselves to the views expressed.

The Christian contributors are Frances S. Adeney, Mary Frohlich, Paul O. Ingram, Ursula King, Donald W. Mitchell, Terry C. Muck, and Bradwell Smith.

The Buddhist contributors are Robert Aitken, Grace Burford, Mahinda Deegallee, Rita M. Gross, Kenneth K. Tanaka, Robert Thurman, and Taitetsu Unno.